EDWIN DILLER STARBUCK

Pioneer in the Psychology of Religion

Howard J. Booth

UNIVERSITY
PRESS OF
AMERICA

Copyright © 1981 by

University Press of America, Inc.™

P.O. Box 19101, Washington, D.C. 20036

ISBN (Perfect): 0-8191-1703-X

ISBN (Cloth): 0-8191-1702-1

LCN: 80-5731

Dedicated to Bonita,
Gevin and Darin, whose
support has always been
a crucial factor in any-
thing I have attempted

ACKNOWLEDGMENTS

Appreciation is expressed for permission to use the following previously published material:

The editors of the Journal of Psychology and Theology for excerpts from the author's article, "Pioneering Literature in the Psychology of Religion: A Reminder," Journal of Psychology and Theology, 6:46-53, Winter 1978.

TABLE OF CONTENTS

Page

LIST OF FIGURES   ix

INTRODUCTION   1

Chapter
  I. BACKGROUND   5

      Psychology of Religion   5
      A View of the Literature   13
      Development of the Field   24
      Starbuck's Place in the Field.   40

 II. A BIOGRAPHICAL PERSPECTIVE: PERSONAL. .   57

      Family Background   57
      Educational Background   66
      Religious Orientation   73
      Personal Background   88

III. A BIOGRAPHICAL PERSPECTIVE: CAREER . .   113

      Beginning.   114
      University of Iowa (1906-1930)   117
      University of Southern California
        (1930-1943)   157
      Summary and Analysis   164

 IV. SIGNIFICANT CONTRIBUTIONS   177

      Writings   177
        Chronological Survey   178
          Phase One: 1897-1906   178
          Phase Two: 1907-1921   182
          Phase Three: 1922-1945   188
        Major Themes   195
        A Pioneering Classic   209
      Projects   216
        The Iowa Plan   218
        Institute for Research in Character .   232
        Conclusion   250

Page

V. SUMMARY AND CONCLUSION 261

APPENDICES. 271

    APPENDIX A: SELECTED SURVEYS OF THE
                 LITERATURE 271
    APPENDIX B: SELECTED DEVELOPMENTAL
                 SURVEYS 273
    APPENDIX C: GENERAL QUESTIONNAIRE OF
                 CONVERSION. 277
    APPENDIX D: QUESTIONNAIRE ON AGE OF
                 CONVERSION. 281

STARBUCK'S WORKS 282

LIST OF FIGURES

Figure   Page

1. The Threefold Re-centering 220

2. Showing the Nascencies of Development
    and the Centres of Ethical Emphasis . . . 224

3. Suggestions of Projects and Problems to
    Enrich A Character Training Curriculum . . 225

4. Self-Measurement Scale 227

5. A Self-Measurement Scale for
    Children, Grades V to VIII 229

6. A Character Test for Primary Children. . . 230

7. A Character Test for Children,
    Grades III and IV 231

INTRODUCTION

In 1949, a ph.D. dissertation, dealing with
the contribution of George Albert Coe to the psychology of religion, was completed. The author of this
work specified a relative deficiency of historical
study in the psychology of religion, as contrasted
with other fields of investigation. He also indicated the paucity of serious studies of the foremost
"thinkers and pioneers" in this field, and called
for an examination of those individuals whose contributions were particularly significant to the
development of the psychology of religion.1 Since
that time a number of major studies, dealing with
the relationship of psychology and religion, have
been produced. However, to this date, we have no
definitive history of this field. Nor has there
been an increasing number of studies written dealing with the life and contibution of the leading
psycholgists of religion.

Our first serious introduction to this field
and its exponents occurred in a course, titled
"Pioneers in the Psychology of Religion," offered
by Dr. David Belgum in the Department of Religion
at the University of Iowa. It became apparent
that few critical evaluations had been made of these
early contributors, and that there existed a legitimate need for such studies. In light of the early
role Edwin Diller Starbuck assumes in the field of
psychology of religion, and his impact particularly
in the study of religious experience, and in the
areas of religious education and character education;
and considering that, to this date, no extensive
biographical treatment or systematic critique of
his work has been attempted, the need for our study
seems clearly evident.

Starbuck's life spans a period of convulsion
and rapid change in the world, and particularly in
America, an era in which demand for the "pioneering
spirit" was great. The study of Starbuck's life
and contribution in his particular field cannot
be understood apart from such a significant time

1

of transition. Until the 1890's, there is no indication, as recorded in the history of psychology,
of any systematic use of the empirical methods of
research in the study of religious phenomena. But
in that decade, a number of contributions were made,
not the least of these being Starbuck's classic study
of conversion. We intend to validate the act of
numbering Starbuck among the pioneers of psychology
of religion and related fields; and consequently,
we can agree wholeheartedly with Vergilius Ferm's
analysis:

> "Were one to list the pioneers
> in the twentieth-century born science
> of religious psychology, one would
> unhesitantly name. . . . Coe, Leuba, and
> Starbuck /my Italics7. Were one to
> mention the names of those whose re-
> searches have opened up new vistas in
> the fields of religious education and
> so-called character education, one
> would think of George Albert Coe and
> Edwin Diller Starbuck /my Italics/."[2]

The purpose of our study includes an attempt to
demonstrate the authenticity of this statement
with regard to Starbuck's specific contributions.

It is our contention that Starbuck must be listed
among those who, in effect, brought the psychology
of religion, as a field, into existence. Not only
do we intend to describe his contribution to this
field, as well as that of character education; our
objective also is to evaluate critically the merits
of his work in light of its uniqueness, its practical
application, and the nature of its influence. Further,
we will endeavor to reveal a continuity, that we
believe exists, between Starbuck's early study of
the phenomena of religious experience and his later
work in character education. In the process we hope
to uncover some of the insights of Starbuck which
have been forgotten, and desire to reawaken an
appreciation of his values, as so creatively expressed by him.

2

An attempt will also be made to place Starbuck's thought and career within its historical and ideological context. We will search for those influences in his life, in terms of personal heritage and educational pursuits, which helped to fashion his thought and motivate his behavior. A biographical perspective is presented to deal with this latter concern.

The general arrangement of the material for this study is based primarily upon the chronological sequence of Starbuck's life and career. Chapter I is designed to provide a setting for our view of Starbuck's contribution to the psychology of religion. A general examination of the development of the field will establish the context for an interpretation of the significance of Starbuck's role. For a better understanding of the major influences which play upon Starbuck's life, Chapter II focuses upon his personal background and development. Chapter III discusses Starbuck's career attempting to analyze interpretatively the nature of his principal interests and involvements. In Chapter IV, a critical evalutation of his writings and major projects is made. The most significant themes of his written works are analyzed, as well as his attempts to implement in practical ways his major interests. Finally, in Chapter V, a summary and conclusions are presented.

NOTES

1. David Henry Bremer, "George Albert Coe's Contribution to the Psychology of Religion" (unpublished Ph.D. thesis, Boston University, 1949), p. 7.
2. Vergilius Ferm, ed., Religion in Transition (London: George Allen & Unwin, 1937), pp. 8-9.

CHAPTER I

BACKGROUND

The study of Edwin Diller Starbuck as a pioneer in the psychology of religion demands a discussion not only of his life and contributions, but consideration as well of the areas or fields in which the investment of his life was made. The purpose of this chapter, then, is to examine that background against which the activities of Starbuck's life were played. Such an examination will include a definition of the psychology of religion in terms of this particular study, a brief survey of the literature, and a limited discussion of the development of the field, especially as it relates to Starbuck's contribution.

Psychology of Religion

In simple terms, the psychology of religion basically is an attempt to understand religion by the study of its psychological meanings and functions. Such a definition precludes any form of psychologizing which seeks to explain away religious experience. Rather its aim is for understanding and appreciation of the meaning and value of religion in life, supplying the principles from which practical applications may emerge.

The key to our consideration of the psychology of religion is to be seen in its relationship to psychology proper. It is our contention that it is but an extension of the general field of psychology; for there is no religious psychology, per se, that is, a peculiar "religious" way of doing psychology. In fact, what distinguishes the psychology of religion as a descriptive science is that it turns aside from primarily philosophical or theological inquiry and endeavors to employ the resources of scientific psychology. The aim has been to study religious man not in terms of religious presuppositions alone, but from the perspective of secular psychology. John Baillie, in his The Interpretation

of Religion, comments, "What has above all characterized the Psychology of Religion has been its desire
to look at its facts from the outside after the
manner of the natural sciences."1 The roots of the
psychology of religion reach far into the past,
but a clear departure from its ancestral heritage
is evidenced around the turn of the century by its
adherence to critical empirical methodology in the
investigation of religion.

While it has been proposed that the psychology
of religion is really a branch of general psychology
and not to be considered in a class all its own,
there are reasons for separate treatment of this
field. George A. Coe, a pioneer in this movement
himself, spoke of them as reasons "of convenience
and of accomodation to existing conditions." The
points he raised early in the century still appear
to be relevant. He gave three reasons for the consideration of psychology of religion separately:
(1) The issues are very basic to human life and the
data is so complex that a thorough treatment of them
is necessary. Such an extensive analysis requires
separate treatment; (2) The religious sensitiveness
and bias which many students and religious bodies
have, works to dissuade psychologists in general
from the discussion of religion, let alone the
serious investigation of it. To deal with such
problems in an interested group rather than throughout the whole body of general psychology seems desireable; and (3) Religion, though a common element of
life, has become "self-conscious." Experiences of
religious life seem to cluster around specific interests and institutions, consequently demanding
particularly close attention. Again separate
psychological investigation appears necessary.2 Just
as a number of other branches of psychology emerged,
such as educational psychology and abnormal psychology,
for the sake of independent investigation, so the
separate treatment of the psychology of religion
appears to be a legitimate development.

Were one to attempt an outline of the work of
the psychology of religion, he probably could do

no better than rephrase James H. Leuba's early presentation, contained in a journal article in 1904. Leuba divides the systematic psychological study of religion into four parts: (1) the examination of the motives of religious life, that is, the needs and desires which are expressed; (2) the study of the "intellectual constituents" of religious life, a conceptual analysis of doctrine, beliefs, and ideas; (3) an exploration of the means used to obtain certain ends in religious life, including the study of worship and religious states; and (4) a critical consideration of the results of religion.[3] Leuba has very adequately presented the nature of its main investigations, portraying briefly what the psychology of religion hopes to accomplish.

Starbuck's approach to the psychology of religion does not differ in any significant way from our attempt to define the field. Paralleling our assertion as to the central importance of scientific methodology, Starbuck wrote at the very beginning of his classical volume, The Psychology of Religion:

> "The Psychology of Religion
> has for its work to carry the well-
> established methods of science into the
> analysis and organization of the facts
> of the religious consciousness, and
> to ascertain the laws which determine
> its growth and character."[4]

At the end of the introductory chapter of this same volume, Starbuck summarized his approach to the field, including, almost without exception, those elements which have been and will be discussed as important to our definition of the psychology of religion. Starbuck proceeded as follows:

> "The psychology of religion is
> a purely inductive study into the
> phenomena of religion as shown in
> individual experience. It differs
> from the methods heretofore employed
> in viewing its facts more objectively

7

. . . The end in view is not to
classify and define the phenomena
of religion, but to see into the
laws and processes at work in the
spiritual life. The fundamental
assumption is that religion is a
real fact of human experience,
and develops according to law.
. . . The service of psychology
to practical religion is to make
possible a harvest of wiser means
in moral and religious culture,
and also to lift religion sufficiently out of the domain of feeling to make it appeal to the understanding, so that it may become
possible, progressively to appreciate its truth and apperceive its
essential elements."[5]

It is quite clear that the psychology of
religion, as it is being defined in this study, was
conceived during Starbuck's day near the turn of
the century. Equally evident is the fact that the
primary impetus for this field was centered in the
scientific spirit of the pioneers of the psychology
of religion, among whom Starbuck is to be numbered.
Generally, although in differing degrees, the
pioneers of the field upheld and employed scientific
methodology, viewing the psychology of religion as
legitimately a part of the science of general psychology.

The psychology of religion has passed through
a number of phases in its development, some of
which have caused it to stray in terms of the
original purposes as defined. Of any contemporary
definition of this field the present writer considers the attempt of Dr. Orlo Strunk, Jr. to be the
most valuable for two reasons: (1) Strunk has
created a definition which appears to be true to
the original interests and purposes of the classical pioneers; and (2) his definition is workable in
terms of acceptable psychological principles.

8

Strunk defines the psychology of religion as "that branch of general psychology which attempts to understand, control, and predict human behavior--both propriate and peripheral--which is perceived as being religious by the individual, and which is susceptible to one or more of the methods of psychological science."[6] This definition would have met with favor certainly in the eyes of Starbuck, and undoubtedly in the view of the majority of the other pioneers. It is feasible that strict adherence to the elements of this defintion would have affected greatly the course of the development of the psychology of religion, going a long way to legitimatize more completely its place in the field of general psychology.

Thus far, we have presented a rather exclusive view of the psychology of religion, especially in terms of the period of its development; but not every participant or observer has approached the field so narrowly. Depending upon the particular interpretation placed upon the psychology of religion, the psychological study of religion can be judged to begin very early in history. For example, Paul E. Johnson, considers psychology to be one of the youngest of modern sciences, but points out that the description and analysis of human experience and behavior has been going on for a considerably long time. And since much of the early recordings are sprinkled through with religious ideas and attitudes, he concludes that "the psychological data of religion are therefore as old as human history." Johnson pushes the premonition of some type of systematic scientific view and the hint of religious psychology as far back as 1375 B.C.[7] He briefly traces this motif found in a variety of historical figures up through the nineteenth century.

John Baillie concedes that the psychology of religion begins in America around 1890, listing Starbuck as one of the early investigators, but he takes exception to the claim that a new method of inquiring in the study of religion had been developed at this time. He spoke of the traditional distinc-

9

tion which had been made between the "old study,"
or theology, and the "new study," the psychology of
religion. It has been accepted that theology used
deductive methods outside the religious consciousness to form its conclusions, while the psychology
of religion drew its conclusions from religious consciousness by the employment of inductive and empirical methods. Baillie contends, however, that the
latter methodology was really first introduced into
theology by Kant and Schleiermacher, that they sought
to understand religion from within. With this framework he perceived the introduction of no new methodology by the American pioneers. Rather their contribution, he felt, was in the type of problems they
studied which had been previously neglected.[8]

Dr. Herbert Searles, in one of the Iowa Studies
in Character, a series edited by Starbuck, took a
similar view to Baillie. In a chapter titled "The
Development Of A Scientific Attitude And Method In
The Study Of Religion," Searles maintained that consideration of the development of a scientific view
and methodology in the psychology of religion depended upon one's interpretation of the psychology
of religion. He went back to Hume, Spinoza, Kant,
Fichte, Lessing, Berkley, and Schleiermacher to
date the beginning of the psychological approach to
religious consciousness. As with Baillie, however,
he acknowledges that the commencement of really serious psychological study of religion is of more recent origin, namely the classical period before the
turn of the century.[9]

G. Stephen Spinks, in his introductory work,
Psychology and Religion, also deals with the history
of the psychologies of religion. While he, too,
believed that the first serious psychologies of religion did not arise until the turn of the century;
still, going back to Plato and Aristotle and tracing
through to the twentieth century, he briefly surveyed Western thought in terms of its approach to
human consciousness. His approach appears to
place his selections within a history of the psychology of religion. Proposing at least a direct relationship to the field he declared that he selected "only
those views which eventually resolved themselves

10

into the psychology of religion."10

Writing about the development of the psychology
of religion, Karl R. Stolz also considers it to be
an "American product." In fact, his chapter devoted
to this topic discusses the various contributions
of seven leading American pioneers to this field.
Not incidental to our study is the fact that Starbuck
heads the list of these pioneers, including George
Coe, William James, James Pratt, Edward Ames, George
Stratton, and James Leuba. Of further interest to
our investigation, however, is that Stolz deals
in the same chapter with the background of the
psychological study of religion. He listed Hume,
Comte, Kant, and Schleiermacher as particularly
astute European "forerunners" or "precursors" to
the American pioneers, holding before us once again
their philosophical and theological inheritance.11

While credit is due to antecedent contributions
and conditions, as has been shown, it is quite clear
that the serious investigation and sophisticated
psychological understanding of religion was not
firmly conceived until the early years of the twentieth century. In this sense, a fairly exclusive
view regarding the demand for an empirical premise
forms the basis for our definition of the psychology
of religion.

One further point seems appropriate regarding
the nature of this field. Its study must of necessity constitute generally an interdisciplinary
approach. The name of the field itself, psychology
of religion, consists of two disciplines, constantly
interacting with one another. Besides this obvious
relationship, however, there is a close relationship
of the psychology of religion to a number of other
fields, which has greatly affected its development.
Starbuck spoke of this relationship in his first
volume on the subject, dealing specifically with
the relation of the psychology of religion to sociology, history, psychology, philosophy of religion
and theology, and religion. Though, in certain
instances he saw the psychology of religion moving

11

in different directions, he recognized the general
indebtedness of the psychology of religion to these
fields. He acknowledged that sociology and history
had provided for his time the primary body of knowledge about the beginning and the development of
religion. Building on this, Starbuck perceived
the task of the psychology of religion as studying
the development of religion also, but in terms of
the stages and principles of development within the
individual life. Starbuck viewed the relationship
of the psychology of religion to psychology proper,
particularly experimental psychology, as one of
alliance, both in terms of subject matter and method.
Methodologically, both were inductive. In terms of
subject matter, Starbuck argued against the sharp
distinction which had been held between the functionings of consciousness labelled religious and those
which were considered to be a part of the "mental
life." All psychic functionings, including such
things as reverance and worship, for example, were
similarly open to psychological investigation.
The psychology of religion, in these terms, then,
was basically a special branch of psychology.
The philosophy of religion and theology, in their
investigations, took a different approach than
that taken by the psychology of religion, but they
were foundational to its deveopment. Starbuck
observed that the philosophy of religion and theology
viewed the problems under study in wholistic terms,
using primarily the methods of introspection,
intuition and logical analysis in its search for
truth. The psychology of religion, on the other
hand, had as its purpose to research smaller units
or facts of religious experience, objectively inspect-
ing them within the context of a more exacting
science. The business of the psychology of religion
at this point was to interpret with some precision
the details of religious experience so as to illuminate the more comprehensive picture of the religious
life of man. According to Starbuck, then, a gap
between the scientist and the philosopher should not
exist. Finally, Starbuck considered the relationship
of psychology of religion to religion itself. Religion, he perceives, is a life which is continually

being expressed regardless of whether or not it is
being studied. But the benefit of applying psychology to religion is like that of medicine to health.
It is clear that Starbuck took seriously, and upheld
for acceptance and understanding, the interdisciplinary context in which the psychology of religion op-
erates.

Not only did Starbuck recognize in his work in
the psychology of religion the theoretical interrelationship of disciplines; he maintained also that there
was a natural continuity between the basic principles
of the psychology of religion and its practical application of these principles of other areas, such as religious education. In considering what religion stood
to gain by the psychological study of its nature and
laws, he expressed at the very beginning of his experimental work in the field, "psychology will contribute
to religion by leading toward greater wisdom in religious education /His Italics/.[12] He was aware very
early in his investigations that religious education
had to be founded upon the best psychological principles available if it was to successfully accomplish
its aims. To illustrate further his conviction in the
interdependence of the psychology of religion and religious education, we refer to the last chapter of his
volume dealing with the growth of the religious life.
Having carefully worked through the empirical data, he
concluded his book with a chapter titled "Some Educational Inferences," spelling out succinctly the need
to apply the principles of his study to the practical
endeavors of religious education.[13]

This is meant to demonstrate that we cannot properly talk about Starbuck's contribution to the psychology of religion without also considering his investment in religious education. And in this particular study we intend to go so far as to include his
work in character research and education as an outgrowth of, and consequently related to, his studies in
the psychology of religion.

A View of the Literature

The second purpose of this chapter, as was

stated earlier, is to introduce the reader to
selected literature of the field, especially as it
pertains to the period when Starbuck was an active
participant. It is not our intention to add another
extended survey to those that have already been
developed.[14] Rather our approach will be to briefly
examine a few of the major pieces of literature
which best typify the work of the early pioneers
in the field.

A word of explanation needs to be made regarding our references. The specific areas of
pastoral counseling or religion and psychiatry are
to be seen as fitting within the broader field of
the psychology of religion, yet references pertain-
ing to these areas are basically viewed as incidental
to our study as Starbuck's relationship to these
areas was negligible. The literature surveys of
the psychology of religion, however, rightly include
references to these areas as one of the practical
outgrowths of the field.

While there are some exceptions, the pioneering
thrust of the psychological study of religion can
be relegated, in general, to the first two decades
of the twentieth century. During these years the
creative classics of the field were produced, those
which inaugurated, though perhaps crude by contemporary standards, the use of empirical methods and
systematic analysis among psychologists in the study
of religion. While other works broadened the bases
for the study of religion, producing additional
data for further examination and evaluation, and
dealt more thoroughly with the practical ends of
such study, these relatively few pioneering
classics set the stage for the field.

Although Granville Stanley Hall authored no
classic exclusive to the psychology of religion,
any consideration of the pioneers in the field
which does not acknowledge his contribution is less
than complete. Hall's interests, as a psychologist,
in adolescence and the religious education of
children, is evidenced as early as the 1880's.[15]

14

As President and director of the graduate program in the newly-founded Clark University, Hall opened the way for numerous pioneering endeavors in the study of adolescence, as well as in the phenomena of religion, and the relationship thereof. He encouraged numbers of students, among which Starbuck and Leuba were the most prominent, in the research of such subjects. His efforts, in fact, were of such substance, that James Pratt, assessing, in 1908, the development of the psychology of religion to date, felt it appropriate to speak of Hall's formation of the "Clark school of religious psychology."[16]

Certainly Hall's thorough treatment of adolescence,[17] establishing the special import of this period, and revealing, with some degree of empirical justification, the nature of the physiological and psychological changes occurring during these years, shaped the direction of the research carried on at Clark particularly through the first decade of the century. He had included in his research the relationship of the phenomena of adolescence to religion and education, clearly denoting his conception of the need and place for such study. Hall, in fact, concluded a relationship between conversion and adolescence, a topic commonly handled among the early pioneers. That Hall's work was especially influential along this line of study is unquestionable. Starbuck had been concentrating on this alliance between conversion and adolescence in his research at Harvard, and made the decision to enter Clark University primarily because of Hall's reputation for supporting such work in religious psychology. While Hall's study of adolescence was comprehensive, his consideration of related religious factors was limited. At this point Starbuck's major contribution in the field, as classically conceived, was made. Although Leuba's study of conversion[18] was actually published nine months earlier than the first of Starbuck's two articles on conversion and religious growth,[19] Starbuck had started researching the subject, while at Harvard, before Leuba. Then, too, Starbuck's treatment of religious phenomena, was more thorough, which makes reasonable the request of London publishers that Starbuck use these articles as the basis for publication. Starbuck was willing; and in 1899 the first volume applying scientific methodology completely to the study of religious phenomena was published.

Starbuck was the first of the pioneers to consider conversion a natural aspect of adolescent phenomena and his 1899 classic stood as the broadest empirically based study extant to substantiate this claim. His use of the questionnaire in studying religious phenomena was imitated, though generally supplemented by other methods, by every one of the representative investigators we have selected. And while later pioneers, at various points, take issue with some of Starbuck's conclusions, and criticize aspects of his data, his study, to this day, is considered insightful into the complexities of the developing religious consciousness, and a substantial portion of his conclusions have been confirmed by other studies.[20]

Although Starbuck wrote numerous articles dealing with many significant features of the psychology of religion, unfortunately, he published no other full-length volume in the field. His interests in the related areas of religious education and character education, during the rest of his life, fostered the pursuit of some of the practical inferences of his earlier work in the psychology of religion, which endeavors proved to be costly to Starbuck in terms of time and energy.

The two pioneers most closely alligned with Starbuck on the subject of conversion, or the religious experience, were George Albert Coe and William James. Chronologically, Coe's work comes first. In his book, The Spiritual Life, published in 1900, Coe investigates, quite independently of Starbuck's study, the nature of conversion as well as other interesting aspects of the religious life. Like Starbuck, Coe believes that conversion,

16

or some form of religious awakening, is a common element of adolescent development. Further agreeing with
Starbuck, Coe concludes, from his own data, that the
average age of conversion is in the sixteenth year.
Unlike Starbuck, however, Coe considers conversion and
puberty concurrent rather than supplemental to each
other.

As with Starbuck, Coe gathers his data for this
book primarily through the use of the questionnaire;
however, he refines, whenever possible, the value of
this instrument through personal interviewing acquain-
tances of the subject, and by observation of some of
the subjects under controlled conditions. In the latter case, the questionnaire is supplemented by experimentation with hypnosis for the purpose of attempting
to establish the degree to which a subject is sugges-
tible and the relation that this fact has to the type
of conversion experienced by the subject. One of
Coe's most important contributions, in this work, was
to empirically substantiate a significant relationship between an individual's temperament and expectations and the nature of his religious experience.
He concludes that Christianity has generally failed
to meet the active, intellectual demands of the cho-
leric temperament by overstressing the place of feelings in the church.

One of Coe's expressed interests was to see the
religious leaders and educators utilize, wherever
beneficial, the results and methods of his labors.
Coe and Starbuck, in fact, are to be singled out as
the two pioneers whose efforts evidence the greatest
concern that the implications of their work affect in
practical ways the programs of religious and educational systems. Both commit the predominant portion
of their careers to the problems of religious education and character education.

The second major publication on religious
experience, after Starbuck's work, and certainly
the most widely known, and consequently a most influential work in the field was William James' The
Varieties of Religious Experience. (1902) For the
most part James ignores institutional religion,
confining himself to the personal religion of the
individual. James' main concern centered about the

17

conversion experience and religious mysticism. His
approach to the subject was principally biographical,
although some of his analyses were based on the use
of some of the respondents' answers to Starbuck's
questionnaire regarding conversion. Unique to
James, and the basis for a certain amount of criticism of his methodology from some quarters, was
his almost exclusive use of extreme cases. To
get at the heart of religious consciousness, James
believed that individuals for whom religion was an
"acute fever" had best be studied, rather than the
typical individual whose religious life shows no
other signs than to be nothing but a "dull habit."

One of the major, and lasting, contributions of
this work is James' classification of religion into
two fundamental categories, "healthy-mindedness"
and "morbid-mindedness." His description of each
as they apply to individual types contributed to
a growing understanding of the significance of a
particular psychological orientation to the nature
of an individual's religious experience. This
aspect of James' study confirms an important point
made by Coe, that the type of religious experience
an individual espouses is conditioned by factors of
temperament.

Since James incorporates some of Starbuck's
findings, it is natural that he would support Starbuck's interpretation of conversion as a normal
fact of adolescent development. According to James,
conversion is an aspect of the sub-conscious maturing
process in individuals leading towards the unifica-
tion of the self. Religion happens to be one of
the various ways to obtain a degree of unity, and
conversion, whether gradual or sudden, is the form.

While James' investigation, as is true also of
every other major pioneer named, yields no evidence
to support the hypothesis of a supernatural origin
to the religious phenomena studied, James himself
does admit in the end to an "over-belief," that
the world, as man sees, describes, and analyzes it,
is really part of a larger spiritual universe.

18

James' use of bizzare cases in the study of religious experience, his informative analyses, and his appealing style, are reasonable grounds for this book to have received wide reading among psychologists and educators; but this final statement of faith, by as renowned a psychologist as James, furnishes conspicuous cause for its appeal to religious apologists as well.

Within the next ten years, the interests of the investigators expanded beyond the early studies of religious experience to broader considerations of religious growth and life, as well as religious origins. A number of psychologists used the data of anthropology and history, along with the questionnaire, in their pursuit of the psychology of religion. Three in particular, made especially distinct contributions: James Bissett Pratt, Edward Scribner Ames, and James Henry Leuba.

James Pratt's The Psychology of Religious Belief appeared in 1907. As Starbuck, Coe, and James had dealt very little with the area of religious belief, Pratt's book, which focused upon this subject, was an especially valuable resource. Pratt analyzes religious belief in terms of types or stages: primitive, intellectual, and emotional. He concludes that a process involving these stages occurs in all religions. According to Pratt, the myths of primitive credulity in religion are broken by the elevation of reason; yet reason never supplies the sense of certainty that man desires, and consequently he looks to the areas of religion which seem to satisfy his instinctive and emotional needs.

Pratt makes use of the questionnaire to gather data regarding the grounds for religious belief in his day. He discovered that, for the average individual, authority and reason were far less important to the development of beliefs than what he experienced and felt. From this, Pratt proposed that religion predicated primarily on reason and authority would increasingly lose its appeal, and that the religion of the future world would have to take into account the central place of feelings in

19

its life, a position not unlike that of James and Starbuck.

For the earliest and most thorough application of functional psychology to the study of religion, Edward Ames' The Psychology of Religious Experience (1910) must be mentioned. Ames' approach is not only exclusively functional, it is also finally biologically oriented. That is, according to Ames, religious consciousness is to be identified with social consciousness or values, which is in turn, basically, the product of the instinctual needs and desires of food and sex.

Regarding the question of origin, Ames proposes that primitive religion arises as a social expression of the most important interests and concerns of the group. Religious ceremonials and rituals emerge in connection with whatever the group most values as fundamental to its existence and welfare.

Although Ames' adherence to functional psychology stresses the social context, he does examine the development of religion in the individual as well. Ames rejects the notion of any innate religious instinct or faculty. He contends, for instance, that religious genius is a product not of heredity but environment. Religion, then, in Ames' view, is perpetuated by the educational process. For this reason, Ames is interested in the principles which the psychology of religion furnishes religious education.

Ames' description of the conversion experience is fundamentally the same as Starbuck's and James'. He agrees with Starbuck's findings that conversion varies in relation to age, sex, and temperament, and that the conversion experience is primarily a product of the manipulation of normal developmental processes in the individual. Ames also holds, like Starbuck, that although conversion may occur either as a seemingly sudden crisis-oriented event or as a normal process, gradual religious growth, without crisis, is the most desirable.

20

Proceeding from his discussion of religious awakening in the individual, Ames attempts to show the extent to which religious beliefs and doctrinal positions are fashioned wholly by the impact of societal experiences. Ames was criticized rather harshly by some of his contemporaries for his assertion that all religion is social, and because they felt he ignored the nature of personal religious experience. Such criticism, however, appears to be a failure to understand Ames' major point, that even man's individual "experience with God" is directly, or, at least, indirectly, conditioned by the total social context of his life.

Unlike the other two members of this triad, whose analyses failed to detract from their sympathetic stand towards religion, James Leuba represents a position much more critical of religion itself. Leuba, who, with Starbuck, studied under Hall at Clark University, was probably the most explicit reactionary, among the early pioneers, to the products of the pietistic tradition. His treatment of religion from the standpoint of naturalism laid bare his contention that the religious life can be explained exclusively in terms of the fundamental principle of general psychology. Using material from anthropology, sociology, and psychology, and incorporating data from private documents and a questionnaire, Leuba in 1912, completed his classic, A Psychological Study of Religion.

In this work, Leuba defines religion primarily in terms of man's behavior, not his feelings. In religion, says Leuba, man searches for a way of satisfying his needs and desires for a better life. Leuba's consideration of the nature of religion includes a thorough analysis of its relation to magic. He conludes that although magic basically has the same aims as religion, its ways of achieving them are different, and its origin is quite independent of religion.

Perhaps more important, even, than Leuba's own attempts to define religion is his inclusion,

as an appendix, of a list of forty-eight different
definitions of religion and their sources. Leuba
has classified these definitions in light of three
types of approaches to religion--the intellectual-
istic, the affectivistic, and the voluntaristic.
Valuable too, as reflective of Leuba's own perspective, are his critical comments and discussion of
the definitions.

As James had done earlier, though affirming
something quite opposite to Leuba's stance, Leuba
ignores, at points, the limited prerogatives of the
scientific method in psychology, and includes bold
ontological statements as a part of his study.
Unlike James who affirmed the reality of a higher
power in life, Leuba firmly declares there is no
objective transcendent agent or source connected
with man's religious experience. And, in looking
to the future of religion, Leuba confidently avows
that the confession of a personal God will, in
time, disintegrate. Nevertheless, in spite of his
biases, Leuba added significantly to the enlarging
scope of religious psychology and provided a unique
and interesting commentary.

Two final works from the classical period must
be cited, George Coe's The Psychology of Religion
(1916), and James Pratt's The Religious Consciousness (1920). They stand as the prominent forerunners among surveys of the entire field. They are
written toward the close of the most significant pioneering, as well as productive, years in the application of psychology to religion.

Coe's book was the earliest attempt to deal
as comprehensively as he did with the problems and
results of the growing field. Like Ames, Coe deals
with religion from the standpoint of functional
psychology, but Coe differs from Ames by refusing
to interpret the data from a purely biological
framework. Coe rejects the act of reducing the
complexity of religion to a simple element or
mechanism. The person, for whom religion is functional, must be studied. This means, according to

Coe, that the psychological study of religion is fundamentally the examination of individuals who are constantly adjusting to their social environment and its values. Religion, then, is defined by Coe as the process of uncovering and structuring, for the sake of unity, life's values.

Every subject which Coe handles in this survey is explicated in terms of his view of religion as natural psychological phenomena. He affirms no innate religious instinct, although he does acknowledge that man appears to be naturally religious, that is, that he normally orders his life around what he considers to be ultimate values. Coe approaches religious consciousness as a form of social consciousness. He contends that ideas about God, for instance, are always related to one's conception of and experience with persons in society. And such a topic as mysticism is explained by Coe as rooted completely in the mystic's background and experience.

Though, as was true also of most of the other pioneers mentioned, Coe dispelled the notion of an extra-human reality as the basis of religious experience, his thorough examination of the phenomena called religious was especially valuable. His investigation was broad, balanced, and critically objective.

The most exhaustive survey of the psychology of religion up to 1920 was Pratt's The Religious Consciousness. The product of twelve years of research, it included every significant aspect of the religious life, although it dealt almost exclusively with highly developed forms of religion. A distinctive feature was Pratt's use of data from Eastern as well as Western religion.

Probably no other pioneering psychologist of religion treated any more fairly and benignly the various phases of such study. He subjected the data to critical analysis, but always for the sake of understanding more clearly the religious perspective of the subjects being studied.

Pratt mediated the extreme positions in the field. He believed, with the majority of other pioneers, for instance, that the phenomena of conversion and mysticism must be viewed in light of the laws of psychology, and that psychology cannot be used to supply conclusive evidence for transcendent reality. However, at the same time, he refused to reduce religion to the subjective response of the individual alone, suggesting there is something to which the response is made. In other words, Pratt does concede an objective as well as subjective content to religious consciousness. Furthermore, in contrast to those who stressed one source to the exclusion of the other, Pratt declares religion to be the consequence of both individual and social factors, and seeks to examine thoroughly the expression of religion in each area. Finally, in conjunction with the first point, Pratt distinguishes between the objective and subjective elements in the religious life. In his study of worship Pratt examines carefully the differences between worship which seeks to affect the ultimate reality upon which man depends, and worship which has as its main concern, the impact upon the worshipper himself. In every case Pratt sought to describe clearly and objectively the natural elements of religious phenomena, but always with an awareness of the limitations of science in attempting to explain the source of man's ultimate concerns.

These works in the psychology of religion represent broadly the direction taken in the pioneering period. Their results firmly establish the importance of a principled approach to the phenomena of religion.

Development of the Field

Having viewed some of the major resources which introduce us to the literature of the field, we shall consider now the third phase of the chapter, the actual growth of the psychology of religion, and Starbuck's place in its development. Initially, it is important to establish some type of boundary for the field, which will delimit the course of our

investigation. For our purposes, the general boundaries for the discussion of the psychology of religion have to do with time and content. First, we
will consider the 1880's as the starting point for
the field under investigation and will be interested
primarily in the field's development during Starbuck's contributing years, although some reference
will be made to the contemporary situation. Second,
our interest in the field generally will center
around the psychological study of religion as classically conceived by Starbuck and the other early
pioneers, as compared with the therapeutic thrust
that later emerged.

A study of the growth of any particular field
cannot ignore the concurrent events and ideologies
of the day, which in varying ways help to shape its
development. The psychology of religion, as a field,
emerged during a troublesome but exciting period in
American history. Two world wars and a depression
were experienced, but in the midst of such trying
events and periodic disillusionment there grew an
ever stronger determination to create a better
future. Programs, many not unrelated to the psychology of religion, were developed to achieve this
end.

Probably, two of the most pervasive influences
upon religion, and consequently upon the psychology
of religion, were evolutionism and pragmatism. In
spite of the fervid attacks on Darwinism, many
religionists, specifically the educated, were vul-
nerable to the new evolutionary ideas. By the close
of the nineteenth century, a majority of the educated Americans had either abandoned totally their
belief in Genesis or had at least de-literal-ized
the story of God's special creation, so as to
allow for some kind of reconciliation with evolutionary theory. John Fiske, for example, an influential teacher of Starbuck, chose the latter
approach. Darwin's work was replete with evidence
that made the rejection of biological evolution
extremely difficult. Darwin's theories demanded
reconsideration of the development of history and

25

mankind. No longer could men unquestioningly accept
an instant creation fashioned by the whimsical edicts
of God; they were now faced with evidence pointing
clearly to a lawful process in the development of
the world and its race. All of this helped pave the
way for a scientific or lawful approach to the study
of religion and to the eventual emergence of the
psychology of religion.

Pragmatism also rooted itself in America near
the turn of the century. It was the predominating
philosophical approach until World War I. This mode
of thought was undoubtedly instrumental in shaping
the direction of the psychology of religion toward
practical ends. Sometimes called empiricism or
instrumentalism, pragmatism is viewed by one source
in the following manner:

> ". . .Believers in pragmatism
> . . . rejected the view of the
> universe as a fixed, final, and
> static Newtonian machine; rather,
> they saw a dynamic world, always
> changing, always growing. They
> refused to accept a theory of
> knowledge rooted in God-implanted
> and innate ideas, substituting
> instead the conviction that know-
> ledge came from experience and
> observation. They insisted that
> there were no external and absolute
> ethical principles but that good
> and bad were relative to time, place,
> and circumstance."21

William James, the so-called "high priest" of pragmatism in America, for example, warred against the
concept of absolutes. He objected particularly to
the idea of approaching absolute truth as something
that was "out there," which had nothing to do with
the perceiver of truth. Rather, James spoke of truth
in terms of the relationship which existed between
the known and the knower. As one of James' students,
Starbuck took a similar approach which had its

26

effects upon his work as will be seen especially in religious education and character education.

The pragmatist emphasized the need for experimentation, for he favored the inductive over the deductive method. His reasoning was a posteriori, rather than a priori. Perhaps this emphasis, more than anything, influenced the thought and work of the early pioneers in the psychology of religion. Experimentation or the scientific study of religion, was certainly a key-note in Starbuck's approach to the field from the very beginning.

Another of the great pragmatists in America during this early period in the twentieth century was John Dewey, whose influence on the educational system can hardly be measured adequately. The effect of his progressive ideas with regard to education made its mark upon the early pioneers in the psychology of religion. In particular, were his ideas incorporated into the research and practical applications in the field of religious education and character education. Starbuck, for example, respected highly the work of Dewey, and many of Starbuck's major concerns about the public schools were not unlike those of John Dewey. One author has assessed Dewey's approach to education as follows:

> "According to Dewey
> education should deal only with
> problems which involve practical
> differences; teaching should be
> adjusted to the natural rhythms
> of the child; learning must exist
> as an active process rather than
> a passive absorption of infor-
> mation; and above all children
> should learn to attack social
> problems cooperatively."[22]

As we shall see later, Starbuck's efforts in character education were fashioned around such principles.

Very few institutions in America were not

27

directly affected by pragmatism. The most radical
changes, as a result of its influence, occurred in
the field of education, but religion was also shaken
by its impact, which in turn affected the direction
of the psychology of religion. The church began to
focus in on "this-worldly" rather than "other-worldly"
concerns. The major task of many in at least the
more liberal religious bodies became not so much the
saving of souls as the educating and healing of minds
and bodies. The effects upon the religious education
curricula were great. And the "social gospel" movement in the early decades of the century demonstrated
a change in religious outlook, from piety to a practical concern for applying Christian principles to
the problems of the world.

With the outbreak of World War I many people
became disillusioned. Their optimistic idealism
had been unexpectedly crushed by a war which they
had thought was inconceivable. A waning of the influence of pragmatism was inevitable under these circumstances, but its influence was not stamped out
completely by any means. There were those who were
only challenged by such catastrophes, whose hopes,
though dimmed for awhile, yet remained to guide them
in constructive efforts toward rebuilding a better
future. Starbuck was such an individual.

While at the University of Iowa in 1918, even
before the war had ended, he chaired a committee on
"Practical Christianity and Reconstruction after the
War," which sought to discover ways that the university could be a center for "awakening intelligent
insight and forceful action" related to the war and
the consequent problems being faced. The committee
decided to establish study groups to discuss the
issues, stating:

> "We are convinced that each
> member of the faculty and student
> body should enter upon a vigorous
> program of self-education in
> world citizenship with a view to
> the discovering of the particular

28

part he can play in deciding
now the fate of democracy."[23]

Such a move was typical of Starbuck's hopeful temper,
and of the pragmatist's view of man as the determiner
of his destiny, and thus responsible for establishing the goals of society and directing it toward
those ends.

One of the best interpretative surveys of the
background for religious growth in the twentieth
century, during the rise of the psychology of religion,
is Herbert W. Schneider's Religion in 20th Century
America.[24] Schneider analyzes the religious life
during this period in terms of three fundamental
reconstructions in religion: Institutional, moral,
and intellectual. A brief consideration of Schneider's
analyses should be helpful to a clearer understanding
and appreciation of the background for the development of the psychology of religion.

Institutional reconstruction, speaking specifically about religious education, affected greatly
the interests of the psychology of religion. Around
the turn of the century, Sunday schools were basically "bible schools"; that is, the curriculum was
almost wholly Bible-centered. Within the first
twenty-five years of the century, however, a fundamental change occurred among most of the major
denominations in their programs of religious education, and this change was not unrelated to the
work taking place in the field of the psychology of
religion. "Graded," comprehensive curricula were
developed, which expanded their objectives to a
consideration of more than Bible stories alone.
Lessons were prepared to deal with church history
and theology, and most important, moral issues and
social problems were introduced. An attempt to
apply many of the principles and methods of secular
education and psychology to the religious studies
was made. Starbuck and Coe were two leading
figures in the psychology of religion who promoted
this approach.

Interdenominational moves also occurred for the purpose of developing better programs of religious education. In 1903 the Religious Education Association was organized. Starbuck, it should be noted, was a charter member of this organization, and was asked to give a major address at its first annual convention in Chicago called by some two-hundred prominent religious and educational leaders in the country. Its influence was felt widely by Protestants, Catholics, and Jews alike; and since 1906 the association has published the Religious Education journal, the only periodical to deal comprehensively and ecumenically with the main problems of religion and education.

The results of the early work of the pioneers in the psychology of religion, especially with regard to conversion and the general lines of religious growth, substantiated the new approach of gradual religious nurture in the curriculum. Starbuck's volume in 1899 was one of the first and leading studies, with results which applied as such to the problem. Also significant, was the fact that during this period Starbuck was intensely involved for two years in the development of a new religious education curriculum for the Unitarian Association, applying there the results of his research in the psychology of religion.

Schneider notes a slight decline during the second quarter of the century in the programs of religious education, suggesting that it was natural for the initial enthusiasm to become somewhat relaxed. A factor to be considered also was the depression of the 1930's which depleted the funding for such programs. Schneider makes a final point about the situation which is related to the interests of character education as well, interest with which Starbuck in particular was associated. Analyzing the situation in the second quarter of the century Schneider concluded:

"The more religion was
related to 'life,' the less

vitality remained in the
distinctive institutions
of religion, and the problem
of religious education was
transferred from the Sunday
Schools to schools in general.
Religion was to be 'studied'
as a normal element in the
subject-matter of general
education. Thus knowledge
about religion threatened
to displace religious training,
and the ecclesiastical in-
centives for liberalized
religious instruction on
which the Sunday School
movement depended, were
secularized by the very
progress made in religious
liberalism."25

Schneider's consideration of moral reconstruction
is also related to the development of the psychology
of religion in America. Around 1900 the predominant
approach to moral training, still taken by religious
bodies in general, was the cooperative endeavor of
the church and the home in rather directly shaping
the child's "knowledge of good and evil." The
experiences in the church and the home were planned to foster this "religious conscience" in
children, which most generally took the form of
some type of conversion experience.

Early in the century, however, as a result of
the studies in the psychology of religion on adolescence, and the consequent interest of religious
educators in this period, a shift in the target
for moral education occurred from childhood to youth
and adulthood. The traditional process of religious
discipline, in time, was replaced, at least among
the more liberal religious bodies, with "religious
education," which was designed to promote religious
nurture on a gradual normal growth basis. The
questions of morality were no longer dealt with

31

predominantly in the context of conversion, but rather in the setting of life after conversion. Such a shift in emphasis appears to have reconciled some of the aims and methods of religious and secular education. Schneider describes the situation as follows:

> "Thus there arose during the twentieth century among religious bodies special organizations of adults to meet special moral and social problems, and those organizations, though they approached problems from the point of view of a religious conscience, cooperated increasingly in methods and contents with secular philanthropic organizations . . . Theoretically . . . the churches can be both traditional and modern, and in practice, too, traditional religious disciplining of children and youth goes on, and conversions are not unheard of, but the characteristic efforts and current aims of organized religion are now closer to secular education and mundane affairs."[26]

It is quite clear, for instance, that Starbuck's interests in character education are not to be viewed as irreligious. Rather, he believed that the aims and methods of religious education should not be foreign to those of character education in the secular context.

Finally, Schneider discusses the intellectual reconstruction which we contend is related not only to the general development of the psychology of religion, but which helps to establish an atmosphere favorable to its emergence as well. Although modernism was perhaps professed by a relatively small percentage of American Christians at the early

part of the present century, its influence was beginning to be rather deeply felt. In the latter
part of the nineteenth century, among liberal
theologians of New England, a so-called "New Theology" arose. Schneider comments:

> "Religion was viewed from
> the perspective of seeing all of
> life as divine. Against the dicho-
> tomized view of certain things being
> done according to natural laws and
> other things happening by Divine in-
> tervention, 'New Theology' saw God's
> actions in terms of continuous, pro-
> gressive change, and according to
> certain laws.[27]

Although such a pioneer as James Leuba was negative
to religion, that is, he considered it a creation
of the mind to assign God as the agent of religious
experience, most of the pioneers in the psychology
of religion, including Starbuck, were attuned to
the stance of "New Theology," and proceeded along
this line in their studies.

This "new theology," or modernism, in the early
decades of this century, began to express itself in
more universal terms than Christian theology had
heretofore allowed. In light of the growing interest
in religions of the world, the willingness to view
Christianity as one religion among others became more
prevalent.

> "It /new theology/ had become,
> as it was later called in retrospect,
> a 'new orthodoxy,' or a 'new dogma-
> tism,' whose chief aim was to rise
> above all theologies, creeds, and
> cults to a universal faith grounded
> in universal evolution."[28]

Studies in the psychology of religion, in the first
decade or so, were made by men who adhered to such a
doctrine. Their main interest in the study of religion centered not in consideration of a particular

33

faith, but rather in the universal religious consciousness.

Schneider suggests that just as 1900-1915 was basically dominated intellectually by modernism, so liberalism prevailed during the period 1915-1930. Foundational to liberalism in America was the developing thought of the German, Albrecht Ritschl. Schneider describes his approach in these terms:

> "Ritschl looked for religious truth neither in natural science nor in pious sentiment, but in the 'Christian consciousness,' that is, in the successive and cumulative revelations of God in the experience of the church or community in its historic development . . . In this process God is revealed and divine judgment takes place, but the revelation is not of God's essence (which transcends human knowledge) but of God's value or meaning in history . . ."29

A number of liberals, however, many in the psychology of religion, skirted the exacting process of historical investigation, and sought to study religious experience, or "Christian consciousness" on an individualistic basis. Theirs was more the investigation of the results of such experience without regard for necessarily determining the source. The union of these two elements of liberalism was described by Schneider as follows:

> "This American version of Christian experience with its openly pragamatic appeal to "fruits," when coupled with the imported Ritschlian appeal to the historical experience of the Christian churches, provided a perfect foundation for liberal theology. The pragmatic empiricism gave it a forward-looking perspective, the historical empiricism

34

a background of tradition;
combined, the two furnished
both scientific method and
religious authority."30

During this same period liberalism also fostered
religious social action, labelled in time the
"social gospel." Probably its greatest, and certainly its most popular exponent, was Walter
Rauschenbusch, whose volume A Theology for the
Social Gospel, published in 1917, spelled out the
theological groundwork for the movement. It is
safe to assume that the direction of religious
education and character education was influenced by
it. Schneider states:

> "During the twenties
> such Christian liberalism
> had its heyday. With a few
> exceptions the leaders of
> theological and of social
> reform within the churches
> combined forces and by organized
> cooperation gave an amazing
> momentum to the movements
> for institutional and moral
> reconstruction . . ."31

The attack of fundamentalism and the response
of neo-orthodoxy to liberalism does not appear to
have significantly affected the course of the psychology of religion.

The growth of the psychology of religion has
been traced and interpreted by competent scholars.
Not only have numerous historical surveys been
written, but several major developmental schemes
have been forwarded as well.32 Against such a
background, we intend only briefly to highlight
some of the primary concerns and stages of the
movement, particularly in the early decades of its
development, and especially as they relate to
Starbuck's contributions.

The study of religious experience, especially conversion, was a dominant interest in the decade prior to the turn of the century. During this period, several articles on the subject were published, all by G. Stanley Hall's graduate students at Clark University. The Clark school produced a majority of the early pioneers in the field, among whom Starbuck was prominent. Many of Hall's students produced works which have stood as classics in the psychological study of religion. Kemp, for instance, in highlighting the first decade of the pioneering period, cites Starbuck's work. He states:

> "The first important
> volume which appeared was
> The Psychology of Religion
> by E. D. Starbuck. It appeared
> in 1899, the year that Dwight L.
> Moody died, and, in a sense,
> marks the transition point from
> the period of revivalism to a more
> psychological interpretation of
> religion."[33]

Starbuck's volume was held in high esteem, as it introduced a methodology and an area for study which was especially productive in the field. His classic was representative of the pioneering efforts to study religious phenomena empirically, and to encourage further the scientific investigation of religious experience.

Starbuck's work was typical of the early efforts during the first decade of the twentieth century. One of the main interests lay in religious experience and growth in individuals. The study of religious belief and mysticism was of special interest, with James Pratt being specifically associated with the former, and Pratt, Leuba, and James with the latter. William James' classic in 1902, Varieties of Religious Experience, stimulated greatly the psychological interest in religion. Borrowing some of Starbuck's cases, as well as examining many others, he analyzed a significant

36

variety of forms of religious experience. As popular a psychologist as James was, it might safely be contended that his contribution to the field offered an important impetus for the acceptance of and continuous work in the psychology of religion.

It is also clear in this first decade that many of the pioneers in the psychology of religion were interested in the implications of their research for education. George A. Coe is probably best known for his work in the psychology of religion as it applies to religious education, but certainly the efforts, expecially of E. S. Ames and Starbuck, are also important in this connection.

As a means of dealing with the origins of religion in society, anthropological investigations were made, a second major concern during the first decade following that of conversion. A treatment of preliterate religious forms was attempted by such studies, aiming toward a better understanding of the genesis of religion.

A final note of importance about the development of the first decade was the founding of the Journal of Religious Psychology, edited by G. S. Hall, first published in 1904. This unique periodical, dedicated completely to the psychological study of religion, lasted through the first decade but ceased to exist at the middle of the second, in 1915. It might be said that the life of the journal, in general, paralleled the life of the most important pioneering work in the psychology of religion, although a few works on both sides of this period were extremely important and would be considered significant to the pioneering efforts.

The second decade did not differ significantly from the first in terms of general interests and problems pursued. Not until this decade, however, was the relationship of psychoanalysis to the psychology of religion really noticed. Sigmund Freud had been invited in 1909, to lecture in America. As a result, American scholars were introduced to

Freud, and literature began to be produced related
to his theory and the psychological study of religion.
Furthermore, Freud himself, became interested in
the application of his theory to the study and
interpretation of religion, as his volume in 1913
confirms.[34] Since then the relationship of psychoanalysis and religion has been studied from a
multitude of perspectives.

The second decade was marked, if in any way it
can be, by an attempt to bring some systematization
to the work that had been done in the field. Coe's
The Psychology of Religion and Pratt's The Religious
Consciousness are outstanding examples of this
attempt to deal systematically with the expanding
subject matter.

By the third decade, the pioneering thrust and
traditional form of the psychology of religion as
a scientific movement had generally dissipated.
It has been suggested, for example, by Hiltner,
that much of the work done in the 1920's was nothing
more than an imitation of the efforts of such pioneers
as James, Starbuck, Pratt, Leuba, Ames and Coe.[35]
The subjects considered and the treatment given to
them were so often lacking in any original research
or insight. While it does not appear unfair to
lable many of the contributors to the field after
the early pioneers as imitators, their work should
not be dismissed as unimportant. In fact, Strunk
suggests that their efforts were extremely important
as they affected greatly the nature and direction
of the psychology of religion in terms of its development toward the means of application.[36]

It appears evident that there was no clear
separation between theory and application, or
between the psychology of religion as a scientific
movement and the practical application of its laws.
No period of application can be screened totally
from the pioneering period, for the pioneers,
genrally, were also practitioners. Starbuck, for
instance, is, from the beginning, interested not
only in the data of the psychology of religion, but

its implications as well for the field of religious
education and pastoral psychology. These practically-
oriented movements served to capture not only the
attention, but also the vocational investments of
many religious psychologists. George A. Coe's move
into religious education is probably one of the
best examples of this occuring. Starbuck's move
into religious education, and then into character
education, also illustrates the point.

Hiltner discerningly notes that not one of the
pioneers in the study of the psychology of religion
approached the field as his major interest. They
were, or became philosophers, religious educators,
or general psychologists. A scan of the responsibilities of the pioneers in the field reveals the
impossiblity of any educational institution allowing
a man to devote full-time to this area. A prime
example of this fact is seen in Starbuck's situation.
Starbuck joined the faculty at the University of
Iowa as a professor of philosophy. He was allowed
to teach a course in the psychology of religion,
but his major work in the field had to be done
in the context of his Institute for Character
Research. This meant that his major efforts in
the psychology of religion had to be performed
outside the realm of the duties for which he was
hired at the university. Such a situation illustrates
the difficulty the psychology of religion had in
developing as a proper field of study. It is
likely, also, that under the pressure of their
discipline's attempt to gain scientific respectability, many psychologists who were particularly
interested in religion felt the need to be cautious
about the extent of their attention to the field.

Such analysis, as presented, reveals the nature
of the problems the psychology of religion has faced
during this century. In one sense, it might be
appropriate to speak of its present status in
terms of extinction. That is, as a field of
scientific inquiry and productive research, it has
not been able to maintain its original impetus as
witnessed in the early pioneers in the field. On

the other hand, one might speak of the development of the psychology of religion in terms of its giving birth to related areas, such as religious education and pastoral psychology, whose practical orientation has served very useful ends. It is true, however, that if the psychology of religion desires to reestablish itself as a legitimate scientific discipline, it will have to continue to renew its efforts to conduct non-apologetic, objective studies in the field. Only then might it regain the prestige it acquired in the early years of this century.

Starbuck's Place in the Field

While in the general discussion of the field, we have attempted whenever appropriate, to refer to appraisals of Starbuck's contribution, it seems fitting to conclude this chapter by more specifically interpreting Starbuck's place in the field. As was suggested earlier in the chapter, our consideration of his contribution to the field includes not only his work in the psychology of religion, per se, as pursued in the pioneering period, but also his work in religious and character education. Our discussion of Starbuck's place in the field consequently will involve an overview of the place of his endeavors in these three areas.

A breakdown of Starbuck's involvement in these areas is not easily charted. In fact a clean-cut pattern fails to emerge, although it is possible to refer to general emphases at certain times in his career. Therefore we shall refer to his work, first of all, in the psychology of religion, as traditionally conceived, secondly, in religious education, and thirdly, in character education. And finally, it should be remembered that our intention at this point is to deal broadly with his status in the field, not to survey in detail his contributions, as shall be done later in the study.

Without exception, every major survey or history of the psychology of religion includes Starbuck's name among the pioneers in the field as it developed around the turn of the century in America. Starbuck is cited specifically for his classical work on conversion, published in 1899, The Psychology of Religion. Starbuck gained an attentive audience both in America and Europe with the publication of this volume. Not only did the actual publication of this book have its impact upon the field, but the marks of its preparation were also impressive. Starbuck undertook his empirical studies on this topic in 1893 while a student in graduate school at Harvard. Working under William James at the time, Starbuck did not at first receive approval of his efforts. But as Starbuck pursued his study and results began to come in, James shifted his opinion of Starbuck's research and even wrote the introduction to Starbuck's book. It has been conjectured, and it appears to be a valid suggestion, that James probably would not have written his classical and most popular study, Varieties of Religious Experience, in 1902, without the stimulation of Starbuck's efforts. We might venture to say, too, that the positive response to Starbuck's work appears to have been significantly encouraging to a number of other individuals who also pioneered in the psychological investigation of religion within the first decade or so after his initial book.

Although it is evident that Starbuck was not the first to use the questionnaire method, sometimes called the "question circular," it does appear that Starbuck's use of this newly invented methodology was a pioneering move as he specifically applied it to psychologically approaching the interpretation of religious phenomena. While James Leuba's dissertation, using this methodology, was the first psychologically scientific article published on religious experience, Starbuck's studies had actually begun earlier. Leuba's article entitled "Studies in the Psychology of Religious Phenomena - Conversion," was printed in the American Journal of Psychology in 1896, and Starbuck's two articles, which were the foundation for his 1899 volume were not published until 1897 in the same journal, but Starbuck had initiated his study at Harvard before Leuba began his investigation at Clark University.

41

In his search for data regarding religious experience, Starbuck turned to living subjects. From them, direct information could be obtained through the use of prepared questions. The answers to the questionnaires were then analyzed for the sake of finding significant differences and similarities and developing generalizations.

American pioneers in the psychology of religion quickly secured this method as a technique for approaching the field of religion scientifically. For a time it became the most popular method used in obtaining data for the psychological study of religion. As late as 1926, Edward L. Schaub had this to say about the impact of the questionnaire method: "Abroad, the psychology of religion in America is even yet associated primarily with the use of the questionnaire and of biographical materials."37 He credits Starbuck with the former.

Starbuck had used the questionnaire to gather data which could be scientifically analyzed by the methods of classification and interpretation. The phenomenon of conversion rendered rather easily a descriptive account of its elements. As a result, the first study by Starbuck turned out to be a successful enterprise.

The limitations of this method, however, soon became apparent; and it came to be rather severely criticized in terms of scientific respectability. That Starbuck was aware of the shortcomings of the questionnaire method is clear; however, he was unwilling, because of its limitations, to reject it as unscientific. Writing about the variety of methods employed by the psychology of religion, Starbuck said of the questionnaire:

> "That the questionnaire
> method is faulty, all will admit. It should be said of it,
> however, that there are certain
> kinds of data that it alone can
> reach . . . In dealing with personal confessions . . . one is

42

handling firsthand material
which can be verified by conversation and correspondence."[38]

That Starbuck did not unrealistically idolize this
methodology, although he still upheld its validity,
is indicated elsewhere. He stated:

"This desire to construct
a mosaic of personal growth out
of the pieces taken from many
lives has been the subject of
most trenchant and deserved
criticism. Uren /Recent Religious Psychology, Charles Scribner's Sons: New York, 1929/
decries it and remarks that a
psychology of religion reared on
such fragmentary data is not
scientific. Still, is not every
generalization, every concept,
every fact, even in the "exact"
sciences, a storm center of mani-
fold constructs?"[39]

Clark University, where Starbuck received his
Ph.D., is commonly associated with the beginnings of
religious psychology. In fact, according to James
Pratt, the Clark school contributed nearly half of
the work of any worth in the first decade of this
century.[40] G. Stanley Hall, the first President of
Clark University, and also Professor of Psychology,
naturally must be credited as a central figure influential in the development of religious psychology at
Clark. His educational background had included philosophy, theology, physiology, and physics, and he was
the first person in the United States to receive a
Ph.D. in psychology. While at Clark, it is estimated
that Hall taught a majority of the first generation
of the psychologists trained in America. By 1893,
eleven out of fourteen, and by 1898, thirty out of
the fifty-four Ph.D.'s awarded in psychology were
granted to Hall's students.[41] His interest in religion and his guidance of so many of his students in

research along the lines of the psychological study
of religion make him an important figure in the
development of the field.

While the significance of Hall's contribution
need not be questioned, a strong case for the central
importance of Starbuck's influence should be acknowledged. Hall's work in the latter part of the century had centered around the phenomena of adolescence.
The researches being conducted under him were largely
confined to adolescence and its pedagogical implications. Starbuck's research, however, introduced
a specific interest in the study of religion as it
pertained to adolescence. Thus, as much as Starbuck
was assisted and supported by Hall in his research,
so should it be realized that Starbuck stimulated
Hall and the students at Clark in the direction of
studies in the psychology of religion. This thesis,
which renders Starbuck's role in the Clark school of
religious psychology as fundamental to the school's
contribution in the field, is supported by Karl R.
Stolz, who states:

> "The work of Starbuck
> definitely began a new epoch in
> the history of the study of re-
> ligious experience. He trans-
> ferred his researches to Clark
> University, where his method
> and its results aroused so much
> active interest that within a
> short time a number of fellow-
> graduate students, to say noth-
> ing of President G. Stanley Hall,
> were engaged in the psychologi-
> cal investigation of religious
> experience."42

It is significant, too, that from Clark University came the first journal devoted rather exclusively
to the study of the psychology of religion, the American Journal of Religious Psychology and Education,
first published in 1904. Although this periodical
was founded and edited by Hall, again Starbuck's
place in this development must also be acknowledged.

Starbuck, along with other pioneers such as Coe and Leuba, assisted Hall in this endeavor.

As early as 1897 Starbuck pioneered in offering a college course in the psychology of religion. By 1913 over fifty colleges and universities were offering courses in the psychology of religion, and eighty institutions were conducting courses in the pedagogy of religion, which drew its content from the psychology of religion. A sad commentary, however, was the fact that few institutions were instigating research in the subject. Starbuck's assessment of what had happened to the field by 1913 is especially revealing. He proposes in his own unique style:

> "Although the Psychology of Religion, like the other children of the Science of Religion, has had a healthy birth and babyhood, its defects are many: it has reached the talkative stage, when its ability to discourse is far in excess of its wisdom; it has fits of vanity during which it makes false claims for its achievements; it is over-self-conscious and looks inward too much upon itself and its methods instead of outward upon a great world that wants conquering; it likes the easy lines of self-expression that lead to superficiality in preference to the saving virtue of exacting labor; it sponges too much upon its older cousins--History, Archaeology, Philosophy--instead of working out its own salvation."[43]

Still, Starbuck was hopeful that the psychology of religion would fulfill its potential to develop into a respectable member of the sciences. His warning about the lack of valid research in the field, however, generally went unheeded.

During the spanning years of his career, Starbuck witnessed what he described as the "Scientific
Psychology of Religion on a Tobaggan." The first
decade and a half of the twentieth century had
experienced the creative spirit of psychological
research in the study of religion. But something
changed this temper. Although articles and books
on the psychology of religion were being published
in large numbers, most of them revealed few signs
of new or serious research in their investigations.
Writing in 1937, Starbuck contended that "genuine
research subsided and creativity flattended out,"
although he does consider there were exceptions.
Starbuck, himself, always encouraged his students
to use objective methods, and to reveal in the findings statistical evidence of their work.[44]

Starbuck discusses two incidences, in particular,
which vividly portray the decline of productivity
in the psychology of religion as an academic discipline. The first incident centered around preparations being made for the Seventh International
Philosophical Congress, which was to be held at
Oxford, England, in 1929. At the Sixth International
Congress at Harvard, Starbuck's paper had been the
only one delivered which based its findings on solid
data. Starbuck's presentation was based upon a
study by one of his graduate students at the University of Iowa, Robert Sinclair. It compared 300
"tough-minded" religiously with 300 "tender-minded."
This report, having been well received, prompted a
proposal that at Oxford two years later, a series
of sessions be devoted to empirical studies of
religion. But when the time came, not one student
proposed a report. The second occasion was the
second World's Fair in Chicago. This Century of
Progress Exposition, commemorating the 100th
anniversary of the city's founding, had been planned
for 1933, and held over to 1934. Starbuck received
a request from Dr. Beth of Vienna, editor of
Religious Psychologie, to invite American students
to join Europeans in a Congress of the Psychology
of Religion to be held in connection with the Fair.
Starbuck contacted all those in the United States
who had contributed significantly to the field,

46

asking, from them or their students, for an original research. Other than a few by Starbuck's own students, not another research was ready for presentation.[45]

Although Starbuck's name was prominently associated with the pioneering work in the psychology of religion proper, a large portion of his years were devoted to the related areas of religious education and character education. From the very beginning, Starbuck's interests in the study of religion were conditioned by his concerns about the educational implications. He concluded his volume, The Psychology of Religion, for instance, with a chapter on educational inferences, making very clear the value of the psychological study of religion to religious education.

As a charter member and officer in the Religious Education Association, founded in 1903, Starbuck's influential voice was heard. Perhaps of all the early psychologists of religion, the contributions of Coe and Starbuck to the association and the general movement of religious education were the most notable.

In addition to his numerous articles on the subject of religious education, Starbuck was involved in various ways, often in pioneering endeavors, investigating the relationship of religion and education. The following references are illustrative of his place in the field. In the Conference of Church Workers in State Universities, initially formed in 1908, and designed to examine the implications for religion of current trends in psychology and the sciences, Starbuck was numbered among an array of distinguished personnel who were asked to present a paper and assist in the discussions of this inaugural conference.[46] In 1911, Starbuck was appointed, along with four other members to a commission charged with the responsibility of investigating the preparation of religious leaders in universities and colleges. Their work was centered about the examination of four major questions: (1) What should be undertaken, if anything in this area? (2) What is presently being done along this line? (3) How would this work fit

into the present programs of higher institutions?
(4) What would constitute the course of subjects or
studies? Answers to questionnaires sent out to over
200 presidents of higher institutions were examined
for any significant trends. The prevailing senti-
ment among educators turned out to be very favorable
toward the development of these interests in higher
institutions of education. The committee commended
the plan of the affiliated theological seminary, but
considered that universities of all types, including
those which were state supported, might well undertake such a program and develop a curriculum for the
preparation of religious workers, excepting possibly
ministers. Finally, university graduate departments
were encouraged to creatively develop the scientific
and philosophical aspects of the field.[47] Significantly, Starbuck's work on this committee undoubtedly may be linked with his later concerns about the
study of religion and the development of a School of
Religion at the University of Iowa. A third example
of Starbuck's involvement in the problems of religious education is revealed in a somewhat obscure
but important editorial which Starbuck and Arthur E.
Holt, of the University of Chicago, prepared in 1928.
Its title, "Theological Seminaries and Research,"
had been discussed by the Research Committee of the
Religious Education Association, and it was considered important enough to request Starbuck and Holt,
members of the Committee, to study the matter and
report by way of an editorial. They recommended
that research was a vital need in theological institutions and that funds should be set aside to foster
more serious efforts in this direction.[48] These incidents have been cited as only examples of Starbuck's involvement in something other than the traditional or ordinary work of religious education.

Starbuck's contribution to religious education,
however, was not limited to this type of participation alone. Between 1912 and 1914, Starbuck was
intimately involved in the development of a new
religious education curriculum for the Unitarian
Association. On leave of absence from the University
of Iowa, Starbuck accepted the invitation to serve as
a consulting psychologist. The curriculum revision

was a pioneering effort in a series of curriculum revisions being attempted, also, by several other denominations at this time. Starbuck was the coordinator of these efforts for the Unitarian Association. Their curriculum was to be among the first of the graded curriculums, developed in terms of age levels. And Starbuck directed the work along the lines of a child-centered approach, as compared to the more traditional content or doctrinal orientation. This philosophy, which centered its interests in life situations more than doctrinal principles, was relatively new to the field of religious education, and Starbuck was busily engaged in the task of adapting this philosophy to the concrete development of a curriculum. Although the outcome was not completely successful, again, Starbuck's pioneering style is witnessed, and this time in the work of religious education.

It cannot be denied that common elements of educational theory and practice among various religious denominations have been fostered by such studies in the psychology of religion as Starbuck's. While not all religious groups accepted the common elements, others gladly received this discovery and worked toward the development of religious quality in individuals on the basis of the principles derived from the work of the psychology of religion. Starbuck led in the cultivation of this latter conceptualization and methodology.

Finally, Starbuck is to be closely associated with the movement of character education in the United States. His inquiry into the psychology and pedagogy of character, however, should not be separated entirely from his interest in such studies of religion. As an example, the work for which he is probably best known was conducted in connection with his Institute for Character Research. This Institute, however, was first established in 1922 as the Research Station in Character Education and Religious Education /my italics/.

As early as 1907, Starbuck had made something of a name for himself in the field of character educa-

49

tion. He had entered a national contest for the
best essay on "Moral Training in the Public Schools,"
and although he came in third, his essay, along with
four others, was published in a book by the same
title as the essay topic. A prize of five hundred
dollars for first-place and three hundred dollars
for second-place was offered by an anonymous citizen of California. The offer was widely published
in journals and newspapers throughout the country,
and as a result over three hundred essays were submitted. The judges, selected by the donor, were
Dr. David Starr Jordan, President of Stanford University, Rev. Charles R. Brown of Oakland, California, and Professor Fletcher B. Dresslar of the University of California's Department of Education.
Mr. Charles Edward Rugh, Principal of the Bay School,
Oakland, California, received the first prize, and
the second prize went to Rev. T. P. Stevenson of
Philadelphia. Starbuck's essay stood next in rank,
followed by Frank Cramer's of Palo Alto, California,
and Principal George E. Myers' of the McKinley Manual Training School, Washington, D.C. These latter
three essays were judged to be important enough contributions that they were published along with the
two prize essays. Starbuck's views on character
education were thus produced and distributed through
an early volume designed to be used by those interested in moral education in the public-school system,
as well as by parents, clergymen, and citizens interested in the problem.⁴⁹

    Starbuck's major contributions to the field, how-
ever, did not come until the twenties. During this
decade, Starbuck chaired the Iowa Committee which won
a national contest for the best plan submitted on
methods for character education in the public schools;
Starbuck established and directed an Institute for
Character Research at the University of Iowa, the
first of its kind supported by a state university; on
the basis of several of the better studies being conducted by his graduate students under his supervision,
Starbuck edited a series of four volumes on Studies
in Character; and with his staff Starbuck sought to
lay some scientific foundations for a character training program through an objectively critical selection

of the best literary materials for character training designed to supplement the public school curriculum. The first two volumes, issued as the result of this scientific technique, were published in 1928 and 1930. Volume I, A Guide to Literature for Character Training, surveyed fairy tales, myths, and legends; and Volume II, A Guide to Books for Character, covered fiction. Starbuck envisioned a multitude of volumes or units of the Guide which would classify references on varied subjects and for all school grades, giving teachers access to the choicest character training literature, but unfortunately this dream was unrealistic and this work was never completed. Still, his efforts stimulated greatly the concern for developing better programs of character education in the schools.

There occurred a renaissance of interest in character education following the events of World War I and the great economic depression. These sad marks in history were viewed by many as the direct result of low ideals, indiscriminate values, and unethical exploitations in human relations. Consequently, these major events set the stage for attempts at rebuilding the character of a new generation through the educational process. Starbuck's work must be viewed with some understanding of this concept.

Perhaps the central issue of character education during the period of Starbuck's involvement was the direct - indirect question. Despite the plea by many for direct moral instruction in the schools, Starbuck, from the very beginning emphasized the need for indirect moral education. Starbuck and his collaborators propounded this view in the Iowa Plan for methods in character education, and all of Starbuck's efforts toward the selection of the best pieces of literature for character training was done with this approach in mind. His effort toward the scientific selection of character building materials to be used as a supplement to the general school curriculum, though never fully realized, was seen as one of the most ambitious attempts to organize such materials as a major resource for indirect character education in the schools.

Not only did Starbuck's philosophy of indirectness in the process of character education affect his literary project; as already suggested, it also affected the proposals of the Iowa Plan on character education methods. For this plan was not interested in courses in character education as such, but rather emphasized the need to provide adequate situations wherein the process of ethical decision-making could be learned by being experienced. Such an emphasis on the importance of providing a democratic setting in the school certainly dominated the educational approach to character training in later decades.

Starbuck's contribution to the growth of character education was not limited to his work at the University of Iowa and later at the University of Southern California. For example, he offered his professional services to the work of the National Education Association, serving as a member of the Committee on Character Education. The committee approached the study of character education through the organization of subcommittees. In the year 1924-25, for instance, Starbuck served as the chairman of the "Character Scales and Measurements" subcommittee.[50]

Starbuck's research in character education at the Universities of Iowa and Southern California was not the only work being carried on in this field. Even during his earlier years at Iowa, other universities were conducting research in character education. Still, his work can be listed among the pioneering efforts, and the nature of his studies in character education have to be seen as innovative and influential.

This background chapter has been developed as a foundation for the more thorough exploration of Starbuck's life and his contribution to the psychology of religion as it will be presented in the following chapters. It has been our intention to define the psychology of religion, to survey its literature, and to examine its development in ways that would prove useful to the understanding and interpretation of this great pioneer in the psychology of religion.

NOTES

1. John Baillie, The Interpretation of Religion (New York: Abingdon Press, 1928), p. 135.
2. George A. Coe, The Psychology of Religion (Chicago: The University of Chicago Press, 1916), pp. 6-7.
3. James H. Leuba, "The Field and the Problems of the Psychology of Religion," The American Journal of Religious Psychology and Education, I, No. 2 (November, 1904), pp. 160-161.
4. Edwin Diller Starbuck, The Psychology of Religion: An Empirical Study of the Growth of Religious Consciousness (London: Walter Scott Publishing Co.; New York: Charles Scribner's Sons, 1899), p. 1.
5. Ibid., pp. 16-17.
6. Orlo Strunk, Jr., "The Present Status of the Psychology of Religion," Journal of Bible and Religion, XXV, No. 4 (October, 1957), p. 291.
7. Paul E. Johnson, Psychology of Religion (Revised and Enlarged ed., New York: Abingdon Press, 1959), pp. 14-15.
8. Baillie, The Interpretation of Religion. See Chapter V for a complete discussion of his argument.
9. Herbert Leon Searles, "The Study of Religion in State Universities," University of Iowa Studies in Character, I, No. 3 (Iowa City: University of Iowa, 1928). See especially pp. 23-24.
10. G. Stephen Spinks, Psychology and Religion (Boston: Beacon Press, 1963). See Chapter II, pp. 16-30.
11. Karl R. Stolz, The Psychology of Religious Living (Nashville: Cokesburg Press, 1937). See Chapter III, "The Rise and Development of the Psychology of Religion," pp. 122-133.
12. Starbuck, The Psychology of Religion, p. 8.
13. Ibid., Chap. XXXI, pp. 408-420.
14. See Appendix A for an overview of the surveys.
15. See G. S. Hall, "The Moral and Religious Training of Children," Princeton Review (New Series, ix, 1882), pp. 26-45; and for a related article published almost ten years later, see G. S. Hall, "The Moral and Religious Training of Children and Adolescents," Pedagogical Seminary, I, No. 2 (1891), pp. 196-210.

16. James B. Pratt, "The Psychology of Religion," Harvard Theological Review, I, No. 4 (October, 1908), p. 436.

17. G. S. Hall, Adolescence (two vols.; London and New York: Appleton and Company, 1904). Although this monumental work was not published until 1904, research he was doing as early as the 1880's was not unrelated. Thus, it is appropriate to defend Hall's influence even upon those pioneers in the psychology of religion whose material, including the relationship of religion and adolescence, was published prior to 1904.

18. James H. Leuba, "The Psychology of Religious Phenomena," American Journal of Psychology, VII, No. 3 (April, 1896), pp. 309-370.

19. Edwin Diller Starbuck, "A Study of Conversion," American Journal of Psychology, VIII (January, 1897), pp. 268-308; and "Some Aspects of Religious Growth," American Journal of Psychology, IX (October, 1897), pp. 70-124.

20. See especially Elmer T. Clark, The Psychology of Religious Awakening (New York: Macmillan Co., 1929).

21. Alexander DeConde, Armin Rappaport, William R. Steckel, Patterns in American History, II (Belmont, California: Wadsworth Publishing Co., Inc., 1965), p. 215.

22. Charles Crowe, ed., A Documentary History of American Thought and Society (Boston: Allyn and Bacon, Inc., 1965), p. 339.

23. MEMORANDUM OF THE COMMITTEE ON CONFERENCE AND STUDY GROUPS On Practical Christianity and Reconstruction after the War appointed at Mass Meeting, Commercial Club, Iowa City, February 21, 1918.

24. Herbert Wallace Schneider, Religion in 20th Century America (Revised ed., New York: Atheneum, 1964).

25. Ibid., pp. 48-50.
26. Ibid., pp. 79-80.
27. Ibid., p. 122.
28. Ibid., pp. 125-126.
29. Ibid., p. 130.
30. Ibid., pp. 132-133.
31. Ibid., p. 138.

32. See Appendix B for a review of the especially important works.

33. Kemp, Physicians of the Soul, pp. 100-101.

34. Sigmund Freud, Totem and Tabu (Vienna, 1913).

35. Hiltner, "The Psychological Understanding of Religion," pp. 10-11.

36. Strunk, "The Psychology of Religion: An Historical and Contemporary Survey," pp. 183-184.

37. Edward Schaub, "The Psychology of Religion in America During the Past Quarter-Century," The Journal of Religion, VI, No. 2 (March, 1926), p. 125.

38. Edwin Diller Starbuck, "Hopeful Line of Development of the Psychology of Religion," Religious Education, VIII, No. 5 (December, 1913), pp. 427-428.

39. Edwin Diller Starbuck, "Psychology of Religion," Encyclopedia of Education Research, edited by Walter S. Monroe (New York: Macmillan Co., 1941), p. 866.

40. James Bissett Pratt, "The Psychology of Religion," p. 440.

41. Robert I. Watson, "G. Stanley Hall," International Encyclopedia of the Social Sciences, VI (1968), pp. 311-312.

42. Stolz, The Psychology of Religious Experience, p. 125.

43. Starbuck, "Hopeful Lines of Development of the Psychology of Religion," p. 426.

44. Edwin Diller Starbuck, "Religion's Use of Me," Religion in Transition, edited by Vergilius Ferm (London: George Allen & Unwin LTD, 1937), pp. 249-250.

45. Ibid., pp. 251-252.

46. Milton Carsley Towner, ed., Religion in Higher Education (Chicago: University of Chicago Press, 1931), pp. 250-258.

47. S. C. Mitchell, Harry E. Fosdick, Pres. L. L. Doggett, Artley B. Parsons, and Edwin D. Starbuck, "Report of the Commission Appointed in 1911 to Investigate the Preparation of Religious Leaders in Universities and Colleges." Religious Education, VII, No. 4 (October, 1912), pp. 329-348.

48. Edwin D. Starbuck, and Arthur E. Holt, "Theological Seminaries and Research," Religious Education, XXIII, No. 5 (May, 1928), pp. 404-406.

49. Moral Training in the Public Schools (Boston: Ginn and Co., 1897), pp. iii-iv.

50. Bureau of Education Bulletin, Report of the Committee on Character Education of the National Education Association, No. 7 (Washington, D.C., 1926), pp. iv-v.

CHAPTER II

A BIOGRAPHICAL PERSPECTIVE: PERSONAL

Family Background

Edwin Diller Starbuck,[1] the youngest of ten
children, was born February 20, 1866 to Samuel Starbuck and Luzena Jessup. He was an eighth generation
descendant of the Starbucks in America.

Neither Starbuck's life-style, nor his general
contribution, can be fully appreciated without some
insight into his ancestral heritage. In fact, Starbuck, in reference to an article entitled "Pioneer,
New Style," about his oldest son, Arthur, an aviator,
and himself, noted that "it is in the breed and the
blood, in the tradition."[2] The dynamic pioneering
style of his life bears heavy resemblance to that of
his forefathers.

Alexander Starbuck, in The History of Nantucket,
states that the Starbuck family probably was of
Danish origin, and that the family likely settled in
England during the days of what has historically
been labelled the Danish Invasion.[3]

The first American antecedents of Edwin Diller
Starbuck were whalers who settled on Nantucket Island some thirty miles south of Cape Cod. The history of this little island of 30,000 acres can be
traced to the early part of the seventeenth century.
Alexander Starbuck quotes from Hough, "Papers Relating to the Island of Nantucket," Introduction,
page IX:

> "King James I, in the eigh-
> teenth year of his Reign, created
> the 'Council for the affaires of
> New England,' known as the Plymouth
> Company, and this Council at the
> Request of Charles I, in 1635, con-
> veyed unto William Earl of Sterling,
> Secretary of the Kingdom of Scotland,

57

Pemaquid and its Dependencies on
the Coast of Maine, together with
Long Island, and the adjacent Islands, with Power of judicature . . .

In April 1637, the Earl of
Sterling appointed James Forrett
his Agent or Deputy for settling
the Islands between Cape Cod and
the Hudson River, and in 1641 the
latter sold for £40 to Thomas
Mayhew, his Son the Island of Nantucket, with several islands adjacent."[4]

The first Starbuck in America appears in the
person of Edward Starbuck (1604-1690) who, with his
wife, Katherine, sailed from Derbyshire, England to
Dover, New Hampshire, about 1635.[5] Then in 1659,
during the months of summer, Edward Starbuck accompanied Tristram Coffin, who was in search of a new
place of residence for himself and his family, on
his first voyage to the Island of Nantucket. They
visited Martha's Vineyard first, a small island
west of Nantucket, where they discovered that title
to the Island of Nantucket was vested in Thomas Mayhew. Here they learned of Mayhew's willingness to
part with a majority of his interest in the island,
and consequently set sail for Nantucket with the
purpose of surveying its boundaries and ascertaining
its virtues.[6]

Edward Starbuck was numbered among the Island's
"First Purchasers," as the original twenty owners of
Nantucket were called. Thomas Macy, who is credited
with being the first permanent English settler, and
who was one of the ten original purchasers who selected ten others to be partners, chose Edward to be a
partner. Edward Starbuck appeared to be a man of
"commanding presence." Alexander Starbuck quotes
Nathaniel Barney's description of Edward:

"He was a man of great firm-
ness and his influence among the
Indians was so great that if at

58

any time suspicion or alarm
arose among the early settlers
he was always in requisition
to explain the apparent causes
thereof and suggest a pallia-
tion for their rude and inexpli-
cable action, which served to
allay the fears of the more
timid."[7]

Several times he served as one of the "lot-layers"
of the Island. And in 1643 and 1646 he was Representative in the General Court. He was a man highly
esteemed by his fellow Islanders.

Among these "First Purchasers," Tristram Coffin
was perhaps the most prominent and influential member. He is mentioned because it is his daughter,
Mary, that Nathaniel Starbuck, son of Edward and
Katherine, married. And being the only son of Edward who lived, Nathaniel, with his wife Mary, became the ancestor of all the American Starbucks.
They also had the distinction of being the parents
of the first white child born on Nantucket.[8]

Nathaniel Starbuck (1636-1718) also was numbered
among the "First Purchasers" as he was chosen as a
partner by his father-in-law, Tristram Coffin. This
proved to be a most profitable opportunity, for at
the time of his death Nathaniel was among the wealth-
iest of the men on the island. Like his father,
Nathaniel was considered a man of distinguished ability, a characteristic which appears to be prominent
in the Starbucks to the present generation.

Any serious examination of the First Purchasers,
among whom the Starbucks had a special place, reveals
them to be spirited men of notable competence. It is
recorded: "They were a sturdy, God-fearing race,
everyone of them prominent in the community in which
he lived."[9] Such ancestral distinction of ability
and prominence as forerunners was not to be lost in a
distant forthcoming descendant, namely Edwin Diller
Starbuck.

The story of Starbuck's daring ancestors is not complete without a brief account of whaling in Nantucket. Whaling is first mentioned in the Town Records at a regular meeting on July 13, 1668. As usual the Starbuck name is included in the action. The Records state: "Edward Starbuck and Peter Folger were empowered to make a bargain with the Gardners Concerning all whales that shall come on shore on the Island on the Towns behalf."[10] The second mention of whaling in the Town Records occurs April 5, 1672, when there appears a statement of agreement between a Mr. Loper and the town regarding whaling. Although there is no sound evidence that Mr. Loper ever fulfilled his part of the contract, or became a resident of Nantucket, these records do signify the Town's early interest in Whaling, which was to become one of its principal industries. The Record states: "James Loper doth Ingage to Carry on a Designe of Whale Catching on the Island of Nantucket that is to say James Ingages to be a third in all Respects and some of the Town Ingages Also to carry on the other two thirds with him in like manner." Part of the contract included the agreement that "whoever Kill any whales . . . they are to pay to the Town for every such whale five shillings." There were terms also to attract Mr. Loper: ". . . for the Incouragement of the said James Loper the Town doth grant him ten acres of Land in sume Covenant place that he may Chuse . . . and also liberty for the commonage of three cows and Twenty sheep and one horse with necessary wood and water for his use, on Conditions that he follow the trade of whalling on this Island two years in all the seasons . . ."[11]

Tradition includes some prediction spoken about 1690 regarding the future establishment of the whaling business in Nantucket, when one of the Islanders, standing on the high land, and observing the whales spouting in the sea, points to the ocean and says to some persons standing nearby, "There is a green pasture, where our children's grandchildren, will go for bread."[12] These words were to be prophetic, for the history of whaling on this Island is a story of achievement, of a hearty community's successful

60

efforts in building up and pursuing a business which
demanded great daring and skill. Such efforts were
to eventually make this little Island known to all
parts of the world. And the great dexterity with
which these men of Nantucket worked would cause
DeCrevecoeur to say of them, "These people are become superior to any other whalemen."[13]

The story of religion on the Island is also interesting, and has its place in the soil out of
which Edwin Diller Starbuck grew. It is contrary to
the facts to consider that the settlement of the
Island of Nantucket involved basically a repetition
of the circumstances out of which New England was
settled. While religious persecution began in Massachusetts Bay Colony not more than twenty years
from the arrival of Pilgrims in New England, and in
the midst of intolerance and even violent acts of
oppression, Quakers were banished from the colony,
the early settlers were not Quakers or Friends who
were fleeing to Nantucket to escape such persecution.
Rather, the facts are clear, as Alexander Starbuck
states, "that it was nearly fifty years after the
first English settlement in Nantucket before there
seems to be any evidence of a church among the English residents."[14] In fact, it was years after the
death of both Thomas Macy and Edward Starbuck before
any kind of English church was established on Nantucket.

The fact that the parents of Edwin Diller Starbuck were Quakers is not unrelated to the history of
the Quakers or Society of Friends on Nantucket.
While there were a number of other English churches
eventually established, the Quakers were the first
and appear to be the most influential group on the
Island. It is significant that the Starbuck name is
associated with the first Conversion and Meeting
Place on the Island.

The earliest recorded visit of Friends to the
Island, was made by Thomas Chalkley in the Spring of
1698. During this first visit, Mary Starbuck, the
wife of Nathaniel, one of the First Purchasers, was
convinced of the Truth. She was to live and die a

61

Quaker, and an eminent servant and minister for
Christ on the Island.

Mary Starbuck seems to have been a woman of un-
excelled judgment, whose reputation for her understanding of religion was so great throughout the
Island that the Islanders viewed her as "an Oracle
among them on that account, insomuch that they would
not do anything without her advice and consent therein."[15] Appearing to have been one of the ablest
women who ever lived on the Island, it is not difficult to see why she was considered the "leading
Spirit in the organization of the Society of Friends."[16]

In 1701, a second visit was made to the Island by
a Friend, named John Richardson. And the next visit,
and probably most important one, was made by Thomas
Story, in 1704. From Story's autobiography we learned
of the growing attraction to Quakerism, both in the
Starbuck family and in others on the Island. Alexander Starbuck quotes Story's description of a meeting
held May 19th:

> "We had another large good meet-
> ing at Nathaniel Starbuck's, the elder,
> his Wife, Mary, as before hinted, being
> the first on that Island who had any
> Regard to the Way of Truth as among us;
> but now her three Sons and Daughters,
> and Sons Wives, are all in a hopeful
> Way to the Knowledge of Truth, and
> Liberty of the Sons of God, with sever-
> al other tender People at this time on
> that small Island."[17]

On May 23, another large open Meeting was held at
Nathaniel Starbuck's home. Here Story records[18] that
he "laid a Charge upon her (Mary Starbuck) to endeavor to have a Meeting established in their Family,
once a week at least, to wait upon the Lord, with all
who were convinced of Truth in the Neighborhood, and
in the Island, as they had conveniency." He states
further: "And accordingly, some time after we depar-
ted the Island, they did meet, and the Lord did visit
them, and gathered many there unto himself; and they

62

became a large and living Meeting in him, and several living and able Ministers were raised by the Lord in that Family."

During the eighteenth century this sect grew readily but by the end of the nineteenth century, and after a number of cleavages, the Sect on the Island became practically extinct. Alexander Starbuck raises a legitimate question at this point: "Who can say, however, that although they have ceased to exist as a distinct body, that the impress of their lives is not even now a traceable factor in the every day life of our people?"[19] And who is to say that the impress of such a heritage was not a traceable factor in the life of Edwin Diller Starbuck?

Mary Eliza Starbuck, whose father, Charles E. Starbuck, captained ships in the whaling grounds of the Pacific Ocean in the 1850's, reveals in her description of the Islanders of her day a continuity of character with their ancestors. She maintains "whether they were at home or abroad, whether widely known or only locally, they were felt to be men of grasp, of power, and of individuality."[20] This continuity of "grasp" and "power" and "individuality" is also to be found in the subject of our study. And when Mary Starbuck characterizes the intentions of the Islanders, as "destined to carry on the work of leavening the world bequeathed to them by their ancestors,"[21] she could just as well have been describing the forthcoming actions of Edwin Diller Starbuck.

All of the Starbucks were not to remain on the Island of Nantucket. In the 1770's and 80's the Starbucks were numbered among the general migration from Nantucket to North Carolina. Hezekiah Starbuck (1749-1830) and his wife, Mary Coffin Thurston, a fifth generation family, moved from Nantucket to North Carolina in 1785. A sixth generation family, that of Matthew Starbuck, was also part of the large Migration to North Carolina, which eventually spread through East Tennessee and on to the middle west. Another sixth generation family, Gayer Starbuck (1777-1866) and his wife, Susanna Dillon, moved on from North Carolina to Ohio in 1807.[22] With them was their son,

Samuel Starbuck, the father of Edwin Diller Starbuck. Samuel Starbuck later moved to Indiana where
he settled and raised his family.

An eventful union occurred on March 23, 1848.
Samuel Starbuck and Luzena Jessup were married. In
a small Quaker community, approximately twelve miles
southwest of Indianapolis, Samuel Starbuck became a
"prominent citizen" and "successful farmer." The
chief interest of his wife, Luzena, seemed to be
children, as the extent of their family suggests.

Between 1849 and 1867 Samuel and Luzena had ten
children, the last of which was Edwin Eli Starbuck,
the name of our subject at birth. Edwin Starbuck
had seven brothers and two sisters, named in order
of birth, Issac, Asa, Anna, Levi, Calvin, Ella, Alva,
Elwood, and William. Only Calvin, born in 1857 and
who died at an early age, would not have been known
by Edwin. Most, if not all, of his brothers and
sisters would have still lived at home when Edwin
Eli was born.[23]

Edwin Starbuck's home, during his childhood
years, was in the country, seemingly located at the
center of five Quaker communities not more than
three or four miles from each other. Starbuck describes his community as "being only a few miles from
everywhere." Consequently, it was called "Centre
Neighborhood." Samuel Starbuck's farm was a large
place. He had built the buildings on his land, himself, when he got to Indiana. Their home, located
near a perpetual spring of clear water, seemed to
be the popular place for neighborly visits. Here
was the heart of five communities where "nearly
everybody knew and liked everyone." Starbuck speaks
fondly of this environment.[24]

The early childhood years of Starbuck appear to
be pleasant ones, although, since his concern lay
with the future rather than in an indulgence in
reminiscence, we have but the slightest recollection
of those years. Starbuck kept no known memoirs for
our perusal. His family was relatively affluent,
enough so, at least, to be comfortable. There is no

indication, however, that theirs was a life of ease.
The family shared the goods of life, but they also
worked together and learned early to assume some of
life's basic responsibilities. A practical application of this principle is discovered in Edwin's participation, while quite young, in driving cucumbers
into town where they were sold to a pickle factory.
Starbuck earned his first money in this manner.[25]

The pleasantries of these friendly Quaker communities were many, though the piety of Quakerism
had its effects on the kinds of leisurely activities
in which the people indulged. But the setting, as
Starbuck describes it, would have spelled joy for
any young person of his day.

> "There was much visiting and
> banqueting, especially on First Day
> after meeting. There were happy,
> informal games on that day, but no
> organized sports, or croquet, or
> swimming, for these would desecrate
> the sacredness of the day. On week-
> days there were sports of many kinds.
> Evenings might bring sociables with
> charades and old-fashioned games.
> Authors but never cards. The Vir-
> ginia Reel, and other simple steps
> to the music of the 'fiddle' but no
> dancing, which was sinful. There
> were corn-huskings, log-rollings,
> barn-raisings, and many other fes-
> tive occasions."[26]

A subtle molding occurred in Quaker families.
Very few direct demands were uttered to the children.
Seldom did the situation require words to directly
encourage a conscientious sense of obligation. There
was no need for the children to be told to be helpful
It was rather understood that all were to participate
gladly in the common life. The chores were endless,
but Starbuck and his brothers and sisters tackled the
work that was theirs almost playfully. There was
little quarreling among them, and as a consequence
little need for punishment. Such was the nature of

Starbuck's family experience, a nurturing in which "moral laws were usually not 'observed,' they were written on the heart."[27]   Little could his parents realize how significant an impact was this early influence to have upon their youngest son's contribution to the world.

When he was fifteen Starbuck entered a Quaker academy near his home where he remained for two years. His last two years in high school were spent at a school further away, but with a reputation for fine teachers. Starbuck describes, briefly but informatively, this period in his life:

> "These were rich though uneventful years, with the usual adolescent foolishness, chums, sociability, intra-mural and inter-academic athletics, artistic effusions stimulated by literary societies, and the usual absorption in studies that were made inviting."

In the same source, Starbuck summarily refers to his religious heritage, again, supplying us with information regarding that foundational experience which would so naturally shape the nature of his religious persuasion in later years. To be noted is the freedom, the rationalism, and the universalism of his experience:

> "Religiously, the atmosphere was entirely free. It was gentle, sincere, and distinctly non-evangelistic. There was a note of personal responsibility that contained something of a universal note."[28]

His teen-age days appear to represent a rather smooth and balanced progression towards maturity.

Educational Background

The immediate ensuing years are to be character-

66

ized by an intense pursuit of higher education. This journey was to last eleven years, and it would take Starbuck to several outstanding institutions before he would finally receive the Ph.D. at Clark University in 1897. Starbuck was expected to go to college and had to earn enough to pay for the expenses himself. In 1884 he turned to teaching in the public schools, first, in a neighboring school, and then, in a school in his own home territory; and for two years he worked diligently attempting to live up to the standards and expectations his family and neighbors set for him. A teacher was judged, both within and without the classroom, a spiritual leader in the community.

This was a time for searching, a time of questioning for Starbuck. A struggle was going on in his thinking. A battle was emerging, between "Adam and the monkey." Starbuck noted that Earlham College was clearly on the side of evolutionism. Two of his brothers and a sister had attended Earlham. But Starbuck was destined to go to Indiana University, where David Starr Jordon, a radical freethinker, served as president, and heated discussions of evolution were frequent. Starbuck describes the university as the "storm-centre" of the "new thinking." Here, among his subjects, Starbuck studied geology under Jordan and descriptive and experimental biology under Kingsley and the facts of evolution appeared evident to him.

A basis for Starbuck's world view was being formed. Not a revolutionary struggle, but a rather "profound reconstruction" was taking place. In this process of dismantling the garb of traditionalism, Starbuck discovered the hazards of moving in such a direction. He was being labelled "atheist" and "infidel" by neighbors and friends at home. These labels would remain with him throughout his life-time, to be repeated by the conservative religionists of his day. But Starbuck, neither now, nor later, would be daunted by such name calling. He had been trying to create truth, but now he viewed that one can only discover truth, and if it is accepted, then one must be willing to bear the consequences.[29]

Starbuck constantly felt tempted to uproot the weeds

of superstition, wherever he found them, but that
urge, natural as it may be, was almost always curbed
by his unfeigned regard for persons with whom he associated. And later throughout his career, he remained highly sensitive to the religious thoughts
and feelings of his friends, particularly his students, resolving to never purposefully injure their
"religious sensibilities." This is substantiated by
the comments made by Dr. Lonzo Jones, a former student of Starbuck's: "I liked his classes and his
careful consideration of each student's cherished
beliefs." In the same vein, Dr. Jones respectfully
recalls that Starbuck was "a man who enlarged my
perspectives and did so without destroying any goodness in my own faith or my love for my own religious
people."[30]

In his growing world of values, ideas of "naturalism" and a "New Humanism" were taking shape. In
the free atmosphere of the University, Starbuck
formed, with some other students, an intimate group
called "B H C," which stood for "Browning Heretic
Club." They met weekly for study and discussion.
Browning became the departure point for analyzing
many different fields of culture.

Another example of the effects of this philosophy
or religion of Humanism can be seen in Starbuck's
relationship to the Y.M.C.A. Before Starbuck, the
Y.M.C.A. society had held a significant position in
the university. Starbuck considered the association
to be too "Bible-centered," too "evangelical," and
too "sectarian" for the "new age" that was dawning.
Disuniting themselves with the local Y.M.C.A. association, Starbuck and some of his friends, established
the "Indiana University Religious Association," an
organization open to anyone, regardless of their faith
or lack of it, yet appealing in particular to those
individuals whose basic commitments had to do with the
welfare of humanity. This movement took the place of
the Y.M.C.A. while Starbuck was at the university.

In the meantime, Starbuck had chosen philosophy
as a major and under William Lowe Bryan, among other
teachers, there was emerging, as he puts it, " a

religion of philosophy and a philosophy of religion."
By the time of his graduation in 1890 from Indiana
University, Starbuck was interpreting the events and
experiences of his life as pointing to a career in
philosophical studies, including a "special emphasis
on religion."[31]

Upon graduation, with a Bachelor's degree, Starbuck accepted a position at Spiceland Academy, in
Indiana, to teach Latin and mathematics. It was not
surprising that he was asked to teach these subjects,
for his classwork in high school and college included
seven years of mathematics and six years of Latin.[32]
The following year he accepted the offer of professor-
ship in mathematics at Vincennes University, in Indiana, where he taught advanced algebra, calculus, surveying, and astronomy. Here Starbuck eagerly employed
the opportunity to teach as an "art," an "exact
science," an ideal that had been placed before him
while at Indiana University by Rufus Green and Joseph
Swaim.

These were busy years, but Starbuck found time to
read, widely, works of religion and philosophy. His
interest in psychology was also beginning to dominate
his passion for knowledge. Starbuck studied cata-
logues of the leading universities but found offerings
along the lines of his interests slight. While other
universities offered courses in religion, only at
Harvard did the study of religion, as well as philosophy and psychology, appear to be dispassionate
enough to be appealing to Starbuck. Thus, in 1893,
Starbuck entered Harvard.

The years at Harvard were stimulating ones for
Starbuck. The atmosphere was conducive to serious
study. His teachers were "seasoned scholars," including admirable men in the fields of philosophy and
psychology. While there, Starbuck joined a Philosophy
Club, consisting of both faculty members and students,
and also participated in the philosophical discussions of another smaller, more intimate club.

For the purpose of learning about techniques and
methods for the study of religion, Starbuck took two

courses in psychology, one descriptive and the other experimental, from Munsterberg and William James. Starbuck's keen interest in the scientific method was satisfied by a course and a seminar under Emerton, whose wholehearted respect for fact would be exemplified by Starbuck throughout his lifetime.

It was impossible for Starbuck to give his undivided attention to the psychology of religion, since at Harvard credit was given for work done only in courses. Still, he did a great deal of work in this area on the side. Starbuck's classical study on conversion for instance, was begun at Harvard.

Surprisingly to Starbuck, his work seemed generally accepted. The response of faculty members varied from encouragement, mostly, to vexation with the topic and the approach Starbuck was taking. Some professors offered more help than others. Dr. James, for instance, extended more than a wish for success. He examined carefully Starbuck's initial draft of the questionnaire on conversions and volunteered a number of valuable suggestions. Interestingly though, it appears questionable that James favored Starbuck's work from the very beginning. This is substantiated, though in a generalized fashion, by a reference made, in a letter from one of Starbuck's graduate students, related to this point. "You may be interested to know that he /Starbuck/ told Dr. William James that he wanted to study the Psychology of Religion for his M.A. and that Dr. James told him that it could not be done but he convinced him so completely that he (James) wrote 'The Varieties of Religious Experience' . . . ."[33] Dr. A. Rudolph Uren, in his book, Recent Religious Psychology, concurs with this notion. He states: "It is probable that Professor W. James' Varieties of Religious Experience would never have been written had Starbuck's study not appeared."[34]

In the middle of the second year of his study, during the winter of 1894-95, several significant consistencies came into view, especially in the conversion study. Dean C. C. Everett was interested enough to ask Starbuck to report on his work in his philosophy of religion class. After the presentation, a discussion ensued, which revealed both strong opposition and friendly endorsement to this "babe newly born into the family of academic subjects." Among all the members of the class that day, however, the presence of one lone figure stood out most plainly. She was to become Starbuck's bride. He fondly recalls his impression of her response to his presentation. "There in that class sat Anna Diller, profound student, musician-artist. She warmed towards it and took it to her bosom as she was later to take the whole oncoming Starbuck brood."35

During Starbuck's two years at Harvard he had earned a Master's degree and had been granted a generous fellowship. But his interest lay exclusively with the psychology of religion, for which he could receive no credit toward the Ph.D. Consequently, when he was told of the unusually open program of independent study at Clark University, he was serious enough to make a visit to Worcester in the spring of 1895. He met with President G. Stanley Hall, and a number of his collegues, who were all agreed that Starbuck's transfer to Clark would be fully acceptable. Starbuck was granted a fellowship, and the move was made.

Starbuck's two years at Clark were relatively "happy" and "profitable." For the most part, his professors were quite helpful to him in his special study. But Starbuck found that his intention to be a serious student of religion was not to go unchallenged. Hall, himself, encouraged Starbuck to switch to another area. Starbuck would not be dissuaded, however, for this had been his primary purpose in coming to Clark.

Starbuck comments about Hall's actions:

"While he was dissuading me, he was at the same time assem-

71

> bling periodically a half-
> dozen students . . . picturing
> the possiblities of the application
> of psychology to religion and
> saying that the next ten years
> at Clark University might well be
> devoted to studies in that field."[36]

Starbuck recalls that the spring before his going
to Clark, Frank Drew, previously an old college
mate at Indiana University and now a graduate
student at Clark, had taken a pile of Starbuck's
questionnaires back to Clark to be filled out by
the students there. They were not returned, and
when Starbuck went to Worcester that spring he
discovered that a student had prepared a syllabus,
the basis of his doctoral dissertation, which was
practically a reproduction of Starbuck's original
one on conversion. Starbuck also discovered that
Hall had received his questionnaire and was ready
to distribute it as his own creation, however,
Starbuck was able to prevent its publication. As
might logically be supposed, Starbuck would not
number Hall among his most ardent supporters in
this field of religion.

Starbuck's remarks about Hall's life are not
meant to be degrading, however, for he considered
that Hall possessed one of the most inspiring minds
he had ever known, and he says further of Hall,
almost, as if to justify his actions:

> "His was probably the most
> dynamic, passionate and high-strung
> personality among the psychologists
> of the world, and at the same time,
> as is characteristic of genius,
> fuller of contradiction. Every
> apparent weakness is only the
> offside of some greater strength
> . . . It was as impossible in
> the midst of that surging mentality
> for him to see the minor things
> in perspective as for a mighty

72

swollen river to feel out the
sources of its many waters and
its why and whither.[37]

Starbuck continued to expand and perfect his
questionnaire studies, and finally in the spring of
1897, he received his Ph.D. degree.

Religious Orientation

The nature of Edwin Starbuck's life commitments
can best be understood by attempting to examine his
religious background. In a brief autobiographical
work, Starbuck refers to the foundational influence
of his "heritage and upbringing," and briefly characterizes its quality:

> "It has seemed certain that
> the heritage and upbringing of the
> subject of this sketch directly
> accounts for nearly everything that
> has happened--tastes, attitudes,
> aptitudes, tempermental eccentrici-
> ties, religious peculiarities. The
> mental and spiritual weathers in
> which he was immersed were intense,
> pervasive, impelling, and inviting."[38]

Starbuck was a "birthright" member of the Society of
Friends. The focal point for the life of the Quaker
community, in which he was reared, was the "meeting-
house." Here Starbuck and his family, and most of
the neighbors around them, met on "First Day morn-
ing" and also gathered for a prayer-meeting in the
evening and a mid-week meeting on "Fourth Day morn-
ing."

In the home, daily devotions were held, usually
after breakfast. Such devotions consisted of Bible
readings and occasionally a few words of inspiration,
after which each member of the family would depart to
go his separate way into the world of work and education.[39]

While it appears that Starbuck, in general, re-

flects warmly upon this religious milieu, he is not
prepared to defend every aspect of the Quakers' experience. Regarding their belief in the function of
the Holy Spirit, he notes the general struggle of
participating vocally in a primitive Quaker meeting.
Even Starbuck's parents wrestled with this problem.
Starbuck recalls watching the "play of emotions" on
the face of his father, who usually sat as head of
the meeting. Starbuck describes the experience of
his father:

> "Really being a gentle, modest man
> he would have much preferred that
> the Spirit would let him alone.
> In spite of himself the lips would
> begin to move, the body to show
> signs of restlessness, and not in-
> frequently did the Spirit win
> against the reluctant flesh."[40]

While his father frequently succumbed, though reluc-
tantly, to this indwelling of the Holy Spirit, Starbuck's mother seems to have succeeded usually in
warding off this penetration.

Starbuck also recalls his own reluctance to
participate in this kind of experience, where silence
was to be broken only by the Spirit's utterance. He
reviews the stress of his own experience:

> "I knew myself the awfulness of that
> struggle. Having as a youth borne
> testimony a couple of times in a
> fairly acceptable manner . . . Some-
> time in looking ahead to a forthcom-
> ing meeting I experienced a luscious
> pain, mingled with nine parts dread,
> that was hard to bear."[41]

It was quite apparent that Starbuck was not to accept
the traditional premise of supernaturalism, upon
which the conservative members of Quakerism built
their faith. Starbuck's approach later was to be
labelled "positivistic" as compared with "metaphysical."[42]

The "unspoken eloquence of the Quakers," as
Starbuck describes it, would have its impact upon
his thought, as later he would develop a subtle
methodology for character education. Starbuck remembers an early experience which occurred after he
and his parents had visited some friends. On the
way home, his mother noticed a smooth stone in Starbuck's hand and asked where he had found it. Upon
confession that he had brought it from the friend's
home, without one word being spoken, the horses
were turned back and they returned to their friend's
home. Without being asked, Starbuck returned the
stone, and they resumed their journey home in general silence. Starbuck recalls, "A hundred sermons on
respect for property never could have sunk so deep."[43]

Perhaps the most fundamental influence of this
Quaker environment was Starbuck's first-hand observance of so many human examples of religious living.
He came to know and love a people who were predominantly anything but religious hypocrites. In their
midst he experienced the reality of transcendence
beyond the level of religious verbalization. He
witnessed the consequences of a convicted people
whose living was a prime illustration of their faith.
As Starbuck notes, "Those simple-minded Quaker folk
didn't talk much about religion; they took it for
granted . . . they lived it."[44] The major efforts
of Starbuck's life could be characterized as an attempt to shape a society of such religious men. He
was ever concerned about the application of religion.
As one of his students comments, "He was dedicated
to a religion of good conduct."[45]

After graduation from high-school Starbuck turned
to teaching in order to raise enough money to pay his
way through college. During his second year of teaching, in 1885, an event occurred which reveals something of the tension and pressure Starbuck must have
felt as a young man, not quite twenty years old, to
act out the traditional forms of religious development.
As was expected of him, he publicly accepted Christianity, which, in his case, was an overt expression of
faith unparalleled by any inner certainty of belief.
One of the true marks of authenticity as a Quaker was

the experience of a definite conversion. In the wake of the spread of Revivalism in Starbuck's community, he underwent his "conversion." Starbuck describes his experience and candidly analyzes its effects:

> "In the heat of the revival at centre meetings I went through the forms of this public acceptance, not feeling at the moment the negative implication that my heart had not been on the whole 'given to the Lord' during the preceding months. It gave the revivalists the pleasure of counting one more recruit, and it gave the devotee the satisfaction of trying to play the game with earnest people."[46]

Although, once leaving home, Starbuck no longer was affiliated with the Society of Friends, he never once denounced his Quaker heritage. Though emerging as a sophisticated, rationalistic, discerning figure, he did not belittle his simple, humble beginnings. He ever trusted and respected the character of these people. This is illustrated by the fact that when the Starbucks lived in Iowa City, although, never affiliated with the Quaker fellowship, they would always seek out Quaker families, in West Branch, Iowa, to care for their children during the summer months when they were traveling.[47]

It can be said, too, that the fundamental principles which Quakers uphold are not unlike those Starbuck maintained. Rachel Knight, in writing about the causes for which Quakers fought, listed, "Liberty, equality of opportunity, education, righteousness, truth, toleration," causes, all for which Starbuck also battled.[48]

Starbuck cannot be accused of losing his faith in college. He was beginning to bring into question the conservative elements of religious belief much earlier. In fact, he describes his doubts as "deepen-

76

ing" before he even entered college. Serious doubts had been shaping regarding the authority of the Old Testament, the miracle stories, the birth, life and mission of Jesus, among many other problems he could see. Still, in the earlier years of his life, Starbuck chose not to disassociate himself from organized religion. In his last three years in Indiana University, he worked in the United Presbyterian Church, where he led the choir and participated in many other activities of the church. Starbuck also served as a Sunday-school teacher for a while; however, as a result of his concern for "fairness to their traditions," he had to abandon, in good conscience, his teaching role.[49]

It appears that in his middle and latter years Starbuck rarely attended church.[50] He had become rather disillusioned with the church as an organization. A student of his recalls his initial contact with Starbuck in 1920: "By the time I met him he was completely dis-associated from any organized church affiliation, although, his wife continued as organist at the Unitarian church."[51] Yet this was a personal view which he seemingly never attempted to infectiously transmit to others. One of his daughters tells of a time in the early years of her marriage when she wrote to her father that she and her husband could see no reason for attending a church. Several ministers of churches in their community had visited them, however, they had decided that they would rather not become involved. Starbuck's daughter was interested in her father's response to their decision. He replied that there was real value in identifying with such a group and that the church was an important social institution that could provide meaningful experience.[52]

During the latter part of Starbuck's stay at Indiana University, he discovered James Freeman Clarke's book, Ten Great Religions, which Starbuck said "cleared the skies and precipitated afresh the sense of the Universal Soul of religion."[53] Clarke's work was especially appealing to Starbuck, and in his senior year he directed a Sunday afternoon study group using Clarke's books as discussion material.

77

Starbuck's interest in comparative religion and the fact that he later taught world religions, seem to have taken root in Clarke's work. The aim of this study reveals an approach which Starbuck would also uphold:

> "It is an attempt to compare the great religions of the world with each other. When completed, this comparison ought to show us what each is, what it contains, wherein it resembles the others, wherein it differs from the others; its origin and development, its place in universal history; its positive and negative qualities, its truths and errors, and its influence, past, present, or future, on the welfare of mankind."[54]

A fair and objective study of the facts, and comparison of the data, as Clarke attempted, were essential factors in Starbuck's work also.

The general results of Clarke's survey instilled in Starbuck's thought the universality of religion in human behavior. As one of the results is stated,

> ". . . this survey must have impressed on every mind the fact that man is eminently a religious being. We have found religion to be his supreme and engrossing interest on every continent, in every millenium of historic time, and in every stage of human civilization."[55]

Starbuck's growing interest in the study of religion and philosophy, and his insistence upon the science of observation and analysis might hypothetically be linked quite significantly, to the impact of Clarke, and more particularly to the following passage from his book. It may have provided the emotional charge for some of Starbuck's serious pursuits in the field of religion.

> "Theology and religion
> today, instead of disappearing
> in science, philosophy, and
> theology are all advancing
> together, a noble sisterhood
> of thought. And, looking at facts,
> we may ask, In what age or time
> was religion more of a living
> force, acting on human affairs,
> than it is at present?"56

Starbuck devoured Clarke's food for thought.
Clarke's humanistic and evolutionary approach to
religion implanted its mark in Starbuck's work.
Clarke notes: "Fulness of life . . . as the essential character of Christianity, should produce a
constant development and progress; and this we
find to be the case."57 With this perspective,
Starbuck could wholeheartedly agree. His studies
would later support this thesis also. Clarke's
pragmatic approach to religion, and Christianity
in particular, was especially appealing to Starbuck,
too. The following statement, from Clarke's book,
undoubtedly provided special encouragement to
Starbuck in terms of his interests in the application
of religion: "Christianity is becoming more and
more practical, and its application to life is
constantly growing more vigorous and wise."58

The interim period, between his graduation
from Indiana University in 1890 and his entrance
into Harvard in 1893 for graduate work, was a
profitable time for Starbuck. Although busy as
a teacher, first at Spiceland Academy, for a year,
and then at Vincennes University, he scheduled time
for serious reading in the areas of religion and
philosophy. Perhaps the book which most profoundly
influenced Starbuck at this time was Max Muller's
Lectures on the Science of Religion, lectures
delivered at the Royal Institution, in February of
1870, but not published in book form until 1893.

In the fourth and final lecture, Muller,
Professor of Comparative Philology in the University

of Oxford, reiterates the major objective of his work:

> "I chiefly wanted to show in what sense a truly scientific study of religion was possible, what materials there are to enable us to gain a trustworthy knowledge of the principal religions of the world, and according to what principles these religions may be classified."[59]

Muller readily admitted that the Science of Religion, or comparative study of the religions of the world, "jars on the ears of many persons." He wisely conceded, also, that this approach could not be taken without a price; yet, he defends the larger benefits. Muller states:

> "I do not say that the Science of Religion is all gain. No; it entails losses and losses of many things which we hold dear. But this I will say, that, as far as my humble judgment goes, it does not entail the loss of anything that is essential to true religion, and that if we strike the balance honestly, the gain is immeasurably greater than the loss."[60]

Starbuck could identify with this description, since it contained a truth about religious growth which was so personally familiar to him.

Starbuck became a serious student of religions of the world, and for a number of years he taught a course in comparative religion. One of his students recalls the proficiency with which Starbuck handled one of his classes in this field:

> "I remember that in one

80

of his classes was a Chinese,
a Hindu, and a German student
along with me and a half-a-dozen
other American students. He was
familiar with the religions and
philosophical background of
each of those foreign students
and could illuminate the discussion with quotations from
the choice literature of their
own hand."61

It is likely that Starbuck's keen interest in
world religions can be traced back to the impact
of Muller's significant work in this field.

In 1893 Starbuck entered Harvard, where not
only would he develop his study of the conversion
experience, but where also he experienced what he
calls "a metaphysical illumination." For over
six years Starbuck had accepted Evolutionism
completely. He asserts, "Absentee Gods and tran-
scendental reals, as magical repositories from
which to draw explanatory concepts, had been banished
never to return."62 Yet, while he had felt the
impact of Berkeley, Kant, and Hume, and had studied
in the physical sciences and even taught astronomy,
still, he constantly found himself returning to a
type of "Cartesian dualism." Descartes, a seventeenth century philosopher-psychologist, distinguished
animal behavior from human behavior. Animals
simply operated mechanically on the basis of reflex
action. Human behavior was approached by Descartes
quite differently however. He asserted a dualism,
a distinction between soul and body in man. Gardner
Murphy, in his Historical Introduction to Modern
Psychology, describes Descartes' dualistic explanation
of human acts:

"These acts Descartes divided
into two groups, those of a mechanical nature and those of a rational
nature. The rational acts were
utterly distinct from the mechanical,

81

and made possible judgment,
choice, and will . . . Descartes
retained the soul as an entity
outside the spatial order."[63]

Starbuck had been searching for an intellectual synthesis, a resolution for the considerations with
which he had been grappling. Referring briefly to
these considerations, he says,

"sensation-perceptions are not the
raw data of mentality but are later
developing specifications of the
wisdom of the organism; creative
imagination, and not thought, is
the Hamlet of the mental drama; concepts are only the patterned forms
of the imagination and symbolize
rather than represent 'objective'
reality. The most stubborn concepts,
such as the categories, can be
viewed truly either as ejects of the
mind or as representations of an external order; hence no necessary
dualism."[64]

In the midst of this search for the realities
and meaning of life, Starbuck experienced an illumination, a "religious experience," which served to provide an inner peace in his struggle to understand the
mysteries of life. He describes this experience as
follows:

"On one of my strolls on a side
street near the observatory the resolution of these focalized considerations came instantaneously. It was
like a recoil from disturbing ten-
sions, an uprush of animation, a
sunburst of illumination . . .
Words burst forth spontaneously:
'I see it! I have it!' Translated
into sober English these words meant:
'I, a mind, a bodymind, am in and
of a universe of meaning. The
values of art, religion, human

82

> relations, and ideal striv-
> ings are at one descriptively,
> with the formalized objects
> of thought and perception."[65]

The insight of this experience, with its sense of "at-home-ness in the universe," would deepen with the years.

While at Clark University, and after graduation during his early years in the teaching profession, Starbuck continued to pursue studies pertinent to the psychology of religion and religious education.

In 1906, Starbuck joined the faculty of the University of Iowa as a member of the combined division of philosophy and psychology. While there, he and his family were affiliated with the Unitarian Church, although Starbuck, himself, rarely attended.[66] In 1912, the year of his sabbatical leave, he was asked by the American Unitarian Association to serve as a consulting psychologist to help prepare a new religious education curriculum. Starbuck could not have been too disillusioned with the institutional church at this point, for he accepted this position, moved to Boston, and worked enthusiastically in the Religious Association for two years, having asked for a second year's leave. Although he helped to produce a number of texts and manuals, conservative elements in the American Unitarian Association impeded the work and the series was never completed. Undoubtedly, his opinion of religious institutional machinery must have suffered as a result of such maneuvers.

As late as 1929, however, Starbuck remained willing to participate in the church institution. In a letter, likely from Starbuck's secretary, to J. M. Ambruster, a clergyman, reference is made about possible preaching appointments for Starbuck in Chicago where he would be staying for several days. On the conservative-liberal continuum, he had progressively moved to the liberal end; and, this is taken into account by a qualifying statement regarding his services. The secretary writes:

> "Of course it would not
> do to assign Professor Starbuck
> to an extremely conservative
> church, but in any church of
> liberal or moderate tendencies
> he would render good service . . ."[67]

Forms of ecumenism were not unfamiliar to
Starbuck. While at the University of Southern California, where he went from Iowa, an interesting
program was initiated. In 1933, Starbuck started
an inter-church where various issues were discussed
by a Presbyterian minister, a Jewish rabbi, and
himself. The meetings, held regularly on a monthly
basis, were open to the public. Its popularity was
attested to not only by excellent attendance, but
also by the fact that it was broadcast over the
radio.[68]

Starbuck's thoughts about religion reveal something of the personality of the man, for he, himself,
wrote that in the area of religion "one best catches
the whole person in the act of thinking and feeling
most vitally."[69] Writing in 1937, Starbuck characterizes his religious inquiry as an "obsession,"
a compelling force which persistently affected
the crucial directions in his life. In the following
passage he discloses the general nature of that
drive:

> "In the first place
> it is hardly correct to say
> that I have worked at the
> Psychology of Religion. The
> greater truth is the other
> way about. It has worked at
> me. Since adolescence there
> has been an irresistable urge
> --a driving force acting some-
> times outside of the personality,
> sometimes as a part of the
> very selfhood, impelling in
> that direction. My 'mission'
> --it has always felt like a sort

84

of 'calling'--has been to
try to render thinkable
and usable the illusive
reals of religion. This
obsession has shifted along
the years through many phases:
zeal for understanding,
teaching, and expounding
the Old and New Testament--
a zeal that found an outlet as
teacher of Sunday School;
missionary enthusiasms; the
application of scientific
concepts to the wonder
tales and miracles; historical
and sociological orientation;
philosophical revaluation;
psychological analysis and
synthesis based upon an
immediate study of the facts
of personal experience.
Regardless of the particular
outlet for expression, the
obsession is always present
and gains momentum through
the years."[70]

Secondly, Starbuck confesses to a kind of
"chronic religiosity." In writing to Dr. Daniel
A. Poling, of the J. C. Penney Foundation, to request funds for his character research project, he
submits, "I suspect you know that I have never
entertained any lively passions that were not actu-
ated by fundamentally religious motives."[71] Even
during his sophomore and junior years in college,
when doubts were prevalent and the process of dis-
mantaling traditional beliefs was so conspicuous,
there yet remained a constructive posture which
enabled him to continue to participate in various
Christian associations, including the United
Presbyterian church.

An "ineradicable mysticism" is also acknowledged
by Starbuck, a quality pointed out by friends and

85

critics alike. Regardless of the nature of his involvement, in it he attested to a sense of "all-over-
ishness" or "all-throughishness." Paralleling this
feeling is a kind of theological or philosophical
asseveration which Starbuck describes as follows:

> "Along with the mystical im-
> mediacy of the religious experi-
> ence and its 'mighty inwardness,'
> there has run through the years
> a philosophy or theology to match.
> It might be described as a sort
> of pantheism--or panpsychism or
> pankalonism--a sense of an Inter-
> fusing Presence . . . In child-
> hood there were floating images:
> a flaming sword, tablets of stone,
> parting of waters, healing of
> diseases. These pictures, how-
> ever, seemed evanescent and fanci-
> ful, while the feeling of a
> Presence has had body and sub-
> stance."[72]

Despite this recondite faith, Starbuck maintained a sound scepticism of any radical forms of
mysticism, and never gave up the struggle for intellectual comprehension and honesty. He declares
himself to be a most "persistent and stubborn
doubter;" however, he quickly adds, "The negations
have never been altogether, not even predominantly,
destructive, for they have been held in check by
insatiable hungers reaching in every direction, including the wish sufficiently to rationalize religion as to make of it thinkable, understandable,
and controllable."[73]

Starbuck's approach to religion is a study in
the art of synthesis. Ever open, ever searching
for parts that would enhance the whole, Starbuck
always attempted to incorporate that which brought
fuller understanding. As a student of world religions, for instance, he declares a rather universal
indebtedness: "Not one of the great religions

and hardly one of the minor cults has failed to furnish some sort of sustenance to the spiritual life."[74] While constantly in search for a "new order," he remained realistically cognizant of the reality of unsettledness and disharmony which preceded any sort of synthesis. This dynamic tension was characteristic of his own experience. He could readily concur with Clarke's "law of human life" which stated,

> "that the development of
> differences must precede their
> reconciliation. Variety must
> precede harmony, analysis must
> prepare the way for synthesis,
> opposition must go before union."[75]

When Starbuck was selected to be one of the six commencement orators, at his graduation from Indiana University, he addressed himself to the topic, "The Unity of Opposites," affirming concisely, "Out of strife and conflict, /there came/ the higher harmony."[76]

Finally, if we are to analyze Starbuck's relationship to the psychology of religion, it is essential that we understand his conception of religion. In 1913, while serving in the religious education department of the Unitarian association, Starbuck gave twelve lectures at Meadville Theological School, following the convention of the Religious Education Association at Cleveland. In these lectures he developed his conception of religion as "man's complete response to reality, a whole-minded harmony of all our instincts in their refined and spiritualized form."[77] Rachel Knight, a graduate student of Starbuck's in her book The Founder of Quakerism, which she dedicated to Starbuck, supplies us with his definition of religion, as delivered in an unpublished lecture.[78] She writes that

> "he defined religion as
> 'centering in one's total and
> whole-hearted reaction toward

87

his most vitalizing feeling
for that which has supreme
and absolute worth or value--
towards his most intimate sense
of Reality."[79]

It is directly evident that Starbuck is speaking of
a religion of personal experience, which is at the
center of man's being. This understanding of Starbuck's view of religion is substantiated later in
Knight's book, when she compares the postition of
George Fox with that of her professor, Dr. Starbuck:

"Though Fox gives no
formal definition of religion,
one finds that for him, as for Dr.
Starbuck, the life of religion
means just the whole-hearted
total responding--not alone
in feeling and mental conception,
but in actual daily living--
consistently and harmoniously,
to this Reality which carries with
it this ultimate vitalizing
sense of supreme worth and absolute
value. Religion becomes a widening
stream of conserved and objectified
experience of value, cumulative
through the years. It is not
true religion until it calls forth
the total response, the intimate
and vigorous and meaningful
response, of the whole life."[80]

The nature and quality of Starbuck's life discloses
the utter seriousness with which he affirmed this
conception of religion.

Personal Background

Our picture of Edwin Starbuck is incomplete
without a consideration of his various physical,
intellectual, emotional, and social characteristics.
An attempt will be made to present a fair and accurate

image of his personal and professional life primarily through the use of descriptions made by Starbuck's colleagues, students, friends and sometimes critics. Finally, his marriage, and consequent family life, will be recounted, and their importance in his life examined.

Starbuck's physical appearance was unusually impressive. The name Starbuck has Scandinavian origin and signifies "a person of imposing appearance, great or grand bearing."[81] Starbuck was fully a model of what his name denotes. According to a close student of his, who studied under him in the early, 1920's, he was a large man, over six feet tall, broad shouldered but trimly built. His hair, thick and wavy, was prematurely silvery white by the time of his middle years. His skin was finely textured, "white with a glow of pink that indicated both health and refinement." His features were "kindly," and he had an "easy smile;" yet, there always seemed to be an "air of detached meditation about him." In terms of dress, he is described as having the appearance of always being "freshly cleaned and pressed."[82]

Starbuck was an example of rare physical strength and energy. The same student of his comments: "He played a strenuous game of handball for exercise and was still adept at it when I saw him last at nearly eighty years of age." Starbuck's grandson, George Starbuck, also attests to this vigorous athletic play, even in his grandfather's latter years. He says that his grandfather worked and played very hard; he was a "driver."[83] A student, under Starbuck at the University of Southern California, tells of Starbuck's spirited play in the game of volleyball at least until he was past seventy years old.[84] Another student of his, at Iowa, corroborates his ardent manner, in sports, if not in everything he attempted. "I remember a group of us playing handball during the semester I was there and he was one of the best and most enthusiastic players on the floor."[85]

89

The extent of his intellectual capacity readily matches the range of his physical prowess. His daughter, Helen L. Starbuck, a practicing psychiatrist, upon hearing of my proposed study of her father, wrote, that "a definitive study is long overdue of this rarely endowed, creative man, who was years ahead of his time. In one of his classes in philosophy, we studied persons--through the ages, who might come under the category of 'genius' or 'near genius.'--He, himself, was such a man."[86] A letter from one of his colleagues at the University of Iowa, F. B. Knight, to Professor Herman H. Horne of the College of Education at New York University, regarding the desirablility of Starbuck changing his position, reveals a similar analysis of his abilities.

> "In all frankness I must say that
> Prof. Starbuck's loss to our staff
> would be a matter of real regret
> to me. Those of us who have
> watched his work and are in intimate
> contact with his teaching recognize
> in him a real teacher and a very
> stimulating companion. He would
> be sadly missed on our campus
> not only for his delightful
> social self but also because
> of his mind and its products.
> Starbuck possesses flashes of genius
> and insight which are most
> helpful to all of us."[87]

Futher evidence of Starbuck's capabilities is disclosed in a pointed statement by President John G. Bowman, of the University of Iowa, who in writing to the Trustees of the Kahn Foundation, regarding Starbuck's application for a traveling fellowship, expressed, "Dr. Starbuck combines marked /my Italics/ native ability and unususal physical strength, both of which he has turned to good account."[88] Still, additional attestation to his abilities is exhibited by the fact that he was selected to be one of the commencement speakers at his graduation from both

90

high school and college.

Another daughter of Starbuck's, Margaret, also
rates her father's talents at the "genius" level.
She observes two basic characteristics of his intelligence, one, his keen ability to abstract and to
generalize, and, two, his broad and subtle vocabulary.
Both of these intellectual attributes are markedly
evident in his writings.[89]

The impact of his personality was equally as
impressive. The following valuations substantiate
this statement. Dr. P. R. Hightower, one of Starbuck's
students at Iowa, reflects, "He was one of the most
delightful persons it has been my good fortune to
know. He was gentle, kind, gracious, and lovable
to the greatest degree."[90] Another student concurs.
She says he was "gentle" and "kind" and had a "warm-
hearted personality," which she notes "pervaded
everything."[91] O. V. Jackson, of the Department of
Bible and Religion, at Cornell College, Mt. Vernon,
Iowa, writing to the President of Iowa Universtiy,
Walter A. Jessup, a letter of appreciation for what
he considered to be an outstanding constructive and
inspiring lecture delivered by Starbuck at Cornell
on "Religion in the modern World," comments on more
than the lecture itself. He praises Starbuck:
"His thorough scholarship and charming personality
will bring honor to any institution."[92] Starbuck's
gregariousness is characterized by a student's
comment that he was "always the center of a lively
and jolly dialogue."[93]

Starbuck manifested a wit that was ever present
even in his most common, everyday associations. As
a support for his Research Station in Character
Training and Religious Education at Iowa, from the
Institute of Social and Religious Research, Starbuck
asks President Jessup for a general statement of
recommendation. At the end of his letter to Dr.
Jessup, he jestingly remarks, "It would not do any
great harm to prevaricate a little in the interest
of a great cause."[94] On another occasion, a member
of the Grounds and Buildings Department, at the

University of Iowa, was the recipient of his humor. Starbuck writes this rather unorthodox plea for assistance regarding a maintenance problem:

> "The radiator in E 403 East
> Hall is constantly busy with its
> music. I don't like the tune. I
> think the blooming thing has
> asthma. I wish you would find it
> possible to send a doctor or a
> plumber at your convenience to
> treat it else I shall be driven to
> the Psychopathic."[95]

One of the central aspects of his personality was his keen sensitivity and openness in interpersonal relationships. Although not incapable of anger, his major role seemed to be a supportive one. Such expressions of support, sensitivity, and ingenuousness enabled Starbuck to communicate with persons in depth, but they also caused him some sorrow. William James had informed him that he would suffer most from being so sensitive about individual's responses. Starbuck expected the best from his students, his children and his associates in general and he was hurt when people failed to rise above themselves or to measure up to his expectations.[96]

Starbuck was a man of many interests and passions, although he never allowed himself to be spread so thinly as to hinder the intensity of his energies in the direction of any one endeavor. A close associate comments that he loved life fully, every "golden day," people of all kinds, animals, nature; and he loved growth of all sorts, including its representation in pregnant women.[97]

He was independent, enough to possess a pioneering, unrutted spirit. Yet he was never so radically progressive as to place himself entirely out of the common struggles of the conventional structures of the society and the university. A phrase, befitting Starbuck's image, suggests that

he was "slightly revolutionary, all his life." An
interesting story about Starbuck is recounted by his
daughter, Margaret. While at Harvard, her father
was closely associated with William James, who cate-
gorized individuals as conservatives or radicals.
An incident occurred which caused James to label
Starbuck a radical. Professor James, with a number
of his students, including Starbuck, supposedly
attempted to cross a street, where traffic was approaching. Apparently, only Starbuck ran over to
the other side of the street, while the rest of the
group held back. James reasoned that those who
remained were conservative, but that Starbuck, who
took the risk of crossing, was radical.[98] Perhaps
this is an appropriate analogy for Starbuck's position,
since he surely risked the crossing of many streets;
he was a pioneering street-crosser in the face of
sometimes unfamiliar traffic and even "hit-and-run"
drivers.

Fitting the spirit of such liberal persuasion,
and the fundamental thrust of Starbuck's personality,
is his attitude toward change. Dr. Howard Voss
Meredith, Professor at the University of Iowa, came
to Iowa as a student, and had a couple of interviews
with Starbuck the summer before he left the university
for California. Dr. Meredith recalls, quite vividly,
a favorite phrase of Starbuck's when talking about
change: "We must become aware of the importance of
change as in a category all its own, not just change
for the sake of something or toward something, but
change for the sake of change."[99] He had come to
understand change as so utterly central to one's
experience, that he could extend the meaning of his
concept, and say that, "gradually we are beginning
to see that whatever of reality there is, is itself
in an endless process of change."[100] One further
example, of his positive posture toward change, is
revealed in a conversation Starbuck had with his
daughter, Winifred, who was experiencing the throes
of early adolescence. She reconstructs her fathers
counsel as follows:

"These next years are often

93

called the 'turmoil of adolescense,'
but it doesn't have to be turmoil;
it is just change, /my Italics/ flux--
whenever there is flux there is opportunity to mold, and every change will
be molding into adolescence."[101]

One could not begin to understand some of Starbuck's unique sentiments and conceptualizations; nor
could certain actions of his be understood, without
an awareness of the inner struggle Starbuck faced.
He describes himself as being pulled in many different, and ofttimes, completely opposite directions.
He characterizes this internal rivalry as a battle of
"beasts" in a "menagerie," where some do no more than
have a "jolly tussle," but where others experience
"long-drawn conflicts." The following passage, by
Starbuck, graphically illustrates the dynamic tension
that existed:

"This warring between tenderness
and toughness between acceptance and
doubt, between inner sensitivity and
vigorous intellectuality are only
samples from among a number of con-
flicting eccentricities: dynamic,
heavily muscled for work and play, at
the same time with irresistable cultural urges and a well-developed inner
sanctuary of worth and meaning; an
imagination intrigued with plots,
plans, and programmers--many of them
extending into the long future--and at
the same time a dullness of fancy that
must stubbornly wrestle with a 'problem' almost endlessly before it
reaches clarification; devotion to
both art and the sciences; strong
sensory appeal and keen recognition of
ideal values; optimism and pessimism;
timidity that can hardly face an audience with equanimity, then, when the
inhibitions are off, the voice of an
enthusiast and would-be prophet."[102]

94

Such polarization in Starbuck renders authenticity to the seemingly contradictory act of calling him, simultaneously, a "mystic" and a "scientist."

Finally, we are struck by what Starbuck describes as his "inner confidence in Life, in Truth, in Beauty," which likely receives its impetus, if not origin, from his experience of "illumination" during his college years. He modestly confesses the following resultant characteristics and positions to be "simple human weaknesses;" however, they might just as easily be labelled virtues, and signs of personal liberation:

> ". . . over-conscientious; sensitive,; chronically sympathetic; ridiculously suggestible even to the point of gullibility; shockingly indifferent to wealth and name and fame; no fear of death; no concern about personal continuance; no felt need of the conserving presence of some Absolute."[103]

His sense of "at-home-ness" in the Universe renders these latter questions, crucial to so many persons, rather inconsequential to Starbuck.

To enlarge, even further, our understanding of Starbuck's life, appraisals of his personal contribution, specifically as a scholar and teacher, are presented. A brief feature article, in the Research News, of the University of Southern California, entitled "Edwin Diller Starbuck--An Appreciation," has outstandingly focused in on the major aspects of his contribution. Wilbur Long, the author of this sketch, points to four personal qualities of Starbuck, which he observed:

> "A vivid zest for life; an exhuberant love for knowledge, that has struck fire in the minds of many students, because for him facts have always been vital, full of significance; an unusual breadth of interest, revealed in his teaching career, which included instruction in Latin, mathematics,

95

                    education, religious education,
                    and philosophy; and an essentially
                    pioneering spirit, an urge to
                    break new and important trails."[104]

In the same article, Long perceptively interprets Starbuck's conception of scholarship, and
suggests that this is the key to his contributing
life. He states, "Doctor Starbuck feels that scholarship is not like a star, a thing to dwell apart;
rather it is something to be put to use in the market
place for the abundant service of humanity." It is
anticipated that we shall be able to see not only
how accurately this statement portrays Starbuck's
role as a professional, but also the full legitimacy
of attributing, as Long does in the previous passage,
such personal qualities to his life.

In the Proceedings and Addresses of The American
Philosophical Association, 1947-1948, a memorial for
Starbuck is included. Dr. Herbert L. Searles, who
had been a student of his at Iowa, and later a colleague in the Department of Philosophy at the University of Southern California, submitted the memorial,
which describes Starbuck's distinction as a teacher.
Dr. Searles writes: "His many students remember him
as a master teacher with an unusual capacity for inspiring independence of thought."[105] The recollec-
tions of many of Starbuck's students support this
statement. Mrs. Carol M. Turner, for instance, after
a lapse of four decades, still remembers well her
invigorating experiences in Starbuck's class. She
writes:

                    "My forty-year old impressions
                    of Dr. Starbuck's Esthetics course
                    are vivid yet. With many their
                    obvious and mechanical art of
                    teaching obscures what is being
                    taught. Dr. Starbuck inspired
                    a stronger awareness of appreci-
                    ation of the value of living.
                    I can 'hear' his voice yet--
                    revealing, as did his facial

> expression, his strength, kind-
> ness, and good humor. When he
> looked at us, I felt that he
> joined us in considering realities,
> which from lesser instructors
> would have been mere routine
> abstractions. He could build
> our confidence to express our
> ideals and convince us that
> our uncertain youthful attitudes
> could develop toward truth."[106]

A graduate student of Starbuck's at Iowa, is also
able to lucidly review the distinct influence Starbuck had upon him in class. In referring to a letter
requesting information about his relationship with
and evaluation of Starbuck, Ralph D. Minard responds,

> ". . .it inspired a reappraisal in
> my own consciousness of what the
> challenge of Dr. Starbuck's vibrant
> personality had done in my earlier
> years of susceptible impression,
> to awaken new insights, interests,
> values and objectives. Though I
> may never have been a very illus-
> trative example of Dr. Starbuck's
> teaching and influence he is still
> etched in the unshaken memory of
> recollections as he came bounding
> into the classroom for his daily
> lecture, a powerful and unforget-
> table figure."[107]

Mrs. Carroll E. Nelson, a student of Starbuck's in
1923 emphasized that he was the greatest professor
she had ever had, and that she had been stimulated
more by his ideas than those of anyone else.[108]
Another student declares that Starbuck was one of
the most inspiring persons he had ever known.[109]
And yet another student of his refers to Starbuck
as "a modern Socrates, bringing to birth the souls
of his students."[110]

Not every student could agree with such totally
praiseworthy evaluation, however. One person, a
student of Starbuck's during his latter years of
teaching, at the University of California, comments
on a seminar he attended. His evaluation has Starbuck
appearing considerably less than inspirational.
He remembers:

> "I was a little bored by the
> informal bull-session atmosphere.
> He lectured very well in the
> philosophy forum but never in
> class. In fact he was quite
> unsystematic in discussion
> plan and in assignments."111

He does confess, though, that this assessment may
have been affected by the fact that he was not
highly interested in the particular course subject.

Undoubtedly, there were particular courses less
interesting than others, and there were certain
lectures delivered or periods of time that lapsed
in which Starbuck's offerings were less than outstanding. Even a close associate of his proposes
that his performance was not consistent, and that
out of the humdrum he would then move into something
great.112 Still, in general, his courses appear
to have been dynamic, and seem to have dealt with
significant issues. One of his colleagues at Iowa
in referring to the response of Starbuck's graduate
students, says they "speak with uniform respect
for his guidance and frequently reveal real affection
for him."113 This appraisal, or one very similar
to it, appears to be rather universal among Starbuck's
students.

Starbuck spent most of his years as a professor
at the University of Iowa. His value, to the institution, as a scholar, was most significant. One of
his graduate students asserts: "His scholarship
was profound and wide." In continuing, he even
declares: "It was his outstanding abilitiy as a
psychologist that took me to the University of Iowa"114

Others have acknowledged the major impact of Starbuck upon the university. One such voice was raised in 1930, in reaction to the possibility of losing Starbuck's services at Iowa University. Herbert Martin, an associate of his in the Philosophy Department, writes:

> "From my viewpoint few others have added such luster to her good name and fame. . . While still a stranger to the campus, to me and to others, the name Starbuck was a synonym for the University. . .He has today the public ear and eye as never before. People from near and far look to him and Iowa for light and leading."[115]

In the face of imminent mandatory retirement at Iowa, however, Starbuck did leave the university that very year.

One of Starbuck's haunting regrets, as a professional, was that he failed to write enough. He had succumbed to his passion for people; consequently, a significant portion of his time had been spent with students and colleagues. His daughter, Margaret, writes, regarding this point:

> "Like so many of the great professors of his time, father's great sorrow was his inability to set aside time for serious writing; he had the sense of having managed poorly because his ideas must live in the lives of students, collaborators, and friends--and not in the covers of books."[116]

It is plainly our loss that Starbuck was unable to create any more time for publications.

Dr. Starbuck was a member of numerous professional organizations including the American Philosophical Association, American Psychological Association, Religious Education Association, International

99

Gesellschaft fur Religionpsychologie, National Society for Scientific Study of Education, Pacific Geographical Society, Phi Beta Kappa, and Pi Epsilon Theta. He was also a fellow of the American Association for the Advancement of Science.[117] One other source adds, to this lengthy list, his membership in the National Education Association.[118]

On August 5, 1896,[119] a step was taken which would have foremost significance in the ensuing years of Starbuck's life. He was married in Lancaster, Pennsylvania, to Anna Maria Diller, one of eight children, the daughter of a merchant, Issac Diller.

Starbuck met Anna Maria at Harvard University, where both were attending. She was one of the first two women to study at Harvard. She and the President of Radcliffe petitioned Harvard for this purpose, and were informed that if they came together they would be accepted. Both Starbuck and his wife-to-be studied under William James and Josiah Royce, but it was in Dean Everett's class that they met.[120]

Very close friends of the family suggest that Starbuck's wife was the "inspiration behind him, the prime mover," and that he depended upon her greatly.[121] She seems to have possessed the rare gift of being able to establish rapport with practically everyone. She had a profound love for music, and could so capably offer people insight into its beauty. Almost blind as a young girl, from spinal meningitis, she went to a private school in Ontario, Canada, where she was able to develop her special interest in music. Later she was sent to Leipzig to study with Hershift, a student of Franz Liszt, who studied under Schumann. She became one of the first to use seriously the technique of Leschetizky (sensitive touch).

Anna Diller Starbuck was on the faculty in the music department at Iowa University until her death in 1929. She apparently was rather timid, but lectured beautifully before her classes.[122] Perhaps she was best known for her lecture recitals which took her to many of the leading musical centers in the United States. In a promotional brochure, designed to des-

cribe her abilities and her availability as a concert pianist, a special aspect of her work is noted.

> "A valuable feature of Mrs.
> Starbuck's recitals that is much
> appreciated is that, when desired,
> she explains her musical numbers
> beforehand in an informal way,
> sometimes analyzing them and play-
> ing the chief motives. Her ren-
> ditions thus afford a rare oppor-
> tunity for persons not musically
> trained, to learn really to enjoy
> the beauties of classic music."[123]

Starbuck's thorough interest in his wife's work
is illustrated in a letter he wrote to President Bowman, of Iowa, regarding his wife's musical involvement in the university. Unknown to her, he was inquiring about any possible official connection she
might have with the university as a teacher. Writing
from Boston, while on sabbatical leave from the university, he refers to Bowman's wish that Starbuck
continue to stay at Iowa. Starbuck raises some concern about salary, but cites an interest in his wife's
happiness as the crucial problem. He states: "The
more important consideration from my standpoint is
that Mrs. Starbuck is not finding in Iowa City a fitting outlet for musical expression. I am not willing
to live where she is not properly used and appreciated."[124]

They did remain at the university, however, and
Anna Starbuck found a sense of fulfillment in her
association with the university. She lived life fully
and richly, and was well received by members of the
faculty. At her death, on February 12, 1929, they
drew up several resolutions in memorial to her life.
These are quoted by Starbuck in a letter he writes to
her intimate friends and relatives. From those quotes
the following excerpts are taken:

> "For over a score of years were
> members of the faculty privileged to
> enjoy the quiet kindliness of her

friendly personality; for two
score years or more were students. . .granted a rare interpretation of beautiful messages
from some of the master minds
of music. . .

Apostle of art, composer
of music and poetry, exampler
of human peace and friendship,
builder of a splendid home,
mother of devoted children,
partner of a worshipful husband--
Anna Diller Starbuck--we now re-
vere her memory."[125]

Starbuck reveals something of the poise with
which he accepted the death of his beloved wife,
when he penned these eloquent words to her friends
and relatives:

"I am sure we, with you,
shall all feel more closely
drawn together through our
mutual reverence for that rare
life and that insofar as we
have been able to enter into it
we belong to the rich fellowship
of those who have gotten their
birth into the Soul of Beauty."

Between 1897 and 1912 Edwin and Anna had their
family. They were blessed with eight children, four
boys and four girls, although their first child
Alonzo died in infancy, and their third child, Edwin
Eli, died at the age of two. The children named in
order of their birth, were Alonzo, Arthur Diller,
Edwin Eli, Anna Margaret, Helen Lillian, Winifred,
Dorothea Ansley, and Edmund Osborne.[126]

The happiness that Starbuck's marriage and
children brought to him could hardly be measured. A
friend of the family, while at Iowa, commented that
the Starbuck's led her list of the happiest married
people she had ever known. She vividly recalls a

102

statement Starbuck once made to her, "Everyday is a poem with my wife and children."127 In a letter to this same associate of the family, and student of Starbuck's, he encloses an analysis, in poetic form, of his reasons for the ever fuller and richer experiences of his family life through the years.

"Friends, playfellows, mates,
lovers. Scarcely a day that wasn't
right. Why? It all seems so clear
and simple. Both, emancipated pagans.
Each finding in the other a devotee
to the soul of life, or, as my Blessed One sometimes called it, the
Spirit of the Universe. Taking liber-
ties with Tennyson one might say:
'We saw through life and death,
through good and evil. Each saw thro'
the others soul. The marvel of the
Everlasting Will an open scroll. Living together with a vitalizing sense
of Permanent Values, then little
things are little; love is religion;
mating, a sacrament; children are
music and poetry; work is a joy; and
life is Sweet."128

The elegant beauty of such relationship is evidenced in the total family experience. Friends of the family commonly observed their home as an inspirational example of interpersonal freedom, respect, cooperation and genuine love. One of Starbuck's students at Iowa, who had not been on the campus very long before he and his wife were invited to the Starbuck's home, comments:

"Dr. Starbuck's home was one of
if not the most delightful that it
has been my great delight to visit.
Each member of the family seemed most
interested in the welfare of all the
other members. It was /a/ delight to
behold."129

This atmosphere created a sense of belonging to

103

the family. Another student recalls the generous
gesture of the Starbuck's during the first summer
he came to Iowa in 1920. He and his wife were invited to live in the Starbuck home without cost,
while the Starbuck family was on vacation. They
were made to feel that they were doing the Starbuck's a favor. He describes his memory of the family, and his response to their alliance.

> "Among them all there was an open
> display of affection,--hugging,
> kissing, caressing, (the father
> and mother too)--all of which had
> been carefully tabooed in my puri-
> tanical background. But with them
> it was genuine and unrestrained."[130]

The Starbuck home was always open to students
and friends. Dinner guests were unending; they were
continually entertaining. Sunday evening became a
special drop-in time, when refreshments were served,
and a social atmosphere of casual interchange pre-
dominated.[131]

Their home was the epitome of culture, a haven
for art, literature, music, and distinguished friendship. There was nurture, with little indoctrination.
Values were not preached to the children, but never
was this a sign of unconcern. Rather, the human
examples of their parents became the childrens'
natural incentive for good conduct. An interesting
observation of the subtle role of influence Edwin
and Anna had upon their children is made by their
daughter, Margaret:

> "Neither mother nor father were
> aware that they were any different
> from anybody else, nor did we dis-
> cover from them how much they were
> honored and respected. We were
> just simple, busy people who had a
> lot of fun doing what we loved to
> do."[132]

The children were left to explore on their own,

104

to experiment, to question, even to deny values. In
this liberated process, they learned to come to grips
with life's meanings and values. One of Starbuck's
students, who had spent some time with the Starbuck
family, said he saw, for the first time, a parent-
child relationship, of the kind which is today called
"permissive." He recalls, "there were no reprimands
and when one criticized another it was usually in
good-humored banter."[133] The freedom, permitted the
children in thought and action, amazed him, but he
grew to thoroughly appreciate the sound value of this
approach, as exemplified in the inner- and interrela-
tionships of the Starbuck family.

Mrs. Starbuck became a convinced Quaker because
she wanted the children to have "birthright" membership as Quakers, or Friends; however, in Iowa City,
the children were taken to the Sunday school of the
Unitarian association, where Anna played the organ.
Dr. Starbuck rarely attended the church at this time,
but it was important to Mrs. Starbuck to have meaningful "church experience."[134] An interesting, perceptive observation is made, that attests to more
than denominational affiliation, as the Starbuck's
would have wished. It is stated, "Mostly they had
church in their hearts and minds."[135]

Starbuck would have retired at the age of 65,
but he was asked to take his Institute of Character
Research to the University of Southern California,
and he accepted the invitation. Shortly after the
death of his wife, in 1930, he moved to California,
where he did not retire from active teaching until
1943.

Starbuck regretted that he had not spent more
of his time in religion, especially at the University
of Southern California, where he had served as Professor of Philosophy and Psychology. In the field of
religion, he had sensed a possession of unusual perception. On an occasion, in one of the latter years
of his life, while staying with his daughter, Winifred, in Conneticut, he visited Yale's library.
When his daughter came to pick him up. Starbuck had
before him a catalogue tray, including cards on the

psychology of religion, and he reflected, "Perhaps I should have stayed with that. There has been so little done since."[136] We share this regret with him, but also recognize that so much of his work was related to the field of religion or the application thereof.

On November 18, 1947, four years after he retired, Dr. Edwin Diller Starbuck, a pioneer in living, died.

NOTES

1. He was born Edwin Eli Starbuck but changed his middle name when married to Diller in deference to his wife, Anna Maria Diller.
2. Edwin Diller Starbuck, "Religion's Use of Me," Religion in Transition, edited by Vergilius Ferm (London: George Allen & Unwin LTD, 1937), p. 212.
3. Alexander Starbuck, The History of Nantucket: County, Island and Town (Boston: C. E. Goodspeed & Co., 1924), p. 656 in a footnote.
4. Ibid., p. 13.
5. Flora Starbuck James, publisher, A Geneology of the Descendants of Samuel and Luzena Starbuck (Palo Alto, California, June, 1962).
6. Starbuck, The History of Nantucket, p. 17.
7. Ibid., p. 802.
8. A Geneology of the Descendants of Samuel and Luzena Starbuck, p. 59.
9. Starbuck, The History of Nantucket, pp. 666-667.
10. Ibid., p. 351.
11. Ibid., p. 32.
12. Ibid., p. 352 (The quote is from Macy's History, p. 33).
13. Ibid., p. 353.
14. Ibid., p. 546.
15. Ibid., p. 665.
16. Ibid., p. 803 (This quote is from the footnote).
17. Ibid., p. 528.
18. Ibid., pp. 529-530.
19. Ibid., p. 546.
20. Mary Eliza Starbuck, My House and I: A Chronological of Nantucket (Boston: Houghton Mifflin Co., 1929), pp. 25-26.
21. Ibid., p. 172.
22. A Geneology of the Descendants of Samuel and Luzena Starbuck, pp. 60-61.
23. Ibid., pp. 1-2.
24. Starbuck, "Religion's Use of Me," pp. 207-208.
25. From a conversation with Edwin Diller Starbuck's daughter, Margaret Starbuck, December 30, 1968, in Los Angeles.
26. Starbuck, "Religion's Use of Me," p. 208.
27. Ibid., p. 211.

28. Ibid., pp. 212-213.
29. Ibid., pp. 213-215.
30. In a letter dated March 31, 1969, received from Dr. Lonzo Jones, of Terre Haute, Indiana.
31. Starbuck, "Religion's Use of Me," pp. 217-219.
32. Ibid., p. 205.
33. In a personal letter from Dr. P. R. Hightower, who studied under Starbuck at the University of Iowa, dated April 1, 1969.
34. A. Rudolph Uren, Recent Religious Psychology (New York: Charles Scribner's Sons, 1928), p. 51.
35. Starbuck, "Religion's Use of Me," pp. 226-227.
36. Ibid., p. 230.
37. Ibid., pp. 232-233.
38. Ibid., p. 207.
39. Ibid., pp. 208-209.
40. Ibid., p. 209.
41. Ibid., pp. 209-210.
42. In a letter dated February 25, 1969, received from Dr. Albion Ray King, Mt. Vernon, Iowa, one of Starbuck's graduate students.
43. Starbuck, "Religion's Use of Me," p. 210.
44. Ibid., p. 209.
45. In a letter, received from Dr. Lonzo Jones, dated March 3, 1969.
46. Starbuck, "Religion's Use of Me," p. 215.
47. Told to me in an interview with George Starbuck, grandson of Edwin Diller, at University of Iowa, June 25, 1968.
48. Rachel Knight, The Founder of Quakerism (London: Swarthmore Press, 1922), p. 256.
49. Starbuck, "Religion's Use of Me," pp. 215-217.
50. Told to me in an interview with Margaret Starbuck Lee in Los Angeles, December 30, 1968.
51. Letter from Dr. Lonzo Jones, dated March 3, 1969. Other references, however, take issue with this point, indicating there was not complete disaffiliation.
52. Interview with Dr. Winifred Scott, Starbuck's daughter, in Los Angeles, December 30, 1968.
53. Starbuck, "Religion's Use of Me," pp. 219-220.
54. James Freeman Clarke, Ten Great Religions (Boston: Houghton Mifflin Co., 1871), p. 1.
55. Ibid., p. 489.
56. Ibid., p. 490.
57. Ibid., p. 507.

58. Ibid., p. 509.
59. Friedrich Max Müller, Lectures on the Science of Religion (New York: Charles Scribner's Sons, 1893), p. 100.
60. Ibid., p. 7.
61. Letter from Dr. Lonzo Jones, dated March 3, 1969.
62. Starbuck, "Religion's Use of Me," p. 227.
63. Gardner Murphy, Historical Introduction to Modern Psychology, (New York: Harcourt, Brace and Co., 1949), p. 18.
64. Starbuck, "Religion's Use of Me," p. 228.
65. Ibid. This experience took place between 1893 and 1895.
66. Interview with Margaret Starbuck Lee in Los Angeles, December 30, 1968.
67. Letter from MWL to J. M. Ambruster, in Chicago, dated May 7, 1929.
68. Interview with Starbuck's daughters, Margaret and Winifred, December 30, 1968.
69. Starbuck, "Religion's Use of Me," p. 201.
70. Ibid., pp. 202-203.
71. Letter from Starbuck to Dr. Daniel A. Poling, of the J. C. Penney Foundation and Mrs. Leonard Elmhirst, dated March 12, 1928.
72. Starbuck, Religion's Use of Me," pp. 204-205.
73. Ibid., p. 205.
74. Ibid., p. 206.
75. Clarke, Ten Great Religions, p. 509.
76. Starbuck, "Religion's Use of Me., p. 219.
77. From a scrapbook kept by officers in the Unitarian Religious Association while Starbuck served there, included in a letter to me from Elizzbeth H. Lasselle, Associate Editor of the American Unitarian Association and the Unitarian Sunday School Society, dated November 20, 1968.
78. Lecture Starbuck delivered at the Conference of Religious Workers at the Summer School, University of Iowa, 1918.
79. Knight, The Founder of Quakerism, p. 258.
80. Ibid., p. 265.
81. The History of Nantucket, p. 656.
82. A letter received from Dr. Lonzo Jones, dated March 3, 1969.
83. Interview with George Starbuck on June 25, 1968.

84.   Letter received from Albion King, dated February 25, 1969.

85.   Letter received from Dr. P. R. Hightower, Frankfort, Indiana, dated April 1, 1969.

86.   Letter received from Helen L. Starbuck, M.D., Starbuck's daughter, San Francisco, dated October 9, 1968.

87.   Letter from F. B. Knight, Iowa City, to Professor Herman H. Horne, College of Education, New York University, Washington Square, New York City, dated March 15, 1927.

88.   Letter from President John G. Bowman, University of Iowa, to the Trustees of the Kahn Foundation, Columbia University, New York City, dated February 27, 1912.

89.   Interview with Margaret Starbuck, December 30, 1968.

90.   Letter received from Dr. P. R. Hightower, April 1, 1969.

91.   Interview with Mrs. Carroll E. Nelson, October 12, 1968.

92.   Letter from O. V. Jackson, Department of Bible and Religion, Cornell College, Mt. Vernon, Iowa, to Walter A. Jessup, President of the University of Iowa, dated December 7, 1929.

93.   Letter received from Albion King, dated February 25, 1969.

94.   Letter from Starbuck to Walter A. Jessup, dated May 27, 1924.

95.   Letter from Starbuck to E. L. Bright, of the Grounds and Building Department, University of Iowa, dated April 26, 1930.

96.   Interview with Margaret Starbuck, December 30, 1968.

97.   Interview with Dr. Herbert and Mrs. Anna Searles, December 27, 1968.

98.   Interview with Starbuck's daughters, December 30, 1968.

99.   Interview with Dr. Howard Voss Meredith, in Iowa City, Summer, 1968.

100.   Quoted in a letter received from Dr. Lonzo Jones, March 3, 1969.

101.   Interview with Starbuck's daughter, December 30, 1968.

102.   Starbuck, "Religion's Use of Me," p. 206.

103. Ibid., p. 207.
104. Wilbur Long, "Edwin Diller Starbuck--An Appreciation," Research News II, No. 1 (Los Angeles: University of Southern California, Graduate School, 1936), p. 1.
105. Proceedings and Addresses of the American Philosophical Association, XXI (1947-1948), reprinted from The Philosophical Review, LVII, No. 4 (July, 1948), p. 380.
106. Letter received from Mrs. Carol M. Turner, Victoria, British Columbia, Canada, dated November 21, 1968.
107. Letter received from Ralph D. Minard, Truro, Iowa, March 4, 1969.
108. Interview with Mrs. Carroll E. Nelson, October 12, 1968.
109. Letter received from Albion King, February 25, 1969.
110. Letter received from Lonzo Jones, March 3, 1969.
111. Letter received from Albion King, February 25, 1969.
112. Interview with the Searles, December 27, 1968.
113. Letter from F. B. Knight to Professor Herman H. Horne dated March 15, 1927.
114. Letter received from Dr. P. R. Hightower, April 1, 1969.
115. Letter from Herbert Martin, Philosophy Department to President Walter A. Jessup, dated May 25, 1930.
116. Letter received from Margaret Starbuck, dated October 9, 1968.
117. The National Encyclopedia of American Biography, vol. E, 1937-38 (New York: James T. White and Co., 1938), p. 319.
118. Robert D. Runes, ed. Who's Who in Philosophy, MCMXLII (Philosophical Library, 1942) p. 256.
119. The National Encyclopedia of American Biography, p. 319. There is a discrepancy between this source and A Geneology of the Descendants of Samuel and Luzena Starbuck, p. 51, which has the date of August 6 instead.
120. Interview with Starbuck's daughter, December 30, 1968. Margaret Starbuck said that her parents met in Münsterberg's class, however, it is likely that Starbuck's own recollection is correct. See Starbuck, Religion's Use of Me, p. 226.

121. Interview with the Searles, December 27, 1968.
122. Interview with Starbuck's daughters, December 30, 1968.
123. Brochure on Anna Diller Starbuck, Concert Pianist, Teacher in the School of Music, University of Iowa. This is in the author's possession.
124. Letter from Starbuck in Boston to President Bowman, University of Iowa, dated February 17, 1913.
125. Letter from Starbuck sent to the Intimate Friends and Relatives of Anna Diller, dated February 19, 1929.
126. A Geneology of the Descendants of Samuel and Luzena Starbuck, p. 51.
127. Interview with Mrs. Carroll E. Nelson, October 12, 1968.
128. In a letter received from Mrs. Carroll E. Nelson, October 12, 1968. The quote comes from a letter she received from Starbuck, December 9, 1931, at the University of Southern California, Los Angeles.
129. Letter received from Dr. P. R. Hightower, April 1, 1969.
130. Letter received from Lonzo Jones, March 3, 1969.
131. Interview with Starbuck's daughter, December 30, 1968.
132. Letter received from Margaret Starbuck, October 24, 1968.
133. Letter from Lonzo Jones, March 3, 1969.
134. Interview with Starbuck's daughters, December 30, 1968.
135. Interview with Mrs. Carroll E. Nelson, October 12, 1968.
136. Interview with Starbuck's daughters, December 30, 1968.

CHAPTER III

A BIOGRAPHICAL PERSPECTIVE: CAREER

One of the commonly accepted definitions of the term "career," the "course of a person's life, especially in some particular pursuit,"[1] has special application to the life of Edwin Diller Starbuck. Perhaps his distinguished career can best be described as the perpetual pursuance of measuring, analyzing, and developing functional guidelines for behavior. The shape of his career, however, though characterized by this singular quest, was multi-faceted. This is notably evidenced by his serious interest and work in a number of fields, such as philosophy, psychology, education, and religion. He invested practically a half-century of his life in the field of education, dealing during that time with many of the major philosophical, psychological, and educational issues of his day. And from the very beginning of his career and throughout, his interest in the study of religion, and related areas of ethics and character education was emphatic. In recounting his special interest in psychology and education, Starbuck hastens to add, "In the study of religion there has been a similar omniverous appetite and catholicity of sympathy."[2] Clearly, Starbuck was not intensely interested in the forms of institutionalized religion, but he did seek to examine the functions and effects of personal religion, or values, in human living.

A student of philosophy, psychology, education and religion, this "intellectual pioneer" exemplified in his approach not only the significance, but also the validity of conceiving a relatedness in the fields of education. Undoubtedly, his early analysis of religious experience in psychological terms shocked many of the "divines" but this and other such studies consequently proved to be appropriate and useful to members in the fields of both psychology and religion. Starbuck had no sympathy for intellectual or academic isolationism. As one colleague at the University of Southern California appraised Starbuck, "Never at home in traditional grooves, he has always revolted

113

against the conventional barriers that mutually isolate the divisions of human interest."[3] It is natural, then, that the book jacket for <u>Look to This Day</u>,
a composite of selected works of Starbuck, should
emphasize this characteristic. Starbuck was designated as "the interpreter of religion and education
in the light of the latest psychological research,
/and7 the interpreter of philosophy from the viewpoint of scientific, social and ethical values."[4]
Certainly these statements attest to Starbuck's interdisciplinary orientation in the endeavor of education.

In examining the concrete products of Starbuck's
career, two factors must be considered if we are to
understand fairly the nature of his contribution.
First, as one of his closer associates commented about
Starbuck, "His passion was people."[5] As a result, his
writings are less than extensive, especially in book
form. Second, and certainly not unrelated, a major
investment of his time was made in connection with
group projects, such as his Institutes for character
research and education, and consequently his time for
personal publications was greatly limited. It is interesting to note, however, that between 1897, when
he took his first college teaching position after receiving his Ph.D., and 1947, the year of his death, a
career span of fifty years, in addition to his major
character education and literature projects, Starbuck
managed to have at least one, and at times, three or
four articles published per year, during thirty of
those fifty years, in numerous philosophical, psychological, educational and religious journals. Of
interest, too, is the fact that between 1910 and 1940,
twenty of Starbuck's addresses, delivered throughout
the country at various conferences and gatherings,
were published in current journals.[6]

Beginning

In the view of the present writer, Starbuck's
career actually begins with the preparation and publication of his classical study of religious conversion,
<u>Psychology of Religion</u>. By virtue of this work Star-
buck established himself as a pioneer in the field of

114

the psychology of religion and as a scholar in the academic arena. In 1908, James Bissett Pratt, whose name is also associated with early research in this field, made the following observation about Starbuck's 1899 publication: "The book deserves the wide reading which it has received, and is one of the two or three most important contributions to the psychology of religion that have yet been made."[7] Starbuck's part in the development of a scientific study of religion from the point of psychological investigation could not fail to influence the direction and extent of his subsequent contributions.

In 1897, the same year that he published the two major articles in the American Journal of Psychology which were to serve as the foundation for his single volume Psychology of Religion, Starbuck was offered a position as Assistant Professor of Education at Leland Stanford Junior University, now Stanford University, one of the best known universities in the country. He was invited to Stanford by David Starr Jordan, then the president of the university, but earlier the president of Indiana University where Starbuck did his undergraduate work, which included the study of geology under Jordan. Starbuck was asked to try something new, to bring together the fields of education and psychology in interdisciplinary study. He was even given the liberty to conduct courses in the psychology of religion. This was significant, for Starbuck considered that at that time there was "not one chance in a thousand for securing a position as teacher of the psychology of religion."[8] Starbuck conducted a seminar in this field for seniors and graduate students. During the first two years, their research centered around the study of conversion, adolescent religious phenomena, and related themes. During Starbuck's remaining four years at Stanford much of the research in the seminar dealt with the origin and development of the "God-idea" and the "God-experience."[9] Although, almost all of the raw data of this study was lost in shipment, later students at the University of Iowa, under Starbuck's direction, picked up and conserved much of this work. In fact, part of a doctor's dissertation by E. Leigh Mudge, a doctoral candidate under Starbuck, was published under the title The God Experience.[10]

115

While at Stanford, Starbuck participated in a number of innovative ventures.[11] Probably the first university course ever offered in educational psychology was taught there by Starbuck. In 1898 he introduced a course in character education, again, it appears, the first such course ever offered in a college or university.

With Dr. William Freeman Snow, a professor of hygiene, Dr. Starbuck offered a course entitled "Applied Physiology and Psycho-Physics," in which experimental tests were used to determine mental and physical variables. It was felt that this data would supply some answers as to the children's capacities and needs, and consequently, would prove useful in the development of better educational programs. Today, such a course is called "Tests and Measurements." Though a common course in the fields of education and psychology today, this was truly a pioneering effort at the time Starbuck was experimenting with it.[12] Interestingly, shortly after his early work in testing at Stanford, the Binet-Simon tests were introduced into the world, a revolutionary event in the history of psychological measurement.

Starbuck spent seven years at Stanford, and in 1903 was given a sabbatical leave. In the winter of that year Starbuck and his family traveled to Switzerland, where at the University of Zürich, Starbuck studied under Professor Ernst Meumann. A student of the founder of experimental psychology, Wilhelm Wundt, Meumann became the leader of the movement in experimental education and educational psychology.[13] Starbuck's laboratory research, under Meumann, dealt with the relationship of bodily functions and mental processes. The assumption of such research was that examining the rate and form of certain physiological processes provided a means of measuring to some extent the condition and changes of consciousness. Emotions, for instance, such as fear and fatigue, were being examined by studying changes occurring in the circulatory system. Starbuck, himself, sought to master the "sphygmomanometer," an instrument designed to measure arterial blood pressure.

Although Starbuck's interest in experimental research is evidenced by his year's sabbatical in the laboratory at Zürich, the ensuing years do not find Starbuck investing himself primarily in this direction. Starbuck did not return to Stanford at the end of his year's leave; rather, he was invited to Earlham College, where, as professor of education, he taught from 1904 to 1906.[14] Earlham College, a liberal arts institution located at Richmond, Indiana, was operated by the Society of Friends. Starbuck had two brothers and sisters who were alumni of the college, and before finally deciding to go to Indiana University, he, too, had thought seriously about going to Earlham for his undergraduate work. Starbuck had been asked to direct and develop a new school of education in the college, and although there is little record of these years, it appears that the challenge of developing a new program could not be turned down by him. The anticipated endowments for this program never materialized, however, nor were these years fruitful in terms of research. It is not surprising, then, that Starbuck changed his residence and accepted a new position. This move, to Iowa City, proved to be more permanent, however, for he remained at the University of Iowa for nearly a quarter-century.

University of Iowa (1906-1930)

Starbuck joined the faculty of the University of Iowa as a full professor in philosophy. He was a member of the combined division of philosophy and psychology until 1927 when an independent department of philosophy was established. Starbuck became the first head of that department, and held that position until 1930 when he left Iowa for an appointment in the philosophy department at the University of Southern California.

While at the University of Iowa an event occurred which basically determined the nature and direction of Starbuck's professional career. He served as the chairman of the Iowa state committee which in 1921 won a $20,000 national award for research in character education for public schools.[15] Starbuck's work at the

117

university can be divided into two general phases, the period prior to this award, and the period of his involvement afterwards. The most far-reaching result of "The Iowa Plan" was the emergence of an Institute in Character research,[16] which served generally to dominate his interest and time, not only through his remaining years at Iowa, but similarly, during his years at the University of Southern California as well.

Starbuck's earlier years at Iowa, prior to this winning study in character education, were filled with many of the typical obligations of a professional educator. Yet he assumed these responsibilities with unusual capacity and drive and quickly gained a reputation for intellectual competence. A representative statement is made by a friend of the family, who attended classes at the university with Starbuck's daughter, Helen. She describes Starbuck's influence upon the university in terms of "major impact" due to his scholarship and reputation for brilliance.[17] And he was described by numbers of his students and associates as truly an inspirational teacher.

There is little record of the events in Starbuck's career during his first six or seven years at the University of Iowa, but it does appear that he performed his work with great vigor, and with eagerness to explore in breadth and depth the academic fields of his interest. He taught by choice, practically every philosophy course offered at the university, and usually had a course or seminar in the psychology of religion. During the 1906-07 school year, for example, his first year of teaching at Iowa, Starbuck taught Logic, History of Philosophy, Logic of Debating, Genetic Psychology, Philosophy and Psychology of Religion, Aesthetics, Kant, Problems in Philosophy, and Philosophical Systems in India. During the summer session of that same school year he taught Introduction to Philosophy, and Public Lectures on the Interpretation of Religion.[18] It is incredible that Starbuck's accomplishments were not limited completely to his preparations for such an array of courses.

118

In 1912, the year of his sabbatical from the University of Iowa, Dr. Starbuck accepted a position in Boston with the Unitarian Sunday School Society.[19] He served as a consulting psychologist in connection with the development of a new religious education curriculum for the Society. Starbuck eagerly accepted the challenge of helping to prepare an educational program for children and youth, since he had proclaimed for some time that the hopes of the world lay with the proper training and education of the youth.

It is not surprising that Starbuck was invited to serve in this capacity. His first major work, Psychology of Religion, had revealed his keen interest in the establishment of sound religious education programs in light of an understanding of the lines of religious growth. He had written a number of articles dealing with various facets of the question of religious education.[20] Representative of his concern is a statement Starbuck made at the beginning of one of these articles: "I have a profound wish, as deep-going as my hope for the perfection of the human kind, that our children should have the right spiritual nourishment."[21]

Not to go unnoticed, too, was Starbuck's early involement in the Religious Education Association, organized in 1903. This organization sought to raise the standards of religious and moral education in church and school, through its national conventions, seminars, workshops, and its bimonthly journal, Religious Education, first published in 1906. Starbuck, both a member[22] and an officer[23] of the association from the very beginning, addressed its first annual convention held in Chicago, February 10-12, in 1903, with other such notables as George Albert Coe and John Dewey. Starbuck spoke on the topic "Religious Education as a Part of General Education."[24] In 1905, at the third annual convention, held in Boston, Starbuck was invited to address the group again, this time in reference to the general theme, "The Aims of Religious Education."[25] It is not likely that the Unitarian Sunday School Society

119

overlooked Starbuck's involvement in such affairs when contemplating his services.

Starbuck began his work with the Unitarian Association in September. In the preceeding month a news item was distributed throughout the church relating Starbuck's educational background and professional accomplishments. It noted that he was "one of the few religious educators of the first rank in America." And as if to defend his place in their program, the feature concludes:

> "He is a birthright member of
> the Society of Friends, but has for
> several years been an active supporter
> of the Unitarian Church in Iowa City.
> He is thus fitted by training and
> by close sympathy with our work
> and ideals to become a leader
> in our educational movement."[26]

Charged with the formulation of a new course of study in religion for Unitarian Sunday schools, Starbuck undertook this task with serious devotion. A series of thirty texts and manuals were to be produced under his direction. It was to be more comprehensive than any other program of religious education previously offered by the denomination, and was to be developed with the most modern pedagogical guidelines and liberal views in mind.

The scope of this work, and consequently Starbuck's responsibilities, was enormous. One denominational report assessed the work as follows:

> "This is a task of no ordinary
> difficulty. To formulate the
> general scheme; to adapt topics
> to the changing needs of develop-
> ing life; to secure authors
> who are pre-eminently fitted to
> prepare the vaious books; to
> bring about the close cooperation
> of these authors and assimilate

120

their various contributions into
one systematic whole; to edit
their manuals, providing in many
instances other books for teachers
and in every instance helps for
both teachers and pupils, and
finally to embody all these
into actual books, with due
consideration to binding, paper,
type, pictures, and maps, --
all this is a task of no common
magnitude."27

In the same report is revealed the actual extent
to which the Society depended upon Starbuck's direction of the preparation of the courses in this new
curriculum, and the degree of confidence the Society
placed in his abilities. The report states:

"The secretary and the associate secretary of the Department /Department of Religious
Education/ have been from the
first in the closest co-operation
with Dr. Starbuck, and a committee
on manuals, composed of persons
of marked ability and self-
sacrificing devotion, has done a
large amount of work. But all
have looked to Dr. Starbuck
as the initiator of plans and
the final judge in matters
concerned. While there has
been no blind following, no
sluggish acceptance of any one's
dictum, all have willingly
accepted his leadership and
gladly recognized his genius."

On June 4, 1914, Starbuck addressed a convention
of the Unitarian Sunday School Society. He explained
the progress being made on the new course of study
for ages four through twenty-one in Sunday schools;
but most important, he discussed the motives and

121

objectives which were influencing those who were involved in the work. A denominational report briefly summarized his statements as follows:

"The speaker pointed out that those who are preparing the new course aim first of all to make it interesting. Children ought not to find the Sunday school dull and religious themes unattractive. They should approach each lesson with enthusiastic delight. The course, too, is designed to be at every point and on every subject deeply and distinctively religious. It is to relate to the whole self, from the physical to the spiritual, to deepen and vitalize all departments of the life. It will deal with the social impulses of the young, that they may be guided aright into future service for the redemption of the whole of life.

The new course is to be fitted for each year through which the growing soul passes. It will aim intensely toward saving the lives of the young for the church, for great causes, for high ideals. To this end it seeks to make use of the time of awakening between the ages of thirteen and sixteen, by securing at that period the consecration of each life to the highest and best things through the church and allied organizations. This course of study aims to inspire young hearts, and to furnish the knowledge which shall help them to know how best to live and to serve. In short, the new course

takes the whole problem of
the religious life seriously.
Those who are working upon
it believe religious education
to be the most important thing
in life. They seek, therefore,
to supply to the teachers,
parents, and officers in our
Sunday schools a means of
doing this great work
effectively."[28]

At the end of his first year with the Unitarian
Association, Starbuck was asked to take a second
year's leave from the University of Iowa. It was
granted. The work in which Starbuck had been
engaged was at such a stage that members of the Association thought to lose him would have significantly hindered the general progress of their efforts.

Starbuck's involvement was not limited to his
work on the new curriculum. He entered into other
areas of the Unitarian's program. It is estimated
that he held over four-hundred religious education
conferences or institutes, addressing officers and
workers of various churches.[29] He preached in many
pulpits, and lectured extensively before a variety
of audiences, taking him to such notable places as
Andover Seminary in Massachusetts and Meadville
Theological School in Pennsylvania.

At Meadville, a Unitarian institution, emphasis
was being placed on the training of religious educators.
In 1911 the school offered its first regular courses
in this area. Following a convention of the Religious
Education Association, at Cleveland, in 1913, Starbuck was invited and accepted the invitation to
lecture at Meadville. He delivered twelve forenoon
lectures on "The Nature and Meaning of Religion."
Ten afternoon lectures dealt with the topic, "The
Child Mind and the Sunday School." The fact that
Starbuck's lectures were well-received is indicated
by the expressions of Rev. William I. Lawrence,
secretary of the Department of Religious Education,

in a denominational report. Lawrence quotes the
following response to Starbuck:

> "Prof. Starbuck came and
> conquered. He came to the Mead-
> ville Theological School to rein-
> force the teaching of religious
> pedagogy, and he won the delighted
> attention and admiration of the
> school. . .Dr. Starbuck's rich
> culture, his command of technical
> science, his penetrating comprehen-
> sion of what poets have said and
> artists have created and saints
> have discerned, made the hearers
> aware that in such a study, under
> such a guide, there was not only a
> gift to the understanding, but a
> wealth of wisdom and incentive for
> the desire of bringing life to its
> full and perfect activity. Prof.
> Starbuck was the pioneer in an
> undertaking which has proved to be
> America's most fruitful contribution
> to the science of religion, and his
> stimulating expositions of this
> religious psychology create a con-
> viction that here is a rebirth and
> renewal of theology."[30]

At the end of his second year with the Religious
Association, Starbuck returned to the University of
Iowa. In a denominational report on his contribution,
a fitting tribute is made regarding the part Starbuck
played in the development of the proposed curriculum.
It reads: "Although his connection with the work has
now ceased, the new course, when it appears, will bear
the impress of his mind and heart to a degree that
will be fully known only by those who have stood near-
est to him during these initial years."[31] Upon leaving, every good wish was extended to him for his continued success at the university.

At this time, even with Starbuck's departure,
the continuation and eventual completion of the series
of religious manuals was confidently anticipated. In

the same article which featured Dr. Starbuck's contribution, an undespairing appraisal of the destiny of the project was expressed.

> "Work on the new course goes on without interruption. Authors are writing, and materials for teachers' and pupils' use are accumulating. The members of the office staff and of the committee on manuals now take the initiative, and look forward to a prolonged period of intensely interesting activity. Other helpers are being summoned, the Association has extended a generous support, helpful suggestions are coming from every quarter, and the constituency is patiently awaiting results. An unmatched opportunity is to be met with a firm and eager purpose. Within a year, we think our schools will be able to begin using a considerable part of the new course."

Unfortunately, the fruits of their labors did not match their optimism. The series was never completed, though some good manuals were produced.[32] The Religious Association, responsible for the project, was taken over by the main body, the American Unitarian Association, thus giving the latter body control of the funds. As Starbuck put it, "Traditionalism lay heavy across institutionalized religion." He considered the effort "a case of the light that failed."[33] The project, itself, cannot really be considered a failure, however. The volumes that were published served as the graded curriculum for the Unitarian Association for many years.

Starbuck resumed teaching at the University of Iowa in the fall of 1914, the same year educators, interested in character education in American public schools began talking about a business man, whose concern for the nation became centered in his statements regarding the necessity of moral education for

125

all children. After serious consideration, a prize
of five-thousand dollars was offered by this anonymous business man, called "The Donor," for the best
"Children's Code of Morals."

This contest, called "The National $5,000 Mor-
ality Codes Competition," lasted from Washington's
Birthday, February 22, 1916, to his birthday on the
same date in 1917. A field of seventy selected code
writers, at least one from each state, competed for
the prize. Their job was to determine, through researching intelligent public opinion, the moral
ideas thought most desireable for children. The results were to be incorporated in the preparation of
two books to be written for the public school, one
for elementary and the other for high school. These
books, to be revised when needed, would serve as reference works for questions of morality in the
schools.

In the midst of this attempt to formulate some
foundational ideals for conduct, a concern for methods in character education arose. Once the ideals
were established, how were they to be used most
effectively to engender character development? Such
an imposing concern resulted in another national contest. This time the Donor offered a prize of twenty-
thousand dollars, the largest amount ever offered in
an educational competition, for the best research on
methods for character education in the public schools.
The move was an obvious attempt to gather "the best
thinking of the Nation on this phase of education."[34]

In light of Starbuck's professional interest in
character education, an interest which dates back,
early in his career, to his days at Leland Stanford
Junior University, his participation in this contest
could have been safely predicted. Interestingly,
almost three years prior to the beginning of this
competition, Starbuck wrote to the president of the
university about a plan for education. He states,
"I have half developed in my mind, a plan, for the
public schools, for education for permanent peace;
and I need to get it out of my system."[35] It might
be conjectured that perhaps this "half developed plan"

126

was the foundation, in crystallized form, for the later developed "Iowa Plan."

The opportunity to participate in this competition was not open to just anyone interested. Each state was to submit one plan. The research was to be done by a group of selected educators, designated as the "Character Education Collaborators," which was not to exceed nine members in each state. The selection of these research collaborators was made, in each state, by a "Committee of Selection," which usually included the state superintendent, the president of one of the universities or colleges in the state, and a person-at-large, often a woman. While collaborators were selected in most of the states, 432, to be exact, only twenty-six states ultimately submitted a research study.[36]

In Iowa the Committee of Selection was composed of Albert M. Deyoe, State Superintendent, and later State Superintendent P. E. McClenahan; State University of Iowa President, Walter A. Jessup; and the Honorable John Hamill, Attorney at Law. This committee selected the following research collaborators: Edwin D. Starbuck, Professor of Philosophy, at the University of Iowa, who served as the chairman; H. E. Blackmar, Superintendent for the public schools in Ottumwa; C. P. Colegrove, President of Upper Iowa University, at Fayette; Professors Fred D. Cram and A. C. Fuller, both at State Teacher's College Extension, Cedar Falls; Ernest Horn, Professor of Education at the University of Iowa; Herbert Martin, Professor of Philosophy at Drake University; A. T. Hukill, Superintendent of the public schools in Waterloo; and J. D. Stoops, Professor of Philosophy at Grinnell College.[37]

Under Starbuck's direction, the research collaborators began meeting together in 1918, to formulate some strategy for development of the "plan." By their second meeting, held in Cedar Rapids, on April 3rd and 4th, it was apparent that the members could work well together, and were eager to cooperate. Although no form for the "plan" was yet decided, unanimity among the committee members regarding several fundamental

points was evident. Four general points were agreed
upon: (1) "Our 'plan' shall emphasize character education by <u>doing</u>. Organize the school as a real community of persons acting morally."; (2) "In every
way preserve the personal integrity of the pupil.
Use stories, dramatic presentations, biography, history, music, and other things that appeal directly
to the sympathies of the pupil."; (3) "Gradually
emphasize more and more the habits of 'moral thoughtfulness'."; and (4) "The regular studies and occupa-
tions of the school should all be used as moral educational material. Whatever additional materials
are used should find a natural correlation with these."[38]

At the same meeting, a tentative "Characteriza-
tion of the Growth Stages During the School Periods"
was developed. The most distinctive growth features
were listed for kindergarten, primary, intermediate,
junior high, and high school stages. With this in
mind, the members then discussed the advisability of
devoting each of the school years, either predominantly or exclusively, to a particular phase of character
development, or to a certain moral theme or attitude.
A tentative list of suggestions regarding themes for
each year was produced. And finally, each member
agreed to prepare personally a written report on the
following items:

> "(1) The end or goal of moral educa-
> tion as conditioning methods and
> materials; what sort of a man or
> woman have we in mind as a type.
> (2) The characterization of the
> stages in child development.
> (3) With '(2)' in view around what
> supreme interests and activities
> should the work center during each
> year of the curriculum?
> (4) Suggestions toward a real organ-
> ization of the school into a natural
> democratic community."

A memorandum of this meeting was sent to the
president of Iowa university, and Starbuck promptly
received an enthusiastic reply. The president en-
couragingly commented:

> "I am very much interested in
> the information you sent me concern-
> ing the work of the Committee on
> Character Education. I feel that
> you are making splendid progress.
> I am really surprised at the develop-
> ments you have made in these two
> meetings. I think you are going to
> get someplace."[39]

All plans, nation-wide, had to be submitted no
later than February 22, 1921. A designated outsider
received five copies of the plans from each group of
contestants. No names or marks to indicate authors
were to be attached to the plans themselves. A letter accompanied the plans, giving names and addresses
of the authors. The outsider numbered the letter and
one copy of the plan, which he kept himself, forwarded
three copies of the plan to the Executive Committee of
the Character Education Institution and one copy to
the Donor. Each judge, who had been selected from the
members of the Character Education Institution (techni-
cally the "National Institution for Moral Instruction,"
but reincorporated in 1922 as the "Character Education
Institution"), chose the three best plans submitted
and sent the numbers to the Executive Committee of
Washington, D.C. Following this procedure, the judges
received a list of the numbers of the plans receiving
special approval, and voted for a first and second
choice. The prize was awarded, then, to the plan having the highest numerical grade.[40]

When the immense task of judging was finished,
the method plan receiving the highest votes was number
9, certified as the plan from the state of Iowa. Dr.
Starbuck, as the chairman was granted $4,000, and each
collaborator received $2,000 as their individual award.
Starbuck had closely directed the development of the
project, and the other collaborators served as his
counselors or advisors. Starbuck was mainly responsible for the final draft of the plan, although three of
the collaborators made especially significant contributions. Superintendent Blackmar and Professor Ernest
Horn collaborated on the fourth chapter dealing with
the "integrity of the child," and Professor Herbert

129

Martin drafted Chapter XI, which dealt with "cooperating agencies." Others, not on the official committee, assisted the collaborators: Miss Ethel R. Gold-
en who created a course of study for character education; Miss Margaret Starbuck, Dr. Starbuck's daughter,
who served as the general secretary and worked on the
bibliography; and George Mendenhall, a graduate student, who had been studying character rating, and out
of that background, carried the primary responsibility
for developing Chapter IX on self-measurement."[41]
Notwithstanding the worthy and often generous assistance given him, it was largely Dr. Starbuck's drive
and ingenuity that pushed the plan to its completion.[42]

The extent of the influence this plan had upon
the public schools throughout the country is difficult
to ascertain. That the plan had friendly reception
both nationally and internationally is mentioned in a
1926 University of Iowa Service Bulletin, designed to
acquaint the Iowa public with some of the special services of the University. The Bulletin does not substantiate the claim, however, although it does report
the influence of the plan in one part of the country:

> "The Bureau of Education of the
> City of New York has, after three
> years of intensive study by a
> special committee, issued a pam-
> phlet entitled Character Education
> in High Schools, quoting frequently
> from the 'Iowa Plan' and paying
> this tribute: 'It should be read
> and studied by every teacher and
> principal who would have a thorough
> understanding of this question'."[43]

While such information reflects very favorably the
acknowledged value of the plan in one area, significantly, five years after this character plan had been
prepared, a Bulletin, reporting on its progress, only
refers to one incidence of its use in the educational
system.

The fact, at least, of its publication and plans
for wide-spread distribution is revealed in the intro-

duction.   The author writes:

> "Five thousand copies of this
> Iowa Plan for Character Education
> in Public Schools are being pub-
> lished at the expense of the Donor
> for free distribution in the United
> States and abroad, as a means of
> securing letters of criticism and
> advice from educators and others
> toward the maturing of opinion as
> to the best methods of character
> education in public schools, and
> preliminary to extensive experiments.
> All the thinking that seems of im-
> portance in all the other plans sub-
> mitted will be given most serious
> attention in these experiements in
> verification of the results of this
> research. The Institution will loan
> copies of these plans to those who
> want them for study, and will loan
> copies of the Iowa Plan on request."[44]

Such is an example of the extraordinary effort of the
corporation, in the interests of character education
and development, to serve by deed, as well as by word,
not only the schools of the United States, but the
schools of other countries also.

It is interesting, especially in light of the
Donor's seemingly conservative and direct approach to
moral education, that Starbuck's plan won. The Donor
had been searching for the right set of moral ideals,
for the purpose of inculcation. The approach of the
Iowa Plan sought to provide a setting for natural
growth and character development. That winning the
award was a real surprise to the committee is evidenced
by Starbuck's own words:

> "...we had elected to be true to
> our convictions instead of following
> the then predominant custom of indoc-
> trinating children with moral ideas.
> We believed in a more natural approach

in which the integrity of the
child's personality was wholly
respected, one that consisted in
intriguing his imagination, elicit-
ing his active, creative interest,
and stirring his impulses by what
we choose to call a dynamic, or
tactful, or sympathetic or creative
method --- a method that involved
the entire child in his relation to
the whole set-up of the school and
society."[45]

The fact that the award was given to the Iowa team
deepened interest in the field at the university,
and made work in character education appealing to
larger numbers of students. And the response of the
administration to the emergence of an Institute for
character research was undoubtedly influenced greatly
by this event.

If one reads the concluding chapter of the Iowa
Plan carefully, he is struck with the notion that the
work referred to as the task of character education
describes precisely the work of Starbuck in character
research during his remaining years at Iowa. In this
chapter, the author states, "the task of character
education is to try out under controlled conditions
the various projects and methods that have distinct
moral value and to discover others."[46] In addition
to his regular teaching load, the projects, in which
so much of Starbuck's time was invested, were developed toward this end. They inevitably shaped the
course of his career.

In 1929, a monthly review, entitled Childhood
and Character, reported the development of character
research at the University of Iowa, and had this to
say about its origin:

"No one knows when the Institute of Character Research at the
University of Iowa had its beginning. It just naturally happened
as an expression of the spirit of

132

the times and of personal enthusiasm."[47]

The first part of this statement is relatively accurate. It is impossible to establish an actual date
for the formation of the original Institute or "Bureau" of the research in character education at Iowa,
even though it is clear that the "Research Station"
was functioning as early as 1923. In that year the
Research Station in Character Education and Religious
Education was established under the auspices of the
Graduate College and the department of Philosophy and
Psychology. Cooperating with the Station was also
the College of Education and the Child Welfare Station.[48] The latter part of the statement, however,
is not altogether true. While the development of the
Institute certainly was in keeping with the educational interests of this period, it is quite clear that,
without Dr. Starbuck's consuming efforts, it would
not have developed "naturally." And while it is safe
to say that the personal enthusiasm of the collaborators of the Iowa Plan provided a significant amount
of impetus for continuing research in character education, the Institute, itself, did not just happen as a
natural consequence of this enthusiasm. Rather, it
is more realistic to suggest that the enthusiasm and
the times provided a sympathetic setting for the emergence of a research Institute.

While the lines of inquiry and research varied,
they were not unrelated to each other. One article,
reviewing these activities in character research at
the university, had this to say about their kinship:

> "The warm center of interest seems
> to be to describe the world of human
> values, the moral, the religious,
> and the aesthetic; to discover their
> setting in human nature, how they
> function, how they develop, and their
> proper regimen; in other words, to
> understand character or personality,
> its nature and nurture."[49]

Another report describes those lines of research which

are in progress by 1926. In addition to the work of observng children and experimenting with methods and materials in the public schools, four general directions in research are noted:

> "(1) the discovery of the elements, mental and social, which are involved in 'character' or 'personality'; (2) the use of comprehension and other tests to determine the adaptability of various materials to the maturity of pupils, and otherwise laying a foundation for the curriculum; (3) controlled observation and testing to determine in terms of conduct, the relative value of various methods of moral appeal; and (4) the preparation of bibliographies of best character materials in order to enrich the program of the public school and of the church school."[50]

The investment of Starbuck's time in character research at Iowa was centered around three major projects connected with the Institute. These projects were the direct result of the work done by Starbuck, his staff of assistants, and a number of graduate students who worked directly under him. Among these projects, the publication of two volumes, A Guide to Literature for Character Training,[51] and A Guide to Books for Character,[52] represented practically a decade of research on the part of Starbuck and his associates in the systematic evaluation and selection of literature as it applies to character education. The selections in these volumes were not the result of mere individual capriciousness; rather they were guides to the best materials for character training, validated by the technique of scientific control of the judgments made regarding the worth of the items to be included. Not only are the selections judged in terms of their relative worth as character-building literature; specification as to which school grades they are best fitted for, and classification according to the moral situation and attitude involved

134

is made also. The aim was to liberate quality from quantity.

From 1921 through 1930 this was one of the most time consuming of Starbuck's projects. It was an heroic undertaking demanding vision and insight, as well as tremendous perseverance. Williard C. Olson, surveying the field of character education twenty years after the two volumes were published, assessed this project as still the most ambitious attempt to organize stories, biographies and other selections as a curriculum resource for character training in the schools.[53]

The second project of the Institute was not unrelated to the first. It was, in fact, literally the product of the first project. The publication possibilities arising from the literature which had been judged and classified was tremendous, even though far less was published than had been projected. Nevertheless, in this case the projection was realized. In 1930, The Wonder Road, an outgrowth of the work of the Institute, was published. Three volumes comprised this work: Book I Familiar Haunts; Book II Enchanted Paths; and Book III Far Horizons.[54] These volumes consisted of a carefully selected collection of sixty-one of the best fables, myths and fairy tales available for children.

In the meantime, a third related project had been underway, demanding, as usual, the serious attention and direction of Dr. Starbuck. The project itself, was the outgrowth of graduate studies which were done under Starbuck during his years at Iowa. With the help of the Institute, Starbuck, as editor, produced four volumes of the University of Iowa Studies in Character, published during the years 1927 through 1931.[55] All but one of the fourteen studies published were submitted previously, in similar or more detailed form, as Ph.D. dissertations. The other study fulfilled the thesis requirement for an M.A. degree.

In response to Starbuck's initiative, and under his tutelage, the University of Iowa offered ample coursework for those interested in character and religious education. In fact one could pursue a graduate program with a major in character education. In addition to a significant number of philosophy courses, related directly to this major interest, the departments of Sociology, Education, Child Welfare, Psychology, and Religion also offered courses which could directly apply to the major. Some scholarships and stipends were also available to superior graduate students. The graduate program in character education, provided by the University of Iowa during the active years of the Institute, was considered possibly the most comprehensive of any such program offered by other universities.[56]

It has been demonstrated that central to Starbuck's interests while at the University of Iowa was the Institute of Character Research and the projects which comprised its work in character education. The following is presented to substantiate further this claim, as well as to provide a basis for the contention that Starbuck's career was affected adversely by the inordinate amount of time he spent to promote and develop this Institute. That is to say, that Starbuck's energies were exhausted in the process of attempting to raise enough funds to support the work of the Institute. Consequently, the possibilities for personal creative production were never fully realized. To understand the nature and extent of Starbuck's involvement in such activities, and for the sake of presenting an historical overview of the ongoings of the Institute at Iowa, some of Starbuck's correspondence between 1923 and 1930 will be reviewed.[57]

As early as April 23, 1923, Starbuck was corresponding with the University of Iowa President, Walter A. Jessup, regarding a wish to secure financial backing for his "character education project."[58] President Jessup was to meet with Dr. Beardsley Ruml, Director of the Laura Spelman Rockefeller Memorial. Starbuck asked Jessup to impress Ruml with the importance of their character research undertaking, which at the time involved the painstaking preparation of a bibliography of the best character-building literature available.

The following week, apparently after some correspondence or conversation with Dr. Ruml, Starbuck
writes him in some detail about the project. At the
outset, Starbuck explains the place of this smaller
character education project in a larger program.
Starbuck's vision of some type of monumental undertaking is revealed very early in the letter. He
states:

> "I am inviting your support of
> a smaller project which is only a
> patch in the bigger field. The
> greater program involving the cooper-
> ation of several related departments
> and the work of great specialists,
> has been my dream for several years
> and I have been working and planning
> in that direction . . . the problem
> of character education approached
> empirically and with laboratory
> equipment, is only a phase of the
> still greater thing we are going
> sooner or later to compass. This
> great thing . . . will include
> scientific interpretation of aesthe-
> tic and religious values with which
> moral values are so intimately bound
> up. It may not be in bad taste to
> confess that I have correspondence
> going on looking toward a several
> million dollar foundation for the
> permanent encouragement of this big-
> ger project. It has absolutely got
> to come."[59]

To further emphasize the relationship of this smaller
project to the larger one, Starbuck adds, "After we
take this essential preliminary step, I promise you,
we shall be right back at you with a request that will
make this one look like a dime on a collection plate."

Starbuck was asking for an endowment of $13,900
as a minimum budget for the next two years, the amount
of time he estimated it would take to complete the project. This was not granted by the Rockefeller founda-

tion,[60] although five years later the foundation did provide a grant to the Institute for a joint study with the Child Welfare Research Station, at Iowa, on the character developments of pre-school children.[61]

In his letter to Ruml, Starbuck refers to the mistaken notion that he and his associates are unconcerned about the practical use of their plan in the schools. Suggesting that this was a misunderstanding, he added:

> "When you asked me what we were doing
> to try out our schemes and I replied
> that we were not concerned now with
> that phase of it, that confession had
> reference only to the present state of
> affairs. We can't try out our scheme
> until we put it in such shape that
> teachers can have at hand the tools to
> work with."[62]

Starbuck continues, ". . . we must have still the greater part of two years in which to perfect our methods and to put teachers readily in touch with the best materials in biography, story, song, project, drama, and the like, that are now available in the world." Explaining that the practical step of completing the project must be handled before serious experimentation can occur, Starbuck asserts:

> "If you will glance again through
> 'The Iowa Plan' and through the
> budget, you will see that every
> item we have named is necessary
> in doing this clean cut task of
> getting in a position to give
> teachers a workable program. When
> we do that we shall be in a posi-
> tion to open up our laboratories
> in the schools and not until then."

In this same appeal for funds Starbuck finally included two items which he considered added credence to the value of the proposed project and "The Iowa Plan" which formed the basis for its development.

First, it is a pioneering project. Starbuck states: "Strangely, no one has tried to put the teaching profession in possession of the best materials of instruction, much less to organize them into a consecutive program running through the years or directed toward specific character ends." Second, the need for such a program seems to be felt everywhere. Starbuck includes an excerpt from a letter he received from Paul B. Anderson in Russia. He quotes Anderson: "All my Russian associates with whom I have thus far been able to share the book, The Iowa Plan have been quite delighted, answering me that there has been no such thing even thought of in Russia."

Unfortuantely, this particular attempt to secure financial assistance was to no avail; thus, Starbuck turned to other sources for help. Among them, his contact with the Institute of Social and Religious Research in New York City proved to be most profitable. In the latter part of May, 1924, in response to a request of May 5th, Starbuck furnished Mr. Galen M. Fisher, of the Institute of Social and Religious Research, with an extended list of the individuals he might consult regarding the value of the project at Iowa University.[63] In June, C. E. Seashore, then head of the department of Philosophy and psychology, and dean of the graduate college, wrote a letter to Mr. Fisher, supporting Starbuck's request for an appropriation. Seashore expressed confidence in the worth of the character education project, explaining that he had used some of the department's emergency funds for such research but that they were quite inadequate in light of the needs.[64]

The Institute of Social and Religious Research provided the major private funds which made possible the completion of A Guide to Literature for Character and A Guide to Books for Character, finally published in 1928 and 1930 respectively. These funds, however, were not obtained without considerable effort. The foundation, for example, was interested in the university's appraisal of the project, and the degree to which the university itself was willing to provide financial assistance. Consequently, Starbuck operated under the double pressure of both working to attract

the support of private foundations and working to
ensure the continual placement of his project in the
university budget. Such pressure is evidenced in
Starbuck's correspondence with President Jessup on
January 20, 1926. Starbuck wrote:

> "Since I saw you yesterday I
> have been mulling over the temper
> of Mr. Fisher and the hard questions
> he asked last year and is doing
> again now concerning what the univer-
> sity itself is willing to do in fur-
> thering the work in character educa-
> tion.
>
> I have a haunting fear that we
> shall lose again unless you and Dean
> Seashore can think it through and
> assure Mr. Fisher that the university
> will continue during the college year
> 1926-27 to support us essentially to
> the same amount that has been expended
> this year."[65]

Despite Starbuck's fear, however, in this particular
case, a very encouraging response came within a week.
Starbuck was informed by Fisher that in response to
his request and the support given by President Jessup,
Professor Seashore, and others, the Board of Directors
voted to grant, for the 1926 calendar year, a sum of
$15,000.[66]

To illustrate, the constant setbacks Starbuck
faced, however, his correspondence with President
Jessup, one month later, is related. Starbuck thanks
Jessup for telling Mr. Fisher that the university
would support the project during the next year to the
extent of $5,250, but Starbuck notes, with displeasure,
that half of his own salary will be included in this
sum. Starbuck expresses himself rather bluntly:

> "It is too clear to need dis-
> cussing that the work of this Sta-
> tion is a legitimate part of the
> program of the Department of Philo-

140

sophy and Psychology and that
you had expected of course to
continue my salary as a member
of the department and also the
person in charge of this research project. As a legitimate part of the work of the
department and also as a phase
of the program of the Graduate
college you should naturally
expect to carry my entire
salary and also that of Dr.
Shuttleworth."

To emphasize his point further, Starbuck continues:

"It should furthermore be
kept in mind that we have asked
for $42,800 as the least sum
needed to complete this particular project. The Institute has
given us only about one-third
that amount. If, now, we must
cut into that too small a fund
to carry items of expense that
you have found it possible during the present year to support,
that cripples us terribly."[67]

In the midst of Starbuck's efforts on behalf of
his Institute of Character Research, a reorganization
of the philosophy and psychology department was occurring, a move which did not find Starbuck unconcerned.
His views regarding a separate department of philosophy, and concerning his approach to philosophy in
general are succinctly expressed in a letter to Professor G. T. W. Patrick. Starbuck received a copy of
the letter Patrick had sent to George F. Kay, dean of
the department of philosophy and psychology, stating
the needs of the "Department of Philosophy," and ac-
cusing Starbuck of having forsaken the mainstream of
philosophical inquiry. Starbuck's response was two-
fold. In the first instance, he agrees with Patrick's
assessment of philosophy offerings and explains the
reason for their problems. He states:

"You are right in stressing the
fact that we must have a greater number of substantial courses in various
phases of philosophy....Our failure
to live up to our plan is simply because we have never had the courage
to launch into a full fledged department."[68]

To the second point of Patrick's letter, however,
Starbuck takes exception. Not only do his remarks
clearly spell out his general approach to philosophy,
but they cleverly defend the validity of his position.
Starbuck begins:

"In the first place you remark that
my interest is now wholly in religious and character problems. The
fact is that I have never swerved at
all from what my colleagues are
pleased to call 'straight philosophy.'
... That you should suspect me of
apostacy to the philosophical faith
is too much like an attempt to ex-
communicate one of the devout worship-
pers from the communion of saints because he can not so readily rattle off
all the tenets of the Nicene Creed."

Continuing to defend his work as a legitimate philosophical enterprise, he asserts:

"There is very little that I am
working at in the university whose
purpose and passion is not directed
specifically toward pure philosophy,--
but with difference, that I favor a
slight shifting of the field of
philosophy to stress human values
rather than conceptual systems, and
also that my procedure is in tune
with the methodology of the modern
world that employs not simply logical
but experimental and other objective
methods of attacking our vital problems."

142

Patrick submitted a list of courses that he considered were legitimate philosophy offerings. In his outline he excludes a number of courses Starbuck normally taught; and Starbuck responds:

> "It makes me feel quite sad
> to note your oversight of the
> Psychology of Religion and the
> empirical studies in the depart-
> ment of personality in children
> and adults in your outline of
> courses. Surely these are legi-
> timate parts of 'straight philo-
> sophy' if that field is rightly
> defined."

Confining the field to logical or conceptual methodology was not acceptable to Starbuck. He believed that a correct definition of the field includes room for an empirical methodology as well. In fact, he felt that such an admission would bring new life into the field of philosophy. Starbuck wrote to Patrick:

> "If we could all see eye to
> eye on this point of adopting em-
> pirical methods in philosophy as
> a legitimate part of its program
> we would have here such a Renais-
> sance of Philosophy as has never
> been witnessed. There is nothing
> in the older traditions and meth-
> ods that would not be conserved
> but we would move out into a new
> world in Ethics, Logic, Aesthetics
> and Religion that would bring a re-
> birth of these subjects to that
> which came to Physics, Chemistry,
> Biology, and the other sciences."[69]

Two months later, in a letter to Dean Seashore, Starbuck pursues this subject even further. While it appears that by now there is some consideration of the possibility of eventually launching an independent philosophy department, Starbuck is dismayed by the

slowness of action, and asks if they are not now
ready to make this venture. Starbuck asks Seashore
to reconsider, and even expresses his willingness
to leave the university, for the sake of a "complete
reconstruction," if his presence is too disruptive.
Starbuck quickly suggests an alternative, however.
He confidently recommends: "If in spite of being a
disturber of the serenity of the place, I am allowed
to continue, the only correct solution of the depart-
mental problem is that I be requested to assume the
headship."[70]

With the conviction that his work at Iowa, thus
far, was related to a "Renaissance of Philosophy,"
Starbuck declared:

> "I have been preparing, plan-
> ning and hoping for many years
> to do my bit, and along with
> hampering difficulties have, I
> trust, accomplished something.
> But why should I not be set free
> and encouraged in every way? I
> am sure it is an academic mis-
> fortune if philosophy of the
> right sort and with proper tech-
> nique does not blossom out at
> Iowa, and thereby save another
> century or two of staggering and
> blundering.
>
> I have been staying on at
> this institution nursing the con-
> viction that we have here the wise
> leadership that could see a simple
> truth like that I have been hint-
> ing, and that after seeing a bit
> of the fruit of our labors, would
> not only be willing but eager to
> work for the Renaissance of Philo-
> sophy."

A letter to President Jessup, with an enclosed copy
of the letter Starbuck sent to Dean Seashore regarding the "Philosophy-Psychology situation," discloses

144

the apparent recurring discord between Starbuck and
Seashore. Starbuck explains to Jessup that the Dean
has condemned his research in the psychology of character or personality, and his study of types of religious experience, as unscientific. Starbuck also
complains that Dean Seashore has been "undermining
and stealing" some of his better students. As an
illustration of his point, an incident with Thomas
H. Howells, who wrote his dissertation under Starbuck,
was referred to specifically. Starbuck claims that
Dean Seashore advised Howells to drop his study under
Starbuck. Starbuck states:

> "He told him he would have to
> abide hereafter by the stamp he
> placed on himself through his
> doctors dissertation and said
> that he (the Dean) would be
> ashamed to have his name connec-
> ted with the studies that Star-
> buck is directing."[71]

In spite of the conflict, however, there is no evidence that their working relationship was completely
severed.

In the following year, two events occurred in
Starbuck's career which must have given him a sense
of confidence and accomplishment. On July 15, 1927,
Starbuck received word from President Jessup that he
had been appointed head of the newly established
Department of Philosophy.[72] Starbuck remained head
of the department until his departure from the university in 1930. The second event had to do with
Starbuck's work in connection with his Institute.
The work conducted by Starbuck and his associates in
character education was finally officially recognized
by the university in 1927 when President Jessup recommended to the Graduate Council and the Board of Education of the University of Iowa that an "Institute of
Character Research" be legally established within the
university. He also recommended that Starbuck, who
had been in charge of this work since 1921, be given
officially the title "Director" of the Institute.[73]

145

During the Fall of 1927, record of Starbuck's fund raising efforts for the projects of his Institute is again resumed. In November, Starbuck made a formal request to the Julius Rosenwald Foundation, for a $30,000 appropriation that would make possible the preparation of the "third unit" of the "Guide to Character Training Literatures."[74] This proposed third volume of the Guide, "Poetry for Children" was never completed, nor was the appropriation from the foundation granted.

On December 30th, President Jessup received two separate letters from Starbuck regarding his projects. The first letter reiterated the need for financial assistance. Although they were asking for $15,000 from The Institute of Social and Religious Research to complete the second volume of the Guide, "Fiction for Children," and they were asking for an additional $30,000 from the J. C. Penney Foundation to back their production of "Volume III--Poetry for Character Training," Starbuck wrote to Jessup:

> "May I send this memorandum as a reminder during your trip to New York City. We need more resources than we shall ever get."[75]

In the second letter, Starbuck revealed to President Jessup a recent development which created even greater pressure to insure the expeditious progress of their literature project for character training. Starbuck informed Jessup that a joint committee had just been formed out of the American Library Association and the American Association for Adult Education, for the purpose of researching the reading interests of children and adults. Expressing the significance of this in relation to their studies at Iowa, Starbuck wrote:

> "I met Dr. Williamson /who was expected to direct the scientific aspects of the studies for the A. L. A./ last year at Columbia and found him heavy and disappointed that we were already working our way into the field that he

had hoped they would master
themselves. We shall have to
continue a lively pace to keep
ahead of them"[76]

It is certainly clear that the interests of these
associations were related to the aims of Starbuck's
work. They sought to promote the love of books and
reading, and sponsored such research activities and
experimental projects as they considered pertained
to their objectives.

In March of 1928 requests for funds were made
to Dr. Daniel A. Poling of the J. C. Penney Foundation and Mrs. Leonard Elmhirst. Starbuck asked for
a substantial sum, $5,000 to complete Volume II,
"Fiction for Children," and $15,000 to help them
along into the third volume proposed, "Poetry for
Children." In this letter Starbuck assesses their
situation financially and interprets the meaning of
this for the future. Starbuck comments:

"We are moving toward financial competency. The proceeds from
the sale of each volume should support experts who will keep the
Guide constantly revised and make
this enterprise progressively useful."[77]

Unfortunately, Starbuck's analysis was incorrect on
both counts. They never became financially solvent,
nor were the number of volumes sold enough to support
a continuing enterprise.

During the next two months, Starbuck corresponded
with Miss Emily Bax of the Women's City Club in New
York City, regarding funds for his project. Some interesting insights are contained in the interchange
which provide some probable grounds for the ultimate
outcome of Starbuck's project. After having written
her for help on April 10, Miss Bax responds:

"I think the project is very
interesting, but should feel it had

147

more value if something could
be done to make sure that the
Guide had some official standing and would be used by groups
as the A. L. A. /American
Library Association/ and the
schools. If the matter were approached from that angle as well,
the publisher's interest could
be very much stimulated I believe
and sales increased. The ultimate usefulness of the Guide as
an index to children's reading
matter will depend, in large measure, on its distribution. And
if its value becomes apparent to
educators and parents the finan-
cing of the other volumes will be
purely a business adjustment."[78]

Up to that point, Starbuck had not attempted to interest the A. L. A. in his project. Neither had he been
concerned about making contacts with those sources
which might be interested in buying large quantities
for distribution. Starbuck confessess, in a letter
to Miss Bax, that he was probably "over-confident"
that the Guide would sell itself in the book market.
He also concedes that since the cost of each volume
of his project was so high, as a result of their exacting methods which made production extremely slow,
that approximately 125,000 volumes of any unit would
have to be sold to support the preparation of another
one.[79] Clearly, the hopes for such sales were not
realistic without the assurance of help from some
large buyers and distributors, and this assistance was
not secured.

In the same letter Starbuck gave a brief account
of the various contacts for funds that had been made.
In addition to those referred to already, he lists
the following: the Harmon Foundation; and such independently wealthy persons as Mrs. Vanderlip; Mr. Jesse
C. Nichols of Kansas City; William H. Danforth, of
St. Louis; and the Ford family. None of these contacts were promising, however.

The last note in Starbuck's file from Miss Bax refers to contacts she planned to make regarding his project, although she expresses very little optimism about the outcome. As she relates, "Many new foundations are being formed every year, but although I have looked them up I find none that would answer your purpose."[80] Once again, the door of opportunism was closed before him.

Even in the face of rejection and indifference, Starbuck did not abandon at this time his efforts to secure financial support. One of the more interesting individuals with whom Starbuck corresponded was Gamaliel Bradford, an American biographer, who in addition to his biographical studies wrote several volumes of poetry, fiction, and drama. Although praiseworthy of his efforts, Bradford raised several questions about Starbuck's approach, admitting that he was more sceptical than critical. It might be conjectured that though Bradford's remarks were couched in kindly expression, they were likely discouraging to Starbuck. At the beginning of his first letter to Starbuck, Bradford, who had written a biography of D. L. Moody, expressed his gratitude for Starbuck's study of the psychology of religion, which had been helpful to him in his own study of Moody. Referring next to Starbuck's project Bradford wrote:

> "I have examined the book of Fairy Tale, myth, and legend and am immensely impressed with both the labor and the critical skill that have gone into it. I am heartily in sympathy with any amount of scientific investigation and research in such matters, but I confess that I am a little skeptical about theoretical character-building /my Italics/ . . .[81]

Starbuck responded that he was sure they were in agreement, and that he, too, was convinced that "theoretical character-building" is fruitless. He expressed strong disapproval of the "hammer and tongs" method of

149

character building which he considered was so prevalent in his day, but he upheld that children's development ought not to be left purely to chance. Starbuck then interpreted his approach to the problem in the following way:

> "It is true . . . that human personality, like the organism of a plant, will flourish depending upon atmosphere and soil. All we are trying to do is help parents and teachers to clean up both atmosphere and soil in order to give the youngsters a little better chance. I do not see how there is much likelihood of the development of high tastes in children considering the diet on which they feed."[82]

Having viewed Starbuck's pamphlet on "character Education Methods" with interest, and convinced that his approach was "sane" and "rational," nevertheless, Bradford, still was not convinced that Starbuck's approach was workable. Bradford queries:

> "Is it really possible that such an intellectualization and systematization of educational methods will work a radical change in spiritual results? I ask not critically or cynically, but somewhat sceptically I confess. I suppose rule of thumb processes were always crude, misleading, and perhaps in the end thoroughly unsatisfactory, but is such elaborate, persistent, and consistent mapping and scheduling of soul-manipulation really helpful, is it really possible? I wonder."

While Bradford considered their attempt courageous and admirable, he had little faith in the fulfillment of its aims. He confessed to Starbuck:

> "I fear my own primitive barbarism

150

is not quite capable of
apprehending what you aim at,
or rather, since the aim is
as intelligible as it is
noble, I should say I have
a dreary and no doubt
exaggerated sense of the
difficulty of fitting the
magnificently cut and ornamented
garment to the fragile,
timorous, attenuated, frame
of human nature that is
meant to be covered by it."83

Needless to say, no financial assistance was granted
by Bradford.

Two days later, after receiving Bradford's
reply, as well as an unproductive reply from G. A.
Plimpton, on the board of Ginn and Company, publishers in New York City, Starbuck, writing to
President Jessup about his fruitless labor for
financial support, appears to be, for the first time,
utterly disheartened. He hopelessly concludes the
letter with "our days are few."84

Starbuck's efforts to obtain financial backing
for the projects of his Institute were costly.
That Starbuck was aware that these efforts hindered
greatly his direction of the research of the Institute,
is evidenced in a letter to Dean G. F. Kay, of the
psychology department:

". . . I feel much broken in
spirit in trying to carry the
financial burden of the Institute
and am sorely disappointed in
using energy in that direction
that ought to be devoted to
furthering the researches."85

The promises of a new year were anything but
bright. In fact the situation had never appeared
so grave. Just how serious was the financial bind

is revealed in a letter from Starbuck to Frank
Shuttleworth on January 26, 1929. Starbuck had
spent the previous week in New York City, Kansas
City and Chicago trying to raise funds which had
finally broken down even from the Institute of
Social and Religious Research, but his efforts had
not been rewarded. Even an attempt to obtain a
loan from Macmillan Company, using their contracts
as collateral, was refused. Starbuck confessed
that he could no longer ignore the fact that they
were broke. He concluded:

> "Today I am compelled to
> get the readers together and
> look toward scattering our forces
> on February first. It seems to
> me a full sized tragedy."[86]

At the end of February, however, the Institute
was still in operation. Out of loyalty to Starbuck
his staff stayed on, and Starbuck, uplifted by
their sacrifice, was again searching for funds. In
a letter to Mr. Thomas B. Appleget in New York City,
Starbuck asks him to bring the matter to Mr. Rockefeller's personal attention. Starbuck explains
that they are at a critical point between success
and failure. But he is convinced that a "few
thousand dollars invested now would . . . tip the
scales toward perpetuity and real blessing to the
children of the world."[87]

Starbuck's plea to the Rockefeller Foundation
was unheeded, but the next month a small grant was
received in the form of a loan which helped to
carry them along for awhile. A Mr. Lindsay of
Davenport, Iowa loaned them $2,000 which was pooled
into the regular budget of the Institute.[88]

Starbuck was encouraged further, when, just
before the end of the spring semester, he was asked
to speak to the A.L.A. about his project. Upon
returning Starbuck informed President Jessup of his
reception. He wrote:

> "I am pleased to report
> that I received the best possible
> hearing at the American Library
> Association, meeting /in New
> York City/. Although we have not
> enlisted as yet the active
> interest of Mr. Milan, I am
> sure that we enjoy now a far
> more friendly understanding
> on the part of the members of
> the American Library Association
> that may bear fruit in the
> future."[89]

During the next year the work was kept alive, and Volume II of the Guide was published. The three Volumes of The Wonder Road series of selected fairy tales were also published in 1930. Their work was commended from many quarters, and in the midst of a relatively favorable upswing Starbuck wrote President Jessup. "We are going to win if we can keep up with ourselves."[90]

Before the end of the school year substantial financial support was finally guaranteed from the Payne Fund of New York. A telegram from Starbuck to Ella Phillips Crandall on May 2 establishes that Starbuck's staff already was being supported by the funds. Starbuck submitted that excellent progress was being made, and predicted that with a productive summer the proposed third volume of the Guide would be completed during the 1930-31 school year.[91]

Three days later, in a telegram from Crandall assuring Starbuck of a $7500 grant for the 1930-31 work on the biography volume, one brief sentence alluded to the imminent departure of Starbuck from the University of Iowa. It read: "Accept without hesitation your judgment regarding transfer to Southern California."[92] After almost twenty-five years at the University of Iowa Starbuck was seriously contemplating a move.

Before the middle of June, Starbuck's plans were

finalized. He had accepted the invitation to serve
on the faculty of the University of Southern California as Professor of Philosophy. This information
was officially registered in a telegram from President
Jessup to Dean George F. Kay. It read:

> "Professor Starbuck invited
> to accept the Southern California
> position and has asked to be released
> as of September first. He is in
> fine spirits and feels he has
> unusual opportunity to be freed
> from administrative work and to
> join a group of distinguished
> philosophers."[93]

An attempt to establish the significant effect
that winning the national contest in character education methods had upon Starbuck's career in terms
of the emergence of an Institute of Character Research,
required a focusing in on that aspect of Starbuck's
life in the University of Iowa. While at the university, however, the events and interests of Starbuck's
career were not limited only to those already considered. Some of the secondary but important aspects
of his career at Iowa will be discussed briefly at
this juncture.

The first series of events to be considered is
centered around Starbuck's connection with the School
of Religion. It has been established that Starbuck
was a pioneering "force in the opening of the School
of Religion at Iowa."[94] While it does appear that
Starbuck contributed to the eventual development of
the School of Religion, the present writer contends
that Starbuck had in mind a department more in keeping with the nature of his Institute of Character
Research, where religion could be studied scientifically and the results of the research could be
applied practically in terms of religious education
and character development. To support this thesis,
reference is made to a letter Starbuck wrote President Jessup in 1922. It appears that a Professor
Kent had come to Iowa as part of a campaign he was

154

conducting to promote the development of certain
types of schools of religion. Starbuck strongly
recommended that Iowa not accept Kent's program.

Explaining his critical stand, Starbuck wrote:

> "I have come up against
> these lively men for several years,
> and have found them able to see
> only in terms of the single point
> of biblical literature and
> biblical interpretation. There
> is not one among them who is
> a profound psychologist or a
> leader in the principles or
> technique of religious education
> when viewed as a subject of
> university inquiry."[95]

Then Starbuck raised again the desireability
of developing a program which he had advocated for
the university since 1911. Considering the time
ripe for this endeavor, Starbuck suggested:

> "We are in a position, if
> we can clear our hands in regard
> to the matter, to enter on a
> career in religious education that
> is on a sounder academic basis
> than it can possibly be when
> fostered by Mr. Kent and the council
> of church boards of education.
> The secretary of the Y.M.C.A.,
> the student pastors, the members
> of the faculty, and everybody
> except the ones highest in
> authority in the place, are
> ready and anxious to move towards
> a venture that will give us
> a unique place in the United
> States as leaders in the scientific
> and practical interpretation of
> religion."

There can be little doubt that this proposal was related to Starbuck's vision of the practical outgrowth of "The Iowa Plan," which just the year before had been declared the winner over all the other plans for character education submitted in the nation.

To illustrate the breadth of his interests in the university two references among numerous such incidents are related. In the midst of his work on "The Iowa Plan," Starbuck took the time to write President Jessup regarding the proposed site for a new Memorial Building, commenting not only on the appropriateness of the location, but offering some specific suggestions about the type of architecture as well.[96] In the following year he proposed the establishment of an art museum in the university with some particular recommendations concerning the place and setting for such a display.[97]

Among Starbuck's contributions, while at Iowa, to innummerable professional conferences, two require special mention. Both conferences took place outside the United States. The first took place in Oslo, Norway in 1925. Starbuck was invited to participate as a lecturer in The Institute for Comparative Research in Human Culture. The purpose of the Institute, established during the World War, was to bring about new international understanding. Each summer and autumn, four or five scholars, from all over the world, were chosen to lecture in their chosen field. The conference was under the auspices of the five Scandinavian Countries: Norway, Sweden, Denmark, Finland, and Greenland, which sent selected conferees to listen and confer in seminars, at the expense of the governments.[98] Starbuck delivered ten lecures on the topic, "An Introduction to A Science of Religion,"[99] outlining the bases for the scientific procedure in psychology of religion research. An interesting side-light is that Starbuck's presentation, along with that of Franz Boaz, a renown American anthropoligist, were the first lectures ever delivered before this Institution by Americans.[100]

A second conference to which Starbuck was invited convened in Geneva, Switzerland in 1929. This international conference, arranged through the sponsorship of the Y.M.C.A., brought together scholars from various universities and countries in Europe with minimal number of representative scholars from the United States. The conference dealt with the problem of meeting effectively the religious needs of the young men of the world. In the interchange a clear division of attitude ensued. The Europeans, in general, favored a program of "convincement," while the Americans spoke of "enrichment."[101] Starbuck, who was abroad from July 23 to September 12, wrote from Geneva after the conference was over:

> "The conference was carried out in fine spirit but it was straight hard work every inch of the way. It was Europe vs. America. They are addicted to philosophy and theology and think us hopelessly empirical. They want to save the youth of the world from their black skepticism by a head-on authoritative attack. We want to bless the youth through activities that will exercise their spiritual muscles and their sentiments."[102]

Starbuck's years at the University of Iowa were replete with many of the normal events of the professional career of an educator, but his untiring drive and determination to help make a better world thrust him in directions that were anything but normal, in the sense of mediocrity.

University of Southern California (1930-1943)

Dr. Starbuck's invitation in 1930 to the University of Southern California was extremely timely in light of the anticipated end of his active career at Iowa. In keeping with the policies of the Board of Education at the University of Iowa, Starbuck who

was sixty-four years old would have to have retired
shortly from the Directorship of his Institute of
Character Research and as head of the Department
of Philosophy, resulting in a significant reduction
in salary.[103] Instead, Starbuck moved to Los Angeles
where he was an active member of the faculty as
Professor of Philosophy and later of psychology
until 1943 and where, by way of transfer, he was
able to continue the work of the Institute of Character Research.

The attractions of the University of Southern
California were numerous. The school and the philosophy department in particular were well respected.
Dr. Ralph Tyler Flewelling, Director of the School
of Philosophy, was seeking to bring the greats in
the different areas of philosophy together, and
chose Starbuck to teach ethics. Starbuck was permitted to transfer the projects and much of the
equipment of his Institute to Los Angeles where it
was housed in the beautiful new Seeley Wintersmith
Mudd Memorial Hall, occupied also by the School of
Philosophy. With the thought of a rebirth of his
Institute in a new favorable setting, and the
opportunity to continue teaching, not to mention
the fact of a good salary, Starbuck must have headed
for California with a sense of exhilaration.

Starbuck was welcomed by the U.S.C. administration, receiving full cooperation especially from
Dr. Flewelling; Dr. Rufus Bernhard von KleinSmid,
president of the university; and Dr. Frank Charles
Touton, the university vice-president. With their
assistance the organization of the Institute was
maintained. Starbuck was disappointed, however,
that they were not able to provide the financial
support he had understood would be available. Part
of Stabuck's staff at the University of Iowa,
including Mrs. Anna Searles, moved to California
with him. Additional staff members, as well, were
necessary to carry on the projects of the Institute.
In this new situation at U.S.C., the staff received
faculty status. Once again Starbuck was pressed to
find enough funds to continue the work of the Insti-

tute. The projects were carried on mainly by the
grants of the Payne Fund in New York City, and the
support of other friends, such as Mrs. Francis Bolton,
a wealthy Congresswoman of Ohio.[104]

American philosophy had been moving in the
direction of empiricism. The University of Southern
California sought to open the way for this movement.
In its school of Philosophy a place for scientif-
cially controlled studies had been provided in the
program.

In a bulletin describing some of the new developments occurring in the philosophy department of U.
S.C., their work was portrayed as distinctive in
the following three ways: (1) It was vital; that
is, philosophy was studied not for its own sake
alone, but for an understanding of the meaning of
life. (2) The program was cosmopolitan. The faculty
represented a variety of ideological positions,
and exchange professors were continually brought in
for a period of residence to introduce muliple facets
of the culture. (3) The work was specific, meaning
that conceptual investigations were concrete as well
as abstract. They were interested in the practical
as well as the theoretical, and consequently their
methodological approach was empirical as well as
rational. It was with regard to this latter aspect
of the program, in particular, that Starbuck was
invited to serve on the faculty of the philosophy
department.[105]

Starbuck's experience as a faculty member appears to be quite satisfactory, although the university would not approve the granting of graduate
degrees in his major interest, character education.
Starbuck did not desire to teach ethics in the traditional sense. Rather his interests centered in
the teaching of character education. While at the
Universtiy of Iowa, Starbuck's students were able
to receive the Ph.D. degree without fulfilling all
the traditional requirements in philosophy. Education
courses were included in the character education
major. But at U.S.C., with no graduate degree in

character education, the traditional number of courses in philosophy were required for the degree, and no exceptions were made for Starbuck's students. As a result, the Ph.D. was never granted to any of the graduate students working under Starbuck. Many of the students who took character education under Starbuck were educators who didn't obtain a degree in philosophy.[106]

During the first school year at U.S.C., Starbuck's interests in the University of Iowa were anything but dissolved. His major concern pertained to the perpetuation of an Institute for character research at Iowa that would carry on further studies in the area as initiated by Starbuck himself. In the middle of September Starbuck was informed that Dr. Lampe, with the university's School of Religion, had been appointed the acting director of the Institute for one year. Although Dr. Lampe considered his position to be largely nominal, he was asked to study the situation and to offer recommendations for a more permanent arrangement.[107] By March of the next year still no decision had been made about the Institute and character research.[108] In response to this information Starbuck wrote to Dr. James C. Manry, who was dividing his time between the philosophy department and the Institute. Expressing disappointment with the school's failure to act, Starbuck said:

> "What is going to be the final outcome of the messing around of the administration in the Institute? I am impatient to guess. They are as silly as anything one can imagine in not making you the Director. I put that up to the President as strongly as a person could.... I hope you will not let them jostle you about, but hold your ground against any of their mechanicians. I was too devilish patient there for a decade and

160

a half before I began to
fight. The fight was good
and won."109

Starbuck is relatively accurate about considering the fight won while he remained at Iowa, but
with his departure the ultimate battle could be
considered lost. On May 8, Dr. Manry wrote Starbuck
that Dean Seashore had asked about issuing some
numbers of the Iowa Studies in Character by the end
of June. A rather large balance in the publications
fund remained and would have to be spent by the last
of June or it would be returned to the general university treasury. During the year Manry had pressed
for an editor of the series, having in mind the
continuation of the publications; however, until
this meeting he had been ignored. Manry wrote:

> "Dean Seashore wishes me to ask
> you whether you will agree to the
> use of your name as editor of the
> Iowa Studies in Character through
> June 30 of this year /1931/. I
> seem to sense that the Dean's
> plan is to bring the series to a
> grand finale with that date ...
> the continuance of the series is
> uncertain because of the uncertainty
> about the future of the Institute."110

As it turned out, both Starbuck and Manry edited
one each of only two studies published in 1931 in
the fourth volume of the series. This volume, as
Manry had guessed, ended up being the last publication of the Iowa Studies in Character. And the life
of the Institute of Character Research, after an
expenditure of over $85,000,111 died at Iowa with
the close of this series.

As was the case at Iowa, Starbuck's supervision
of the Institute of Character Research at Southern
California was above and beyond his responsibilities
as a faculty member. As usual, however, he managed
to devote a significant amount of time to the Insti-

161

tute's various projects. The major immediate objective of the Institute during Starbuck's early years at California was an extension of the work started at Iowa, that is, supplying children, by an exacting methodology, the best literature, music, and art of the world, for the ultimate purpose of building, though indirectly, character. Starbuck passionately believed in this approach whereby the selected educational gems would be unconsciously absorbed into the imaginative mind of the child, as a result not only stimulating his thought, but also guiding his desires, uplifting his attitudes, and motivating his will for a better life.

Starbuck regarded his plan as the most comprehensive system for character education ever devised. The years had been spent scientifically sifting through the world's offerings in literature, in the field of fairytale, myth, legend, fiction, biography, poetry, art and music. Starbuck envisioned an expansive system of books covering every fundamental phase of character education which would be useful to teachers, parents, and pupils up to the Junior College level. The culmination of his scheme was to be a series of school readers entitled "Living Through Reading,"112 in which the most outstanding selections for reading would be produced for all grades.

In a promotional brochure distributed around 1935 Starbuck spoke of twenty manuscripts which were ready for publication: five volumes of biography; five volumes of poetry; a series of Character Education Readers, presumably, eight; and two volumes dealing with methods, materials and theory of character training. In addition, other materials were being edited and assembled. As was also true at Iowa, it appears that the fundamental barrier to production was the need of adequate funds.

With this need in mind, under the laws of the State of California, the Institute was incorporated as the Institute of Character Research, Inc. The initial stock issue, opened to subscription, consisted

of 500 shares, at $100 per share. This step was pro-
moted not only as a desirable financial investment,
but also as an investment in social and cultural advancement. Starbuck and his staff were ardently
convinced that the most valuable contribution at the
time that anyone could make to society was to aid
the adoption in America of their character education
movement. His was a dream of a substantial contribution to the country:

> "America is beginning to
> climb out of the valley of eco-
> nomic discouragement, and the
> time is ripe to place this vital-
> ly important project on a vigor-
> ously progressive business basis.
> We hope to be in a position to
> supply for publication, at this
> critical period, complete materi-
> als to fulfill the demands of the
> school people and parents of
> America by furnishing every re-
> quirement for a new and vital
> CHARACTER EDUCATION betterment.
>
> We propose to become a perma-
> nent clearing house for CHARACTER
> EDUCATION publications and to es-
> tablish here the chief center of
> expectancy in America along this
> line."113

Starbuck's dream, however, was never fulfilled.
Even with the act of incorporation, funds raised
were inadequate to carry out the proposed scheme.
In fact, it appears that funds were largely exhausted
after the publication of the three volumes, Living
Through Biography, in 1936. This series of readers,
particularly suitable for grades seven to nine, although of universal appeal to a wider range of grades,
offered an outstanding collection of appealing biographies, meant to supplement and enrich the regular
school curriculum.

Besides this biography series, no other materials
of the Institute were published during Starbuck's

years at U.S.C. In 1945, however, two years after Starbuck's retirement from active teaching, Look To This Day,[114] selected writings by Edwin Diller Starbuck, was assembled and edited by the staff of the Institute of Character Research, a final tribute to the one who had been their inspiration.

Summary and Analysis

Such were the efforts and contributions of a rare man, with pioneering spirit, whose career spanned nearly a half century. It has been demonstrated that Starbuck was among the first who prepared the way for later developments in several areas. His doctoral dissertation, later published as the first book to carry the title, Pyschology of Religion, was a classic study of religious experience, which encouraged many other scientific studies in the field of religion. At Stanford University, even before the publication of his book in 1899, Starbuck pioneered in offering psychology of religion courses. Also at Stanford he was the first to offer a course of instruction in character education, in 1898. The pioneering efforts of Starbuck and his students in applying laboratory experimental methods to the study of character must not go unnoticed either. And as a result of these latter efforts, Starbuck and his associates developed the first system of judging literature, expecially for character training, in the context of a scientific, objective methodology. Finally, Starbuck was the first to develop an Institute for character research which was recognized as an official division of the university.

Under no circumstances could Starbuck be labelled an armchair philosopher. His career exhibited a keen interest in the practical application of theoretical insight. Not only was this revealed in the classroom, when he was teaching, but it was evident also in his activities in religious and character education. Starbuck's acceptance of the consultation position with the Unitarian Association for the purpose of developing a new curriculum in religous education is an indication that Starbuck desired to apply to a concrete program the

164

educational inferences he raised in his study, Psychology of Religion. Further, his literary projects
were the practical result of the theoretical and experimental work done in his Institute. He was always
fundamentally interested in the meaning and possible
implications of his research. He was ever an advocate
of experimentation and research not as an isolated
methodology to be preserved and protected, but as a
tool to be used in the practical work of dealing more
effectively with the problems and issues of his day.
There is no better example of this than his attempt
to develop objectively a comprehensive set of readers
for the schools which would supplement their program
especially in terms of character training.

It has been suggested that Starbuck's career has
a dividing point which is the winning of the national
contest for the best character education methods. The
winning of this award with the "Iowa Plan" in 1921
determined significantly the nature of Starbuck's investment of his energies for the next twenty years,
including his prime years at Iowa. The emergence of
an Institute of Character Research to expand the
research of the original project, and to carry on other
studies of importance to character education affected
drastically Starbuck's career and contribution, in
terms of time and direction. His research in other
areas of religious study was curtailed, and the possibility for personal writing and publication in areas
other than those being studied in the Institute was
almost completely sacrificed. And perhaps, most importantly, a vast amount of time was expended regularly
through the years for the purpose of raising funds to
support the work in character research. This was done
to the detriment of other potential contributions.

Any judgment about the success of Starbuck's
career is extremely difficult to make. If success is
defined as achieving one's objectives, then certainly,
in one sense, Starbuck might be considered unsuccessful.
His grand plan for the publication of a comprehensive
set of materials related to character education was
never completed. But if success can be viewed in
terms of the personal satisfaction of facing squarely

the challenges of life, and in the process inspiring those in one's association, then Starbuck was truly successful. For twenty years he maintained two full-time jobs, that of faculty member and directorship of his Institutes. He accepted the ongoings of life not submissively, but courageously. As a teacher he was highly admired and respected not only by his students but also by his colleagues. In the midst of many set-backs and discouragements, especially with regard to his efforts in character training, Starbuck was re-warded with enough praise and support at the appropriate times to keep his vision alive.

There appear to be at least five reasons why Starbuck's proposal for character research and educa-tion was not entirely fulfilled. (1) Starbuck's pro-posal would have required a tremendous staff and or-ganization to produce and continue to revise the vast curriculum of materials he envisioned. Such a large enterprise was not feasible for Starbuck to direct while also serving as a full-time faculty member. (2) The expense of the proposed projects was prohi-bitive. The cost of the completed volumes alone turned out to be between $100,000 and $150,000. Star-buck seemed to have poor judgment about the estimated expenditures of his projects. He was periodically predicting the movement of his work into a self-sus-taining position. But many thousands of dollars more than he estimated to finish a project were needed be-fore it was finally completed, and the distribution of the publications were never large enough to put them on a self-sustaining basis, as he had hoped. It is interesting to conjecture what might have been the out-come of Starbuck's vision, if the anonymous "Donor," or any other foundation, had been willing to underwrite the entire project. (3) By the time enough research and literary judging had been done to prepare the way for actual publications the Depression had hit the country and funds for such purposes, in general, were extremely difficult to obtain. (4) It is apparent that Starbuck was the creative, sustaining force behind the work of the Institute. Neither Institute at Iowa or California was able to continue the momentum with Star-buck gone. When the Institute at Iowa was transfered to California, it was almost ready to begin producing the results of its research, but Starbuck, who was very much the director of the work had reached retirement age and undoubtedly was unable to work at such a pace as before. And finally, (5) Although Starbuck's plan for character education was unique, it was one among other plans and methods which were being introduced and promoted during his day.[115] Starbuck admits in Volume I of his Guide that his project was only one more of the many efforts that had been made, to publish lists of the best literature for children, but he does contend that he considers his venture to be more comprehensive and scientifically objective than those that had preceded him.[116]

Starbuck's career, then, was a fine mixture of success and failure, depending upon the particular period or event in his life to which one points, and depending also upon the criteria by which one judges the worth of a man's endeavors.

NOTES

1. *Webster's New Collegiate Dictionary* (Spring-field, Mass.: G. and C. Merriam Co., Publishers, 1961), p. 125.

2. Edwin D. Starbuck, "Religion's Use of Me," *Religion in Transition*, edited by Vergilius Ferm (London: George Allen & Unwin Ltd, 1937), p. 206.

3. Wilbur Long, "Edwin Diller Starbuck--An Appreciation," *Research News* II, No. 1 (Los Angeles: University of Southern California, Graduate School, 1936), p. 1.

4. Book jacket for *Look To This Day: Selected Writings By Edwin Diller Starbuck*, Assembled and edited by the staff of the Institute of Character Research University of Southern California Press, 1945).

5. Interview with Dr. Herbert and Mrs. Anna Searles, Dec. 27, 1968, Los Angeles. Mrs. Searles made this particular statement.

6. This information was obtained by tabulating chronologically and topically Starbuck's known extant publications.

7. James Bissett Pratt, "The Psychology of Religion," *Harvard Theological Review*, I, No. 4 (October, 1908), p. 439.

8. Starbuck, "Religion's Use of Me," p. 235.

9. *Ibid.*, p. 236.

10. E. Leigh Mudge, *The God-Experience* (Cincinnati: Caxton Press, 1923).

11. Starbuck, "Religion's Use of Me," pp. 237-238.

12. In his experimental work in psycho-physics, Starbuck helped work on establishing norms for measurement. He, with Newell H. Bullocks and a few graduate students, conducted extensive tests on about twenty mental and physical proficiencies on 2,400 schoolchildren in San Jose. Unfortunately, this data was lost, where Starbuck later taught, at the University of Southern California.

13. Edwin G. Boring, *A History of Experimental Psychology* (New York: Appleton-Century-Crofts, Inc., 1957), p. 581.

14. Starbuck, "Religion's Use of Me," p. 240.

15. This study was published in pamphlet form

168

as Character Education Methods: The Iowa Plan
(Washington, D.C.: National Capital Press, Inc.,
1922).

16. A survey of the sources referring to this
Institute reveals that until 1927 when it was officially named Institute of Character Research, it
was variously referred to as the Bureau of Research
in Character Training and Religious Education,
Research Station in Character Education and Religious
Education, or Research Station in Character Education.

17. This appraisal was made by Mrs. Pearl Minor
during a phone interview in Iowa City, Iowa, in the
summer of 1968.

18. State University of Iowa Catalogue, 1906-07.

19. Letter received from Mrs. Elizabeth H. Lasselle, Associate Editor of the Division of Education
and Program, of the Unitarian Universalist Association, and President of the Unitarian Sunday School
Society, dated November 20, 1968.

20. See especially the following: "Reinforcement to the Pulpit from Modern Psychology," The
Homiletic Review, LII, No. 3 (September 1906), pp.
168-172, and No. 6 (December 1906), pp. 418-423;
"The Child-Mind and Child-Religion," The Biblical
World (Chicago: University of Chicago Press). A
series of five articles: Part I: "The Child-Consciousness and Human Progress," XXX, No. 1 (July,
1907), pp. 30-38; Part II: "The Nature of Child
Consciousness," No. 2 (August, 1907), pp. 101-110;
Part III: "The Method of Evolution of Consciousness and of Religion," No. 3 (September, 1907),
pp. 191-201; Part IV: "The Development of Spirituality," No.5 (November, 1907), pp. 352-360; Part
V: "Stages in Religious Growth," XXXI, No. 2
(February, 1908), pp. 101-112; and "The Play Instinct and Religion," The Homiletic Review, LVIII,
No. 4 (October, 1909), pp. 275-278.

21. Starbuck, "Part I: The Child-Consciousness
and Human Progress," p. 30.

22. The Religious Education Association, Proceedings of the First Annual Convention (Chicago,
February 10-12, 1903), p. 356.

23. Ibid., p. 349.

24. Ibid., p. v.

25. The Religious Education Association, Proceedings of the Third Annual Convention (Boston,
February 12-16, 1905), pp. ix and xi.

26. American Unitarian Association, The American
Unitarian Association and the Unitarian Sunday
School Society (August 22, 1912). A xeroxed copy
of this was received from Elizabeth H. Lasselle,
Associate Editor of the Division of Education and
Program.

27. A published report from the files of former
officers of the Unitarian Sunday School Society,
dated September 10, 1914. A xeroxed copy of this
report was received from Elizabeth H. Lasselle,
current President of the Society, in a letter dated
November 20, 1968. It should be noted that annual
reports and old records of meetings of the Sunday
School Society are currently kept in a vault in a
Boston bank and arrangements can be made, through
the Unitarian Universalist Association in Boston,
to see the papers in the Sunday School Society
archives.

28. A published report from the files of former
officers of the Unitarian Sunday School Society,
dated June 4, 1914. A xeroxed copy of this report
was received from Elizabeth H. Lasselle.

29. Starbuck, "Religion's Use of Me," p. 242.

30. A published report from the files of former
officers of the Unitarian Sunday School Society,
dated April 24, 1913. A xeroxed copy of this report
was received from Elizabeth H. Lasselle.

31. A published report from the files of former
officers of the Unitarian Sunday School Society,
dated September 10, 1914.

32. It should be noted that George Herbert Betts
in his volume The Curriculum of Religious Education
(New York: Abingdon Press, 1924), speaks of this
series, which by then is called "The Beacon Course."
He substantiates Starbuck's claim, that the series
was not finished, by suggesting that the materials
had been developing gradually but that several of
the volumes were not yet issued. (p. 429) A hint
is given by Betts as to one of the probable reasons
the effort was not supported fully to its completion.
He states, "Accustomed as the evangelical group

are to approaching ethical conduct through the religious motive, they will not be in accord with the evident purpose of approaching the religious through the ethical, which this series manifestly seeks to do." (pp. 441-442).

33. Starbuck, "Religion's Use of Me," p. 242.
34. Starbuck and Research Collaborators, Character Education Methods, p. iii.
35. A letter from Starbuck to President Jessup of the University of Iowa, December 26, 1916.
36. Starbuck, et al., Character Education Methods, pp. iv-v.
37. Ibid., p. vi.
38. Memorandum of The Second Meeting of the Committee on Character Education, Hotel Montrose, Cedar Rapids, April 3rd and 4th, 1918.
39. Letter from President of the University of Iowa to Starbuck, dated April 16, 1918.
40. Starbuck, et al., Character Education Methods, p. v.
41. Ibid., pp. vi-vii.
42. This assertation is substantiated by a statement made, to this effect, by Margaret Starbuck in an interview with her, December 30, 1968.
43. University of Iowa Service Bulletin, X, No. 20 (May 15, 1926), p. 1.
44. Starbuck, et al., Character Education Methods, p. vii.
45. Starbuck, "Religion's Use of Me," p. 243.
46. Starbuck, et al., Character Education Methods, p. 46.
47. "Character Research at the University of Iowa" (author of the article not stated), Childhood and Character, vii, No. 2 (November, 1929), p. 6.
48. University of Iowa Service Bulletin, X, No. 20 (May 15, 1926), p. 2.
49. Childhood and Character, p. 6.
50. University of Iowa Service Bulletin, X, No. 20 (May 15, 1926), p. 2.
51. Edwin Diller Starbuck, editor; assisted by Frank K. Shuttleworth, et al., A Guide to Literature for Character Training: Volume I Fairy Tale, Myth, and Legend (New York: Macmillan Co., 1928).

52. Edwin Diller Starbuck, editor; et al., A Guide to Books for Character: Volume II Fiction (New York: Macmillan Co., 1930).

53. Williard C. Olson, "Character Education," Encyclopedia of Education Research, Walter S. Monroe, ed. (New York: Macmillan Co., 1950), p. 133.

54. The Wonder Road: Book I: Familiar Haunts, Fairy Tales Selected by Edwin Diller Starbuck, and assistants; Book II: Enchanted Paths, Fairy Tales Selected by Edwin Diller Starbuck and Frank K. Shuttleworth, and assistants; Book III: Far Horizons, Fairy Tales Selected by Edwin Diller Starbuck and Frank K. Shuttleworth, and assistants (3 vols.; New York: Macmillan Co., 1930).

55. Edwin D. Starbuck, gen. ed., University of Iowa Studies in Character, Volume I: No. 1, "World Citizenship: A Measurement of Certain Factors Determining Information and Judgment of International Affairs," by James C. Manry; No. 2, "The Measurement of the Character and Environmental Factors Involved in Scholastic Success," by Frank K. Shuttleworth; No. 3, "The Study of Religion in State University," by Herbert Leon Searles; No. 4, "Untruthfulness in Children: Its Conditioning Factors and Its Setting in Child Nature," by W. E. Slaught; Volume II: No. 1, "Measurement of the Comprehension Difficulty of the Precepts and Parables of Jesus," by Samuel P. Franklin; No. 2, "A Comparative Study of Those Who Accept as Against Those Who Reject Religious Authority," by Thomas H. Howells; No. 3, "A Comparative Study of Those Who Report the Experience of the Divine Presence and Those Who Do Not, by Robert Daniel Sinclair; No. 4, "A Study of the Placement in the Curriculum of Selected Teachings of the Old Testament Prophets," by Ralph Thomas Case; Volume III: No. 1, "The Attitudes of Children Toward Law," by Earl G. Lockhart; No. 2, "Biblical Information in Relation to Character and Conduct," by Pleasant Roscoe Hightower; No. 3, "The Character Value of the Old Testament Stories," by George W. Beiswanger; No. 4, "The Development of Imagination in the Preschool Child," by Elizabeth Gordon Andrews; Volume IV: No. 1, "Information and Certainty in Political Opinions: A Study of University Students

During a Campaign," by Harold S. Carlson; No. 2 /Ñote: James C. Manry, ed./, "Race Attitudes of Iowa Children," by Ralph D. Minard. (4 vols.; Iowa City: University of Iowa, 1927-1931).

56. University of Iowa Service Bulletin, XII, No. 6 (February 11, 1928), p. 6.

57. Note that the correspondence referred to is to be found in the archives of the University of Iowa main library.

58. Letter from Starbuck to President Walter A. Jessup, dated April 23, 1923.

59. Letter from Starbuck to Dr. Deardsley Ruml, Director of the Laura Spelman Rockefeller Memorial, dated May 1, 1923.

60. Letter from Starbuck to President Jessup, dated May 8, 1923.

61. University of Iowa Service Bulletin, (February 11, 1928), p. 6.

62. Letter from Starbuck to Ruml, dated May 1, 1923.

63. Letter from Starbuck to Mr. Galen M. Fisher, Institute of Social and Religious Research, New York City, dated May 27, 1924.

64. Letter from C. E. Seashore to Galen M. Fisher, dated June 13, 1924.

65. Letter from Starbuck to President Jessup, dated January 20, 1926.

66. Letter from Galen M. Fisher to Starbuck, dated January 28, 1926.

67. Letter from Starbuck to President Jessup, dated February 26, 1926.

68. Letter from Starbuck to Professor G. T. W. Patrick, dated June 2, 1926.

69. This and the preceding quotes are from Starbuck's letter to Professor C. T. W. Patrick, dated June 2, 1926.

70. Letter from Starbuck to Dean Seashore, dated August 11, 1926.

71. Letter from Starbuck to President Jessup, dated August 13, 1926.

72. This information contained in a letter of acknowledgment from Starbuck to President Jessup, dated July 16, 1927.

73. Letter from President Jessup to the Graduate

173

Council and the Board of Education of the State University of Iowa, dated May 23, 1927.

74. Letter from Gamaliel Bradford to Starbuck, dated December 15, 1928.

75. First letter from Starbuck to President Jessup Dated December 30, 1927.

76. Second letter from Starbuck to President Jessup, dated December 30, 1927.

77. Letter from Starbuck to Dr. Daniel A. Poling, with the J. C. Penney Foundation, and Mrs. Leonard Elmhirst, dated March 13, 1928.

78. Letter from Miss Emily Bax, Women's City Club, New York City, to Starbuck, dated April 21, 1928.

79. Letter from Starbuck to Miss Emily Bax, dated April 25, 1928.

80. Letter from Emily Bax to Starbuck, dated May 8, 1928.

81. Letter from Professor Gamaliel Bradford, dated November 29, 1928.

82. Letter from Starbuck to Professor Gamaliel Bradford, dated December 4, 1928.

83. Letter from Gamaliel Bradford to Starbuck, dated December 15, 1928.

84. Letter from Starbuck to President Jessup, dated December 17, 1928.

85. Letter from Starbuck to Dean G. F. Kay, dated January 26, 1929.

86. Letter from Starbuck to Dr. Frank K. Shuttleworth, dated January 26, 1929.

87. Letter from Starbuck to Mr. Thomas B. Appleget, dated February 27, 1929.

88. Letter from Starbuck to Mr. H. W. Bates, at the University of Iowa, dated March 25, 1929.

89. Letter from Starbuck to President Jessup, dated May 24, 1929.

90. Letter from Starbuck to President Jessup, dated March 28, 1930.

91. Telegram from Starbuck to Ella Phillips Crandall, of the Payne Fund in New York City, dated May 2, 1930.

92. Telegram from Ella Phillips Crandall to Starbuck, dated May 5, 1930.

93. Telegram from President Jessup to Dean G.

F. Kay, at Stanford University, dated June 11, 1930.

94. Monte Thomas Starkes, "Glimpses of Greatness: O. D. Foster" (Unpublished Ph. D. Dissertation, University of Iowa, 1967), p. 73. See pp. 73-74 for a brief description of Starbuck's pioneering efforts before Foster, and regarding their relationship.

95. Letter from Starbuck to President Jessup, dated October 14, 1922.

96. Letter from Starbuck to President Jessup, dated January 28, 1921.

97. Letter from Starbuck to President Jessup, dated February 21, 1921.

98. Starbuck, "Religion's Use of Me," pp. 244-245.

99. Unfortunately these lectures were never published. An unknown number of outlines of this series of lectures were printed, however. Copies of this outline, it is known, are in the possession of at least the University of Iowa library archive, and Mrs. Anna Searles, of Los Angeles, as well as the present writer.

100. The National Encyclopedia of American Biography, vol. E (New York: James T. White and Co., 1938), p. 319.

101. Starbuck, "Religion's Use of Me," p. 246.

102. Letter from Starbuck to President Jessup, dated August 19, 1929.

103. Memorandum on conference between President Jessup, Dean George Kay, W. H. Cobb and Dr. E. D. Starbuck, dated May 10, 1930.

104. Interview with Dr. Herbert and Mrs. Anna Searles on December 27, 1968, in Los Angeles.

105. A brochure, entitled "New Developments in Philosophy in the University of Southern California." An attractive brochure describing the nature of the studies with which Starbuck was associated, and the place of his work and interests in the department. No copyright date is available, but by virtue of its content, it would have to have been produced sometime between 1931 and 1936.

106. Interview with the Searles, December 27, 1968.

107. Letter from James C. Manry to Starbuck at U.S.C., dated September 16, 1930.

108. Letter from James C. Manry to Starbuck at U.S.C., dated March 11, 1931.

109. Letter from Starbuck to James C. Manry, dated March 11, 1931.

110. Letter from James C. Manry to Starbuck, dated May 8, 1931.

111. Cost sheet entitled "Character Education Summary of Expenditures," dated May 9, 1930. Expenditures from the S.U.I. budget were listed as $38,630.93, and from gifts and loans, as $47,209.50.

112. Some sources refer to this series as "Character Education Readers."

113. Institute of Character Research, Inc., affiliated with the University of Southern California (Los Angeles: George Rice and Sons Printer, n.d.).

114. Look To This Day: Selected Writings by Edwin Diller Starbuck, assembled and Edited by the Staff of the Institute of Character Research (The University of Southern California Press, 1945). Preparing this for publication appears to have been largely the work of Mrs. Anna Searles.

115. Frank C. Sharp, Education for Character (Indianapolis: Bobbs-Merrill Co., 1927). See especially pp. 399-440 for a discussion of these plans.

116. A Guide to Literature for Character Training, pp. viii-ix.

CHAPTER IV

SIGNIFICANT CONTRIBUTIONS

In this chapter, an attempt to deal selectively
with the most representative and pioneering efforts
of Starbuck is made. Our approach is to analyze
Starbuck's most significant theoretical and practical
contributions by way of his writings and the projects
to which he devoted so much of his attention. The
first part, dealing with his writings, will include
an interpretive chronological survey, a discussion of
recurring themes, and a critical review of his 1899
classic. The second part, dealing with his major projects, will evaluate, thoroughly and systematically,
his efforts to implement, in practical terms, some of
his more important visions for a better society.

Writings

Compared to the voluminous output of the average
pioneer in practically any field, Starbuck's legacy
in terms of publications seems somewhat meager, indeed.[1] It has been our contention, throughout this
study, however, that the worth of a person's contributions cannot be relegated completely to the sum
total of his written words. Furthermore, the quantity of a man's writings may readily belie the quality
of his work, as well as the nature of the time and
energy spent in preparation for the final product.
Our inspection of Starbuck's life and career has revealed an image of a man whose ultimate priority of
personal relationships over publications was clearly
evidenced. This glimpse of Starbuck's endeavors has
uncovered also the real extent to which a minimal
number of published volumes, by virtue of the methods
and procedures involved, demanded such a prolonged
effort on Starbuck's part prior to publication. These
two factors, alone, justify the limited magnitude of
Starbuck's writings.

The modest number of publications has enabled
us to examine carefully every work, known to us, which
Starbuck composed himself, or helped to create. Our

research has comprised the perusal of over one hundred items by Starbuck, including books, articles, and materials edited.[2]

Chronological Survey

An overview of the sequence of Starbuck's works fails to disclose a balanced scheme in his series of publications between 1897 and 1945. That is, it is impossible to neatly categorize the nature of his writings during evenly graduated periods of his life. For instance, a division of his publications by decades in terms of special themes or ideas does not fall into place. Nevertheless, certain patterns in his written contributions do emerge, and it is possible to discern not only his basic thoughts as revealed in particular major works, to which we may point; but it is also apparent that specific writings do indicate turning points in the direction of his interests and concerns and that consequent publications, in general, manifest the nature of the direction. Along these lines we will divide his written contributions into three phases: 1897-1906, 1907-1921, and 1922-1945. Phase One: 1897-1906. The two articles published, in 1897, in the distinguished American Journal of Psychology,[3] served to inaugurate Starbuck's writing career. The research for these articles had been undertaken during Starbuck's graduate work at Harvard University and was completed at Clark University where he received his Ph.D. The significance of this work was not to be fully realized, however, until it was used as the core of Starbuck's first published book, The Psychology of Religion, in 1899. This work, more than anything else, gained for Starbuck a reputation as one of the key pioneering figures in the psychology of religion movement in America. In these studies Starbuck clearly established the seriousness of his concern, and the validity thereof, that the methods of inductive science become common-place tools in the study of religion. More than merely an analysis of the religious experience of conversion, this study objectively delineated the normal development of religious growth, and the mental and organic factors that affect that growth.

178

From the very beginning, Starbuck's interest in the relationship of psychology and religion is matched by his concern that the implications of such study be felt in the educational field. His participation in the movements of both secular and religious education substantiates this point, as do the numerous articles he devotes to this subject. The first such article, symbolizing this keen interest in education, as related to religion, appeared as the published product of a major address he delivered at the first annual convention of the Religious Education Association in 1903.[4] In this article Starbuck speaks of three "growing world-conceptions," which he feels need to infiltrate the programs of religious education, as they have to a greater extent the institutions of secular education. He speaks of the universe as involved in the "process of becoming," as "dynamic," rather than "static." As Starbuck puts it, man cannot help but be confronted with the fact "that growth is the method of life; that the divine Life as the reality of the universe is in a process of eternal change, transition, and self-revelation." The implications of this conception for religious education are considerable: religion arises out of the natural development of the stream of life itself; the dichotomy is false which separates religious education from the rest of education; and the final aim of religious education, not unlike secular education, is the "growth of individuals and society." The second conception, to which Starbuck refers, is that of individualism, the matter of the worth of individuals. According to Starbuck, this conception signifies that the purposes of religious education are not to be hitched to the visions of another world, but are to be related to the present needs of the lives of individuals. The final conception involves the sensing of "society as an organism," a recognition that its inter-relatedness, its responsibility for community, will save it for a better future. This will mean, for religious education, some changes in emphasis, such as greater consideration of "social righteousness" as opposed to "personal salvation." Starbuck's hope for the development of social consciousness was an optimistic one, as illustrated in this statement:

"Our chief business today is to live

179

> beautifully and helpfully in this
> present world, trusting God for
> the future; to labor for a perfec-
> ted personal and social life,
> believing that human genius and
> human conscience, in whatever
> sphere we find ourselves, working
> together with Him, can meet and
> master the problem of human des-
> tiny.[5]

The essence of these three conceptions will be reproduced over and again in various forms throughout the structures of Starbuck's work.

The next important article of Starbuck's, "The Feelings and Their Place in Religion," is published the following year.[6] Unlike so many of his works which actually deal with related disciplines, this particular piece examines directly a specific issue in the study of religion. Here Starbuck's concern has to do with the place of feelings in religion, or as Starbuck prefers to speak of it, because of its comprehensiveness, the role of the "affective life." Religion, according to Starbuck, involves those aspects of life, such as, faith, hope, and love, which cannot be reduced, finally, to intellectual terms. He is not replacing the cognitive process with feelings. Rather, he is suggesting that only cognition is a distortion, and that man's response to religion is characterized by the blending of feeling, idea, and volition.

In 1905, Starbuck was invited to speak, again, to the members of the Religious Education Association, holding their third annual convention. Of the two addresses he delivered, one was especially signifi- cant, handling, as it does, the broad relationship be- tween religious education and the public schools.[7] As in 1903, Starbuck's interest remained warm to this issue. He notes the growing controversy over the teaching of religion in public schools, and the conse- quent concern that many in the field of religious edu- cation have regarding a law that appears to be cre- ating a barrier between religion and the children of the country. In Starbuck's analysis of this situation, we learn not only something about his views toward the nature of religion, but also the relation of his concept of religion to education.

At the outset, Starbuck boldly declares that he does not consider the concern over the exclusion of Bible and "religious" teaching from the public schools necessary at all, nor does he believe this means the end to religion in public education. What Starbuck is suggesting is that the exclusion of formal religious instruction in the schools need not avert the promotion of religious development in the students. He offers several suggestions, which provide a philosophical basis for his discussion of the place of religion in public school education, or as he calls it, "spiritualizing the secular schools." In the first place, learning must be related to living, and such learning, according to Starbuck, has consequently to do with religion. Secondly, Starbuck steers clear of reducing religion to a specific set of doctrines or ecclesiastical dogmas. Instead, his appeal is to a view of religion in terms of the whole of life. Seen in this light, the purposes of education cannot be isolated from those of religion. More than a sense of legal permission, the schools, Starbuck believes, ought to feel a responsibility towards the cultivation of the religious life, as so defined.

Thirdly, Starbuck upheld the central place of instinctive gifts in the development of personality and character. The teacher's main task, therefore, is to work with this instinctive structure towards a harmony in personality, a harmony in life not disassociated from the life of religion.

In terms of Starbuck's understanding and defining of the issues, his answer to the question of religion in public education was unqualifiedly affirmative. He concluded:

> "In so far as a dignified sense of God and a reverent appreciation of life shall prevail, and to the extent that we have men and women in the teaching profession who have

come into their own spiritual
heritage, the common school will
become a life-giving and religion developing institution."[8]

Such viewpoints are representative of the thinking that later would carry Starbuck headlong into the
throes of his character education projects, with an
idealism related to the possibilities of improvement
in this field that would not know retirement.

Phase Two: 1907-1921. 1907, the end of the first
decade in Starbuck's writing career, and the year his
essay on "Moral Training in the Public Schools"[9] took
third place in a national contest which received over
three-hundred submitted essays, marks not necessarily
a turning point in his career, for we have already
viewed precursors to this essay in previous articles;
but this event, and this work, does establish unques-
tionably at this early date the strength of his interest in character education, and must have supplied a
certain amount of confidence for future endeavors in
this area. Starbuck's work during the next decade-
and-a-half would include several publications directly
related to character education, although during this
period, still, these would be matched with other subjects in philosophy, psychology, and religion.

An examination of Starbuck's 1907 essay not only
discloses a striking continuity, throughout, with his
1903 address on "The Foundations of Religion and
Morality," but also provides clear evidence of a philosophical approach that prefigures The Iowa Plan,[10] a
signal work produced by Starbuck and his associates
in 1922. One of the central assertations in this
essay, common to Starbuck's other major works in this
field also, is that a direct, moralistic approach to
ethics in the public schools is undesirable. Although
he is not opposed to even formal ethical study, especially in the latter years of the school program, his
main concerns center around those factors which, apart
from the formal approach, stimulate the impulses of
morality already resident in the child. He begins and
ends his essay with this point in mind. Early in the
essay Starbuck states:

182

> "Moral Training will be efficient
> in so far as it influences the
> instincts, motives, tastes, and
> aspirations of children, and not
> so far as it tries to inculate in
> their minds ideas of right and
> wrong." [11]

And he conludes his essay with these words:

> "It has seemed worth our
> while to try to set forth in the
> strongest terms that, during
> the earliest years, character
> formation does not come about
> through definite ethical teach-
> ing, but through influencing the
> deeper sources of life and conduct
> that lie back of the intellect
> and perform the quality of the
> life."[12]

It is interesting to note that Starbuck's proposal for nurturing those "deeper sources" of
personality turns out to be a brief foreshadowing
of his efforts, in the 1920's and 30's, to select
the best character building literature as a supplement to the regular school curriculum. A refinement
of the instincts in children occurred, according
to Starbuck, when the teacher cultivated them through
the use of appropriately selected stories, poems,
fiction, and biographical works of inspiring
individuals. His vision of such supplemental literature would eventually demand an investment of his
life which he could hardly have imagined at the
time.

Between July of 1907 and February of 1908, a
series of five articles by Starbuck, were published,[13]
which brings to greater light his conception of the
nature and development of child consciousness, and
its relationship to religious growth. While they
are written with the problems of religious education
specifically in mind, their content pertains to the

183

interests of character education as well. In the
first article Starbuck deals with the evolutionary
process. He points out that, unlike most of the
lower animals, a human child depends quite entirely
on parental care for the satisfaction of his basic
needs, in fact, for survival. There is no room for
the "laissezfaire" approach in this parental role.
Starbuck's point is that, just as this is true in
terms of the child's biological needs, it is no less
true in terms of religion and morals.

Starbuck concludes that every attempt to discover more about the child must be encouraged, for it
is essential to have more than a loving concern for
their welfare. It is imperative that the work of religious education be performed by educated teachers
and parents, who are knowledgeable about the "facts
of child-consciousness."

Starbuck's second article delves more deeply
into the actual nature of child consciousness. Anyone interested in the perfection of humanity must
have, according to Starbuck, a primary interest in
childhood. But, so often, this has not been the case.
As Starbuck so picturesquely expresses it, those who,
in the past, have envisioned a new and better society
of men have "spent too much time in cultivating old
gnarled orchards and too little in breeding and rear-
ing the seedlings."[14]

Starbuck begins his third article in this series
with the postulation of three basic assumptions:
(1) that there is continuity in a person's mental life,
(2) that a continuity exists between the consciousness
of human and other animals, and (3) that religion is
to be seen as a natural part of the total development
of an individual.[15] The third assumption is especially important to Starbuck. He sees religion as a condition of consciousness. Although men will continue
to view it in terms of a revelating expression of
divine truth, Starbuck would have us also regard it as
"a self-revelation of consciousness to itself."[16]

He concludes the article with a discussion of
the religious impulse, viewing it not as a single
component of consciousness, but rather as a compound,
whose influence upon the totality of consciousness is
significant. The implications of this viewpoint, as
well as of the general contents of this article, are
summed up in Starbuck's final statement:

> "The point of value so
> far is to appreciate that religion
> is not a simple fact that is to
> be administered in set doses to
> children but that both religion
> and the child are complex facts
> that have definite laws of develop-
> ment."[17]

In the fourth article Starbuck investigates
the nature of "spirituality," and its relation to
morality. Whatever else may be included, Starbuck
insists that spirituality involves the natural
development of a child's hereditary gifts. He
speaks of spirituality in terms of the role the
instincts and impulses play in harmonizing the
child to his outside world. That world, with which
the child must learn to relate, includes both
persons and the ideals of self-fulfillment. With
the first, morality is born, and with the latter,
religion.

The final article in this important series
deals specifically with the various stages of
religious growth. Not only are there differences
in religion among individuals; there are also
sigificant changes which occur between the religion
of childhood and the religion of later years.

Starbuck divides this growth in religon into
four basic stages: (1) babyhood, from birth through
the first year, (2) childhood, the second to the
seventh year , (3) youth, the seventh to the thir-
teenth year, and (4) adolescence, from the thir-
teenth year to about the twenty-fourth year.

In a very real sense, Starbuck is subtly

185

pleading in these articles that the stages of growth in the lives of individuals not be ignored. An enhancement of the spiritual life is dependent upon this. As Starbuck concludes:

> "These four stages (if they
> have been rightly described) are
> fixed firmly in the nature of
> the growing life of the world
> and cannot be altered by parents
> and teachers. But they can
> be understood and used."[18]

1910 marks the beginning of a series of eight articles Starbuck was asked to author for the noted Encyclopedia of Religion and Ethics.[19] This encyclopedia, whose first of twelve volumes was published in 1909, introduced each year a new volume until its completion in 1920. Between 1910 and 1919, within the range of the second phase of his writing career, Starbuck contributed articles for seven of the volumes. The subjects witness to his interest in, and reputation for, scholarship in various areas of psychology and religion.

The next important item appears in 1913, when Starbuck writes an article for the Religious Education journal on the Psychology of Religion.[20] Starbuck's sensitive analysis of this movement, which he includes in the larger Science of Religion, hints, even at this early date in its burgeoning development, at the possibilities of degeneration. With the interests of the discipline, itself, and the practical implications, in mind, Starbuck offers several suggestions regarding needed lines of development and methodology. An examination of these points reveals something of the scope of his approach to the study of religion; at the end, he expresses confidence, though with some reserve, in the ability of the psychology of religion to establish itself more soundly among the respected group of sciences. In later years he would experience disappointment with respect to this hope, although he never finally refrained from encouraging such

186

approaches to the study of religion.

One final work, in this second phase of Starbuck's writings, demands consideration. Reminiscent of a thesis in his 1904 articles, to which we have already referred, which states that the affective life is a direct source of knowledge, Starbuck presents an elaboration of the principle in a 1921 article, titled "The Intimate Senses As Sources of Wisdom."[21]

The senses have been customarily classified as "higher," which includes sight and hearing, and "lower," which includes all others; but in this article Starbuck suggests that there be a reclassification of the senses in terms of the manner in which they deal with the data. Those receptors which are able to distinguish qualities in objects and are prone to organize relationships between objects, he chooses to call "defining" senses. Hearing and sight, for instance, have a propensity for definition. Other senses which he calls "intimate senses," Starbuck contends, interpret objects and their qualities without moving through the procedure of definition. The qualities are immediately and directly regarded affirmatively or negatively by the organism. The so-called lower senses generally would be included in this category.

The fact that the intimate senses are predominantly incapable of definition is not reason, Starbuck argues, for degrading these senses by labeling them "lower," or relegating them to a relatively insignificant role in the life processes of an individual. Rather, according to Starbuck, there are certain times when the role of the intimate senses is a primary one, and its place in the life of the individual deeply significant. Although both types of sensory behavior are important, the defining sensory mechanism being especially adept at scientific inquiry and logical analysis, it is the intimate-sense mechanism which, using the language of symbolism, can generate meanings for which there is not adequate description. While

187

the fruits of the defining processes are generally such subjects as science, logic, mathematics, and metaphysics, those of the intimate processes are religion, art, and morality.22

Starbuck's analysis of the intimate senses clearly reveals an aversion towards any form of intellectual absolutism. Rather his approach is cordial to personalism and any other philosophy which views reality in terms of life-processes.

With this article the second phase of Starbuck's writing career comes to an end. A complex of religion/psychology/education subjects has been presented, laying a foundation for even more concerted efforts in religious education and especially in character education during the final phase.

Phase Three: 1922-1945. Over half of the materials edited and written by Starbuck were published during this period. The distinguishing characteristic of this last phase, however, is that, with few exceptions, from this point on, almost every piece of work with which Starbuck is associated deals variously with some aspect of character education and development.

"The Iowa Plan," largely written by Starbuck, with the able assistance of several associates, marks the beginning of this final period. This plan for methods of character education in the public schools, the $20,000 winner of a national contest in 1922, not only symbolized the current interests of Starbuck at that time; in our opinion, it was, perhaps, the key project which actually thrust Starbuck onto an endless road of endeavors in this field for the rest of his life. The victory provided the psychological confidence and impetus for desiring seriously that the ideas be implemented; and the prize money enabled Starbuck to initially fund an Institute for the purpose of concretizing such desired implementation. This latter effort grew into a life-time project, receiving Starbuck's wholehearted commitment, and demanding extraordinary amounts of time and energy throughout the rest of his career.

Starbuck would be drawn through the years to many practical extensions of this project. The basic principles of the character education program were established. It had yet to be completed in detail for all the grades. What had been begun, Starbuck desired to finish, and so, the efforts through the years reveal that attempt. Certainly, the majority of his publications from this time on bear the marks of some aspects of this notable project.

Between 1922 and 1927, when the first volume of the University of Iowa Studies in Character was published, Starbuck managed to produce a dozen major articles in the fields of character education and religious education, the latter field accounting for only two articles, both, incidently, related directly to a consideration of character development. Seven of these articles were published addresses delivered at national or state education conferences.

In the first article published in 1923, to which we shall refer briefly, Starbuck deals specifically with the place of religious education in the development of human nature.[23] He is idealistic enough to suggest that practically anything can be done with human nature, if the laws of mental life are known and observed. But he bluntly alleges that, at the present, religious education is almost incapable of doing anything with human nature, because it knows so little about it. According to Starbuck, it has not taken seriously enough its obligation to study the object of its efforts. With this in the open, Starbuck proceeds to discuss some of the laws of instinctive tendencies and their relationship to individual development.

In 1924, at the 62nd Annual Meeting of the National Education Association, Starbuck delivered an address on "Fundamentals of Character Training."[24] Though not repetitious of any prior single publication of his, it does reinforce and at times reiterate some of the main principles of his combined efforts in the

189

field. Starbuck begins by naming four major opponents of attempts at character education in the schools: "mechanism," "information," "institution," and "tradition." He does suggest, however, that these enemies can be transformed into friends. As Starbuck puts it:

> "Mechanism should live among children instead of slumping in our cellar. He can make of our schools not workshops of devices but houses of efficient service. Information has been converting our schools into museums of curious knowledge. He can transform them into temples of wisdom. Institution is the greatest architect and builder of modern life. He is inclined to forget his true function which is socialization, not organization. It is the high mission of tradition to open up the treasures of the past in order to give spiritual orientation so that our pupils can meet the present work in a spirit of reverence."[25]

Starbuck's point, of course, was that such change would occur only when those responsible for directing the program of education in the public schools, and those responsible for teaching in them, would earnestly endeavor to learn and apply the fundamental principles of character education. With this in mind Starbuck presents the following fundamentals. (1) Abandon any element of the educational system significantly irrelevant to life. (2) Let the school adjust to the interests and needs of children, rather than forcing the children to conform to a rigid educational structure. (3) Recognize the entire school life as the real life of moral experience. Instead of concentrating on the direct promulgation of "virtues," let the natural problems that arise in the school community provide the setting for the process of social adjustment. Let this first-hand experience with demands for moral judgement become one of the major tools for the discovery of the intricacies of moral behavior. (4) Let the objective of character education be internalized by the teacher to the extent that her life shall incarnate the principles rather than her words symbolize them. (5) Let character development be considered the work of the entire school program. In general, compartmentalization of character education in terms of particular time, place, or subject falsifies its relatedness to all of life. The best stories, literature, poems, music, art, and other instruments of culture should be readily available to every teacher of the institution. Starbuck refers to his own work on classified bibliographies as attempting to supply part of this latter need. (6) The range of morality's meaning must be widened. That is, those values fostered by adjustment to the life-situations of the school community must be viewed as one with the moral experiences of the rest of life. (7) The improvement of the educational scene depends greatly upon a deepened understanding of the meaning of character and its development laws. This will come most of all from the results of scientific study and experimentation in this field.[26]

At the same conference, Starbuck wrote and submitted a report of the Sub-Committee of the Character Education Committee on character testing and measurement.[27] Here, Starbuck's concern, that scientific methods be applied to the study of character, is again evidenced. He discussed eleven methods or techniques being employed, and noted that over 150 psychologists and educators were presently conducting such research in the field.

During the next two years, Starbuck delivered two more major addresses, which were published, on the subject of character. The first, "Character Training in the Public School," is given at the 38th Annual Convention of the Washington Education Association,[28] and the second, "Some Fundamental Principles Underlying Religious Education," is presented at the 6th Annual Session of the Ohio State Educational Conference.[29] Careful examination of these articles reveals a fundamental coalescence with the contents of The Iowa Plan.

In 1926 Starbuck, again, was invited to address the National Education Association, this time speaking

191

on "The Challenging Epochs in the Life of A Child--
Abridged."[30] His analysis of the developmental periods
or stages in a child's life is familiar, however he
does offer a new and interesting way of verbally dia-
gramming the educational experience of the child in
terms of constants and variables. Starbuck describes
three constants in perpetual interplay with two variables. The "a" constant stands for "educational authority," the embodiment of the more traditional principles
and objectives of education. The second constant, "b,"
has to do with "educational behavior," or the school
system as it is represented by the institutional machinery designed to perpetuate the proper mechanics of education. The "c" constant stands for the "curriculum,"
that certain body of information which must be fed to
each new generation of pupils. Contending with these
constants are the variables. Starbuck names two. The
first is the "y" variable, symbolizing "youth," which
Starbuck describes as "the growing type of an abstract
somewhat called the developing child." He can be
identified with the constant process of change, both
quantitative and qualitative. The second is the "x"
variable, or "Xenos, the stranger or alien or eccen-
tric one." It stands for the child's individuality,
the capacity for unnumbered forms of variation. Starbuck's main point in the article is that there has been
too much preoccupation with the constants and too little
consideration of the variables. The plea, in this particular case, turns out to be a recognized call of his
for special understanding of the first variable in particular.[31]

For approximately the next ten years, from 1927-
1936, Starbuck's major investment, in terms of publications, was centered around comprehensive editorial
responsibility for several series of volumes dealing
with various aspects of his interest in character education. The first series, with which Starbuck was
associated as general editor, was Studies in Character.[32] Four volumes were issued between 1927 and 1931.
This series consisted of fourteen monographs originally
dissertations, all under the direct supervision of Starbuck, and all related to the work of The Institute for
Character Research at the University of Iowa. The
studies, in general, deal variously with the issues and

questions of character and personality, the methods and techniques of character education, and the constituency and composition of the curriculum. Characteristic of the studies was the application of scientific principles to the multi-faceted examination of character.

The second series included two volumes, A Guide to Literature for Character Training[33] and A Guide to Books for Character,[34] published in 1928 and 1930, respectively. These two works were the product of several laborious years of preparation rendered by Starbuck and his associates of the Institute of Character Research. They constitute, in the first volume, a selection of the best fairy tale literature, myths, legends, and animal stories, and in the second volume, a selected list of the best fiction available for children.

The third series of volumes, edited by Starbuck, was also published in 1930, and the product of The Institute of Research in Character. This series, named The Wonder Road, consisted of three volumes.[35]

The sixty-one stories for children contained in these volumes were considered by Starbuck and his associates as the very best both in terms of literary quality and character education.

The stories of Book I are older classical works of children's literature, while Books II and III contain newer less established stories. This selection resulted from the careful screening of thousands of works by the Institute staff members over a period of several years.

The last series edited by Starbuck, Living Through Biography, was published in 1936, six years after his move to the University of Southern California.[36] Thirty-one of the best biographies available were selected by Starbuck and his Institute staff using the same careful judging techniques as had been employed at Iowa. These selections especially fitted to the interests and level of pupils in grades seven through nine, were included in three volumes: The High Trail,

<u>Actions Speak</u>, and <u>Real Persons</u>.

During this period, when the preparation for the various series Starbuck was editing demanded so much of his time, he still managed to produce a substantial number of articles and essays, focusing, as has been suggested already, on numerous aspects of character education and development.[37]

In 1937 an autobiographical sketch by Starbuck, "Religion's Use of Me," was produced in Vergilius Ferm's <u>Religion in Transition</u>. Ferm chose individuals whom he considered best represented the pioneering spirit of the age in fields related closely to religious philosophy and theology. Starbuck, along with James Leuba and George Coe, was selected by Ferm as most representative of the pioneers of religious psychology, and, in Starbuck's case, religious education and charactor education. Starbuck's essay provides invaluable insight into his personal religious struggle in such a period of transition.

The first empirical studies of religion had been engaged in by Starbuck during the last decade of the 19th century, and the first volume on the psychology of religion had been Starbuck's. Fittingly, almost a half-century later, when Starbuck was seventy-five, he was asked to author the topic "Psychology of Religion" in the <u>Encyclopedia of Educational Research</u>.[38] In this article, Starbuck recounts eight methods by which the field has been approached, with reference to the more significant studies made within each methodological category. Further, he recommends the need for expanded research in seven broad areas. This was, perhaps, Starbuck's last major composition.

1945 marks the final year of publication attributed to Starbuck. His staff of the Institute of Character Research at the University of Southern California edited and had published a selection of Starbuck's writings in the volume titled <u>Look To This Day</u>.[39]

We have attempted to present, in general chronological order, a synthesis of some of Starbuck's major thoughts by way of surveying key publications throughout his writing career. This career was divided into three specific phases. The first phase, 1897-1906, was noted especially for Starbuck's pioneering efforts in the psychology of religion. The implications of these empirical studies of religious experience were dealt with more thoroughly in the second phase, 1907-1921. During this period Starbuck's interests in religious education and character education were heightened. The third phase, 1922-1945, is marked by its almost exclusive attentiveness to the concerns of character development and education. In each phase, as we have indicated, an initial major publication seemed to set the stage for the general direction of Starbuck's work during that period. Now, our intention is to analyze several major themes that highlight Starbuck's work, noting, whenever possible, the nature and extent of their recurrence.

Major Themes

Although, as has been shown, the subjects dealt with by Starbuck were multi-faceted, there are three recurring themes underlying this assortment. It is evident that Starbuck was a moderator between disciplines and ideologies. His endeavors towards mediation or integration are plainly revealed in his consideration of the application of science to the study of religion and character, the relationship of emotion and reason, and the alliance between religion and morality.

Central to Starbuck's interests in the various disciplines with which he was associated, be it religion, psychology, philosophy, or education, was his subscription to the scientific method. This is to be noted especially in his studies of religion and character education. It has been established that Starbuck's classic, The Psychology of Religion, was the first to apply empirical methods to the study of religious experience. Starbuck was fully aware that his attempts to study the facts of religion scientifically would draw criticism from those who chose to

isolate the spiritual realm from the lawful realm of
the world; but he was convinced that all things follow
some form of a cause and effect sequence, and that
every part of the world, including the religious element, was subject to its orderliness. Contrary to the
suspicions of those who may have questioned his motives
as an attempt to invalidate religion by explaining it
away, Starbuck's interest, as a scientist of religion,
was to penetrate for the sake of discerning its insights. He asserted that "the end of our study is not
to resolve the mystery of religion, but to bring
enough of it into orderliness that its facts may appeal
to our understanding."[40]

Starbuck never assumed that science provided absolute answers or explanations. That which is being
studied, he thought is dynamic, always beyond man's
complete grasp, ever, to some extent, unknown; but,
he believed, man can, and must, resolve to find some
degree of consistence and coherence in the flow. In
order to carry religion beyond superstition, to make
its complexities and subtleties intelligible, Starbuck
insisted "it must have a thousand thoughtpaths leading
into its holy of holies."[41] And Starbuck created,
himself, as well as directed the construction of numerous such paths.

Starbuck envisioned a "science" of religious education. While religious education never moved in
this direction with complete success, he constantly
urged disciplined research in this field. In his estimation, as a charter member, the Religious Education
Association had been established precisely for the
sake of such study. On the occasion of the 1927 convention of the R.E.A., in which reports on research in
progress had been presented, Starbuck was asked to
summarize the proceedings. Included in his response
was an evaluative statement, typically representative
of the position he held throughout his career in the
work of religious education. He stated:

> "One or two of the kind to which
> we have listened, if followed up
> by other researchers and tested
> out and then put to work, will do

196

> more for religious education
> than an entire year of spiritual
> fevor undisciplined by thought-
> fulness."[42]

Starbuck was no less interested in the application of the scientific method to the study of character.[43] In the twenties he became almost exclusively
devoted to such study, as symbolized by the publication, at the end of this decade, of the Studies in
Character at the University of Iowa. These four
volumes included completed researches all performed
under the direct supervision of Starbuck. During
this decade he also instigated the creation, under
his direction, of a Research Station in Character
Education at the University of Iowa. And his literary projects, related to character education, demanded
exhaustive research and scientific technique.

The study of character or personality, according
to Starbuck, demanded the objective discipline of empirical research, if, with any sense of validity, it
were to inform education of the needs and possibilities in human development. On one occasion, although
he could have referred to any number of studies performed under his direction, Starbuck pointed to a
specific study in Volume I of Studies in Character by
W. E. Slaught on "Untruthfulness in Children," which
he considered representative of the scientific approach to character, and the value of which he assessed as follows:

> "I submit that one controlled study
> of this kind, in which the factors
> in human experience involved in lying
> are objectively differentiated, is
> worth more in its immediate and re-
> mote effects upon an understanding of
> personality and in its right education
> than a hundred dissertations about the
> moral life done by the technique of
> the essayist and logician."[44]

Starbuck envisioned a growing respectability and use
of research in character, especially in terms of its
implications for education. Looking at its status

today, it is clear that his hopes were vindicated.

Consistent with his procedural approach in other fields, Starbuck urged the adoption of empirical methodology by the students of philosophy. Very early, after the turn of the century, he was expressing the hope that philosophy had passed through the "talkative Stage" in its development. In 1913, Starbuck says, of philosophy: "Now it is learning the joy, not simply of thinking, but of working out, its salvation."[45] As a faculty member of the philosophy department at both the universities of Iowa and Southern California, Starbuck's efforts were marked by a determination to utilize, as much as possible, many of the techniques of empiricism common to the more exact sciences. If philosophy was to enrich life; if it was to inform life of its meanings, then, thought Starbuck, philosophy's conceptual or logical framework must be supported by a scientific emphasis. The studies that took place under Starbuck's direction at Iowa and Southern California attested, in concrete form, to his convincement of the important place of empirical research in the studies of philosophy. Starbuck never wavered in this conviction; however, he came to know real disappointment in the fact that so little scientifically controlled research in philosophy was being performed in the country during his day.

Starbuck was the integrated man, however, which brings us to the second underlying theme, the relation of emotion and reason. His dream of a better world included more than a picture of scientific and intellectual expertise. While in no way would he degrade these important aspects of human existence and development, he recognized the significant worth of other qualities in life as well. Intellectual growth in the human animal, he insisted, does not take place apart from the vital role played by the feelings. One of Starbuck's fundamental pleas, as he approached it from so many different directions, was that we must not ignore the individual as a feeling-thinking human being.

He stressed the confluence of affection and

cognition, and its implications, particularly, for
education and religion. Starbuck felt that this
intersecting affective-cognitive relationship had lost
its sense of equilibrium. The creation of such imbal-
ance had been fostered, in Starbuck's opinion, by the
mistaken notion that the rational factors of man's
life are more important than the emotional factors.
Starbuck's contention, to the contrary, was that little thinking is based upon fact, rather it is more
directly related to our impressions and sentiments.
He believed that any notion that our lives are systematically fashioned by clear thought is primarily a
case of exaggerated conceit. Starbuck describes man
as essentially an "acting--reacting--feelingful" entity, whose ability for clear thinking had not been well
established. Consequently, in various ways, he sought
to revive the balance by reviewing the limitations of
cognition and the potentialities of affection. So
much of his work was motivated by a felt mission to
create that which would speak to the heart as well as
to the mind. Starbuck describes the fundamental nature of knowledge in these concise terms.

> "It has passed through the stage of
> extreme headishness during which it
> would trust to nothing for its gui-
> dance but its rare intellect. It is
> now learning to be more heartful and
> to trust its feelings along with its
> intellect.[46]

While in no way desiring to degrade the capacity and
responsibility of the intellectual processes, Starbuck firmly held that there is a process of gathering
truth immediately and directly, there is a "wisdom"
which emerges, that is not mediated by sets of ideas.
The "truth" that religion and the arts contain, for
instance, is not penetrated finally by the intellect;
rather there is a different source for understanding
and appreciating such values.

Frequently, Starbuck speaks of this source simply
as the "wisdom of the heart," but he does not leave
this crude phrase unexplained. In the first place,
Starbuck viewed the human psychophysical organism as

uniquely endowed with "native wisdom," that is, with
the ability to adapt according to its needs, within
and without. He believed that the mental life of man
was sensitive, beyond full measure, to its surroundings. In fact, he considered its sensitiveness so
incredible that he postulated an integration of knowledge from stimuli or impressions obviously impercep-
tible to the receiver. Starbuck notes:

> "The mind responds in a consistent
> way to stimuli that are entirely
> beneath our power of direction and
> gets out of them results that are
> useful to our behavior. Our minds
> take note of, actually, entirely
> imperceptible things and make use
> of them."[47]

Starbuck contended that the human organism was
so responsive to its environment, even to the slightest of stimuli, that it was impossible for the individual to be conscious always of the nature and extent
of influence. Nevertheless, psychology postulated
that all the responses were conditioning factors in
consciousness, and with this Starbuck agreed. In
fact, the point he sought to make clear, was that
these responses of the organism were not the result
of following intellectual cues; rather, he believed,
the intellectual processes were being greatly conditioned by the type of organic changes taking place.
Such a position profoundly shaped, in particular,
Starbuck's approach to the fields of religion and education.

At this point, a more thorough discussion of the
predominant components of Starbuck's approach to personality, namely, the autonomic nervous system, the
intimate senses and instinct or intuition, is in order.
It is appropriate to consider the sympathetic nervous
system and the intimate, or lower, senses together.
As has been previously mentioned, Starbuck contends
that the fundamental essence of personality is not so
much thought as it is appreciation and conduct. He
was convinced that the responses of an individual to
his experiences were affected more by the autonomic

200

nervous system and organic mechanisms than by the cortex, the supposed seat of intelligence. Although, the center of personality had been traditionally associated with the cortex, Starbuck linked the key to personality with another center. He expressed it anatomically:

> "The live centers of selfhood are in the basal ganglia beneath the cerebrum, which are the seat of the reflexes and other bodily functions, and not in the cerebrum which has been awarded too much the place of honor in life's economy by our books on psychology. Personality lurks in the thalamic and hypothalamic mechanisms beneath the base of the brain which are the high road of coordination between the central and the sympathetic nervous systems and between the skeletal and the visceral muscles."[48]

Emphasizing elsewhere the importance of these mechanisms, he stated:

> "It is the kinaesthetic, the organic, the other lower senses, and the hypersensitive somatic medianisms that direct both the white rat through the maze to the food box and us toward wisdom."[49]

Starbuck suggested that the designation, "higher senses," was quite inappropriate, if this was to imply that the so-called, lower senses, such as pain, temperature, equilibrium, the kinesthetic, and organic, perform a less distinguished role in shaping the responses of the organism. He pointed in various places to those studies which indicate that while conscious discrimination, in time, reaches the level of impossibility, the lower senses continue to inform the organism in ways that carry over into consciousness. The significance of these lower senses to the organism's perception, then, could not be praised too highly by

Starbuck. He declared: "In all matters of art-appreciation and in the interpretation of human relations and contacts with nature they are the higher."[50] Central to Starbuck's epistemology and theory of personality is his inclusion of instinct or intuitional psychology. His definitive work on intuitionalism is found in a 1915 article, by that title, in the Encyclopedia of Religion and Ethics. Here Starbuck defined intuition as that which "symbolizes the conception that one among the sources of knowledge is the direct and immediate apprehension of truth."[51] Being rejected was the idea that wisdom can result only from intellectual processes. Or as Starbuck phrased it elsewhere, and earlier, "the deep things of the heart are to be trusted as well as those that appeal to the intellect."[52]

Starbuck notes that the last half of the 19th century saw intuitionalism fall into general disrepute. The idea of the perpetuation of wisdom through the learning theory of "social heredity" had become rather widely accepted. Starbuck claimed, however, that since approximately the 1890's there had been a revival of a "modified" intuitionalism, based on the study of instinct and feelings. This newer intuitionalism, of which Starbuck was an exponent, rejected the view of the factors of consciousness as primarily determined by intelligence and reasonable judgment. Rather, a continuity is posited between the basal instinctive wisdom of the animal world and the intuitions, generally refined, of mankind. Starbuck refers to this kinship as follows:

> "If the lower and higher kinds,
> including the mind of man, belong
> to a single order, if nature makes
> no leaps, but each 'new' thing is
> but the variation upon and refine-
> ment of some old fact or function,
> then, there is no difference in
> kind between the 'native reactions'
> of simpler organisms and the con-
> scious behavior of men, between the
> instinctive adjustments of animals
> and the logical judgments of a
> scientist."[53]

He is proposing that the processes of intellectual judgment are not finally different in kind from those of instinct or intuition, and that much of the truth or values which man acquires is mined from the recesses of feeling and experiencing. The intellect serves as a tool, as a means of expressing the deep life of the instincts. This is plainly representative of his view towards the central place of feelings in human growth, and provides the philosophical foundation for his interests in developing an educational curriculum which would appeal, by way of the total experience, to the child's impulses as much as to his mind. It appears safe to suggest that Starbuck's concerns, at this point, were a precursor to some of the interests of "confluent education" today.

The integration of emotion and reason, with special emphasis on the place of emotion, is prevalent also in Starbuck's study of religion. Interestingly, though Starbuck is addicted to empirical habits in the process of his investigation, he discovers the preponderance of affection in the life of religion:

> "It must be clear that throughout
> it is a matter of the affective life.
> The end of religion always and every-
> where is to induce a heart and will
> response to the larger things of life
> that lead away towards unconditional
> reality and boundless fulfillment...
> Like music and poetry, although full
> of a sense of conviction and certainty,
> it is incapable of reduction in terms
> of ideation."[54]

To the extent that knowledge arises partially out of the refinement of the instinctual vestiges of the experiences of the human race, the study of religion becomes not so much a search for new truth as it is a quest for validation of the more meaningful religious insights of humanity.[55] And, in so far as the source of knowledge is not to be limited to the exact calculations of the intellect, Starbuck contends that although knowledge of religion cannot

be confined to the boundries of the intellect, nevertheless, the study of religion, and the reports contained therein, are credible. Speaking to this point,
Starbuck writes,

> "Although the kind of knowledge (or
> wisdom) that religion professes
> cannot be couched in the stilted
> terms of the intellect, it has never-
> theless an <u>objective</u> content. We
> have seen how consciousness interprets
> rightly, not only the dreamy un-
> noticed facts that surround it,
> but also those that are entirely
> imperceptible."56

According to Starbuck, the nature of this
reality, to which religion relates, is not to be
labelled; yet,its play upon individual consciousness
can be defined, to some degree. "Revelations" enter
man's domain by way of organic responses to the
multitude of influences bombarding the unconscious
which eventually penetrate to the level of thoughtful
consciousness. Such explanation of the process of
attainment of religious insight was undoubtedly
disturbing to many people, especially in Starbuck's
era. Perhaps, with this in mind, Starbuck sought
to allay potential suspicions that his approach
would eliminate the element of the divine. On the
contrary, Starbuck argued,

> "It only gives us a God that
> is adequate to compass the
> whole of life. It gives glimpses
> of a divine life that not only
> infuses this little span of the
> personal life but a reality
> that extends infinitely beyond
> it after which the personal
> life is feeling."57

Starbuck was sensitive to the schisms that
existed between science and religion. He recognized
that, realistically speaking, there probably never

would be a complete eradication of the breach that
exists between those for whom "merchandise of the
intellect" has greatest appeal and others who prefer
the "spriritual tastes." Nevertheless, such disunity
troubled him greatly for he believed that "all
phases of life have their legitimate function and
tend to make a whole man."[58]

The final underlying theme, to be discussed,
centers around the interrelationship, as conceived
by Starbuck, between religion and morality. Central
to his perspective is the general identification of
life with religion. This theme is carried out by
Starbuck in various places. Early in his career,
he wrote, "Religion is the response of the whole
of life to its fullest sense of reality."[59] Expanding the substance of this statement he later
penned:

>"To live divinely, serenely,
>joyously, with every moment of
>time revealing eternity, with
>every needful part of life shot
>through with a glow of rich
>meanings, with every right
>experience an inlet of the
>all-beautiful, with the life
>in tune with the World Heart,
>that is religion."[60]

Whatever else Starbuck may have been intending,
he sought to bring the religious experience out
of the clouds into the everyday affairs of responsible
human life. This "spiritual re-organization" aimed
at acknowledging the whole of life as sacred. He
rejected, as false, the traditional dichotomy
between sacredness and worldliness. God was the
god of Life, not an absentee observer in the Heavens.
As Starbuck put it so poignantly:

>"Now the veil of separation
>between man and God is being torn
>away, and man is given a clear
>vision of the divine beauty

205

reflected in all things, most
intimately indeed within himself. He is learning that
every bush is a burning bush,
every cliff a tablet of stone,
every place a sacred place, and
every noble institution a City
of God. Here is the whole crux
of the matter: God is not in
the sky more than he is here
and now; He is the Reality of all
phenomena, the Life of all that
is."61

Interestingly, such an interpretation of God in life,
as Starbuck expresses, would not experience disharmony with the later theological developments of
Bonhoeffer's "beyond in our midst" and Tillich's
"ground of our being."

In Starbuck's estimation the goals of religion
could not be reached apart from the work of education. He had noted early in the century, "Salvation
by education is coming to be the great watchward of
this generation."62 The evangelical fervor with
which he undertook the direction of work in religious
education and character education, for so long, indicated just how much he believed in contemporizing
and humanizing, by way of education, the processes of
salvation in human lives.

Starbuck held that religion's tasks and responsibilities were common to those of education. In fact,
he approached religious education as an integral part
of general education. Speaking of this relationship
he wrote:

"The feeling of the unity of
life must lead us to feel
the weakness of the distinction between secular and
religious education. The end
of all education must center
in the deepest and highest

206

         products of development--
         the spiritual life."[63]

The components of this "spiritual life," or moral
life, were, in Starbuck's view, the end of education,
as well as the essential characteristics of religion.
He defined them in terms of (1) the cultivation of
a higher self-realization, (2) the growing valuation
of others besides self, and (3) the integration of
self with the larger values and ideals of the world.[64]
Starbuck believed that almost every aspect of the program and curriculum of public education would be used
to contribute to the development of these three objectives.

     On the surface, one might consider that Star-
buck's interest shifted from religion, at the start
of his career, to character education, in later years.
This ignores, however, his fundamental approach to
these subjects. When Starbuck spoke of religion, he
was not necessarily referring to rituals and dogmas.
Rather he was speaking of a devotion to and meaningful participation in all of life. Any movement
directed toward the development of an appreciation of
one's own life and the larger world about him was, to
Starbuck, a form of character training. Consequently,
when viewed as such, he could refer, approvingly, to
the "cultural equivalent of religion" in the public
schools:

               "This great influence in the
               world will have to be interpreted
               not traditionally nor theologically
               but humanly and universally . . .
               Is it not simply the appreciative
               insight into, and active devotion
               which seems to have relatively
               permanent worth or value. Inter-
               preted in this way there may be
               a religion of Art or the Truth of
               Science, or the Beauty of Nature,
               or Love for Humanity or of Nature
               or any one of the hundred idealisms

                          207

that have stirred the hearts of
earnest and devout human beings
and called by a hundred names such
as Brahma, Allah, Yahweh, Beauty,
Truth, Justice, God, World Order,
Over-Soul, Spirit of the Universe,
or Lord of Life."[65]

Whether referring to religion or morality,
Starbuck meant, by these terms, basically the same
thing. This was true, also, of his conception of
religious education and character education. He
viewed them to be part of fundamentally the same
process. Although numerous examples could be cited,
by far, the best illustration of this point is to
be found in the comparison of two separate items he
wrote early in his career, first, a published article
of an address he delivered to the Religious Education
Association in 1905, titled "The Foundations of
Religion and Morality," and second, an essay he
produced in 1907, with the same title as the book in
which it was published, "Moral Training in the Public
Schools." A careful examination of these two works
reveals several passages from each as practically
identical. Starbuck was speaking of the nature of
religious education and moral training in almost
verbatim terms. There was, however, a definite, and
for our purposes, most significant change at specific
places in these passages. Where, in the first
article, Starbuck spoke of "religion," in the second
essay he actually substituted the term "morality;"
and where he was dealing with the development of
what he called a "religious institution," in the
first instance, he substituted the phrase "character-
building institution" in the latter reference.[66]
Clearly, the willingness to enact such an interchange
revealed his concept of their integration.

Our examination of Starbuck's publications has
disclosed the general chronological flow of his most
important thoughts and a systematic synthesis of
the fundamental subjects with which he dealt.
Although it is quite evident that the extent of his
written contributions was limited, what he did produce

208

was, for the most part, relevant to the needs and issues of his day. His style was direct, flowing, refreshing, and, in general, even his more technical work was popularized for the consumption of the layman as well as the professional. While seldom "the" pioneer of any single concept, he can be numbered among the few, in many instances, who dared to be led by his visions beyond the traditional directions in several important fields.

A Pioneering Classic

As has been noted, the work for which Starbuck is best known, is his first publication in book form, The Psychology of Religion. Starbuck's major interest, in this book, was the religious consciousness of individuals, and the general nature of its development. Without defining the constitution of religious consciousness, or interpreting the source or agent of religion, Starbuck endeavored to investigate thoroughly the verbalized "facts" of religious experience through a systematic analysis of returned questionnaires. He was convinced that religion could be studied scientifically, and that the psychology of religion, through empirical methods, could supply the data for a valid description of not only the characteristics of religious experience, but also, the factors conditioning religious growth.

Starbuck divides his work into three major parts. The first, and longest part, deals with the study of conversion itself. The sources for this study were principally autobiographies written in response to Starbuck's solicitation in the form of a standardized open-ended questionnaire.[67] One hundred ninety-two responses were examined carefully for inclusion in the statistical analysis. The respondents were predominantly Protestant, including more Methodists than other denominations. The second part looks at those lines of religious growth which do not involve conversion, as traditionally conceived. Again, the data for the research comes from autobiographical responses, this time two hundred thirty-seven cases. The respondents, as in the first part, were primarily

Protestant and a significant number attended college.
In the third part, Starbuck compared the nature of
religious growth with and without conversion. And
in addition to his general conclusions about religious
growth, Starbuck discussed their implications for education.

In Part I, as a result of his statistical analysis
of the data, Starbuck was able to make some interesting
observations about conversion. First, conversion was
a phenomenon natural to religious growth. Although the
data revealed that approximately eighty per cent of the
conversions could be connected directly to revivals and
church services, the other twenty per cent occurred
apart from any immediate external influence. Secondly,
the results showed that conversion was distinctively
an adolescent phenomenon, occurring almost exclusively
between the years ten and twenty-five. The average
age for conversion is 16.4 years, although the event
comes earlier for females who experience it most frequently at thirteen and sixteen. It occurs in males
most frequently at seventeen. Thirdly, while there is
a positive correlation between the time of conversion
and the period for the greatest bodily growth, there is
rather a supplemental relationship between conversion
and puberty, conversion coming more frequently just
prior to and after the height of the stage of puberty.

The motives and forces involved in conversion are
examined by Starbuck. The data reveals that, compared
to instinctive considerations, a small role in conversion is assumed by rational factors, although the intellect plays a more prominent role in the conversion
of males than females. Central to the pre-conversion
conditions is the "sense of sin." The process of conversion, consequently, involves more the struggle to
escape sin than straining for righteousness.

The basic types of conversion are pinpointed by
Starbuck. The first involves a sense of escaping from
sin, while the second type, more positive in nature,
is characterized by the struggle for a fuller, more
complete, life, which Starbuck labels "spiritual illumination." In either type the process involves surren-
dering of self, and a sense of forgiveness, as well as
the experience of a seeming spontaneous re-awakening.

210

This "new life" generally calls a person away from his own interests into a larger world of others. Starbuck discovers, in all of this, that conversion, or the new life, while not always explicable, and sometimes seemingly spontaneous, is the manifestation of "natural processes," and involves factors which, though conceivably new to consciousness, are nevertheless latent in the individual.

Starbuck concludes this section with an overview of conversion. Sociologically speaking, the converted individual passes from a state of inward perspective into a larger life of existence, in which he becomes not only aware of others, but sensitive to their needs as well. From a physiological point of view, conversion is conditioned by the psychic awakening taking place in the adolescent. Finally, from the psychological standpoint, in adolescence there are forces striking disunity in consciousness. This struggle between what one actually is, and what one sees as his potential, sets the stage for conversion.

In Part II Starbuck discusses religious growth as a gradual, developing process. In order to view the process with any sense of comprehension, Starbuck observes the characteristics of growth in childhood, adolescence and adulthood. He dealt very briefly with the religion of childhood. One of the most marked features was credulity, as well as unconscious observance. He discovered that a child's relationship with the supernatural involved intimacy rather than awe or fear. And finally, in the sense that children are especially receptive to their surroundings, religion was seen to be something external rather than of internal significance to the child.

Starbuck's handling of the adolescent period is much more extensive. Adolescence is the formative period, a time for great upheaval, but also a time for significant psychological, and intellectual awakening. The data reveals this to be a time for clarification, for new insights, for immediate understanding of right and wrong, accompanied by emotional response to this new awareness. There is a spontaneous awakening, which is religious, occuring. Such awakening, Starbuck ob-

serves, resembles a mild form of conversion. He discovers, in fact, that religious awakenings occur in
wavelets at twelve years, 15½ and nineteen, just prior
to the years when the number of conversions are most
frequently registered. Perhaps one of Starbuck's most
significant conclusions arises out of this information
whereby he suggests that the findings infer not that
conversion is a distinct experience, unique to itself,
but that the experience is paralleled by the normal
events of religious growth.

"Storm and stress," an adolescent phenomena coin-
ciding with this spontaneous awakening, is intensely
experienced by seventy per cent of the females and
fifty-two per cent of the males. This period begins
with females earlier than males, 13.6 years of age as
compared to 16.5 years, although the duration of the
period is less in females than males, about three years
for females as compared to five years for males. Five
distinct types of this phenomena are dilineated by
Starbuck: (1) the feeling of incompleteness or imper-
fection, sometimes emerging as a sense of sin, (2) general depression, (3) anxiety as a result of religious
doubts, (4) conflict with elements of the environment,
and (5) the struggle to control the feelings of passion.

The data also indicated that intense doubt was experienced in adolescence by fifty-three per cent of the
females and seventy-nine per cent of the males. This
phenomenon arises in the midst of great educational
and social influence. Doubt is assigned, generally, to
the latter part of adolescence by Starbuck, following
the period of storm and stress. In comparing males and
females, it is shown that men in adolescence experience
primarily doubt, while women experience primarily storm
and stress.

Alienation is another phenomenon of adolescence
which Starbuck discussed. Over one-third of the females and practically one-half of the males passed
through this period, the duration of which was most
frequently five to six years. Alienation is identified
commonly as a natural derivation of doubt, and the consequence of the storm and stress period. For this

212

reason it usually occurs in the latter part of adolescence. It is important, according to Starbuck that the adolescent face his struggles, in so far as possible, independently, that emancipation be won by, rather than given to, the child.

From the vantage point of this wider research in adolescence, Starbuck was able to designate its central characteristic, the "birth of a larger self." Behind the variety of adolescent phenomena was an awakening to new insights and appreciations, the emergence of a new selfhood. The new self, the "I" can reflect upon its growth beyond the limited perspective of the self of childhood, the "i," as Starbuck calls it. He observes, an important point which he does not thoroughly test, that the variance in the experiences of adolescence is conditioned largely by not only the environmental influences, but also by tempermental factors.

Prior to our consideration of Starbuck's analysis of the adult life, it would be appropriate to discuss briefly his mention of those for whom growth is so even that definite transitions cannot be distinguished. Starbuck interprets this unusually gradual growth as an ideal, rather than a normal situation. He lists the following conditions which appear conducive to such growth: (1) religious surroundings during childhood, which interpret religion in terms of life, (2) no introduction of religious dogma beyond the child's capacity for assimilation, (3) anticipating and attempting to meet the needs of the child as they naturally arise, and (4) the right amalgamation of faith and doubt. All of these points had direct implications for religious education.

The adult life is marked as a time for reconstruction, which occurs most generally, according to Starbuck's research, between the ages of twenty and thirty. He discovered that the tendency for reconstruction to follow the uncertain struggles of adolescence was practically universal. This process of reconstruction involved either the independent development of a new position acceptable to the individual, or the return to former beliefs, revised to some extent. Actually, the

process often involved the blending in various forms
of the two. In terms of belief, the marked tendency
is to sense more appreciatively religion from within.
The religious feelings of adulthood focus upon an appreciation of one's own life as spiritual, that is,
one with God, an awareness of a larger world or life
beyond self, and a new appreciation of the continuity
between one's own life and the larger life of the
world. The tendency, then, is to move from childhood
egocentrism to the mature life of societal-centered-
ness.

Part III deals with a comparison of the lines of
growth involving conversion and those not associated
with this experience. The data shows that there are
more difficulties which accompany conversion, however,
the possibilities for complete alienation are much
less among the conversion-group. Also in the conversion-group the period of storm and stress is more intense, while doubts are less frequent. The approach
to religion is more subjective and emotional in the
conversion-group, resulting in a depreciation of the
intellectual comprehension of religion.

From the fifty-one cases which professed the
experience of sanctification, Starbuck developed a
definition. He described sanctification as that point
where the individual identifies himself finally with
the life of the spirit, a step which at the time of
conversion only was judged as a possibility. Although
it is similar in form to conversion, sanctification
succeeds original conversion in time and consequently
is more the culmination of the appreciation of conversion to the spiritual life.

The education inferences bring Starbuck's book
to a close. He believes that his study reveals that
religious education must take seriously the needs and
situations of every child. Religious education must
know well the nature of the successive stages of
growth from childhood to maturity, thus coming to the
point of being able to intelligently decide upon those
ideals which would best fit those particular stages
of growth.

Perhaps the most significant defects of Starbuck's book have to do with his methodolgy. It is plainly evident that Starbuck's use of the questionnaire, though a major step toward a more consistent and coherent understanding of religious experience, left a great deal to be desired in terms of scientific exactness. The method is limited, first of all, by virtue of the fact that it depends entirely upon introspection for its data. Regardless of the competence of the developer of the questionnaire and the credulity of the respondent, the medium cannot yield entirely quantifiably objective data. There is no way the researcher can be assured that all the respondents have understood the questions in precisely the same way or mean the same thing in terms of their answer. And, secondly, the significance of Starbuck's data is weakened by the narrow range of his respondents background, largely American Methodists. Finally, his questionnaire consisted mainly of loose, open-ended questions, to which most personal and interesting responses could be made, but which sacrifices in degree the capacity for exact and discriminating quantitative analysis. To be fair, however, it must be acknowledged that Starbuck was quite aware of the shortcomings of this approach, but saw it as a useful tool in examining the religious consciousness at least more scientifically than had heretofore been done. As a pioneering work, in fact, Starbuck's study was a valuable contribution to the general movement of the psychology of religion.

Starbuck stirred the interest, and paved the way for others in the field to enter this kind of study. It has already been established that William James would probably not have written his Varieties of Religious Experience without Starbuck's initial study. George A. Coe's book, The Spiritual Life, published in 1900, follows similar lines to those of Starbuck's work. And undoubtedly, Starbuck's work set the stage for other works such as James B. Pratt's The Psychology of Religious Belief in 1907 and James H. Leuba's A Psychological Study of Religion in 1912. Starbuck had established by his study the importance of, from the standpoint of psychology, the investigation of religion as an individual experience. So many of the pioneering works which followed bore the mark of that contribution. Virtually every major work in the psychology of religion in the early decades of the century, in fact, quoted Starbuck's work or at least referred to his study.

In spite of the defects of the methodology this work offers an impressive mass of useful data regarding religious experience which has been fairly treated by Starbuck. It proved to be valuable for theoretical and practical purposes. Certainly, Starbuck's classification of the types of conversion, the volitional, the self-surrender, and the spontaneous awakening, stands as a classical codification. It is evident, too, that subsequent studies reveal little deviation from Starbuck's findings.

Projects

Starbuck was irrevocably committed to the notion that there is no real progress in the world except through education. More specifically, he was convinced that the potential for the development of the human race was directly linked to the education of children. In short, his aims for education were emphatically child-centered. This ran counter to an adult-centered emphasis, with major efforts in education being pointed to the more mature minds, but Starbuck insisted that hope for a better world lay primarily with childhood. Almost chidingly, Starbuck spoke of a method of human progress which he unhappily contended had not been seriously tried, a method of child-centeredness. He wrote:

> "Were there a conscious, intelligent, persistent program of eliciting friendly responses in children from the earliest days filling their minds with examples of cultivated and considerate behavior, enticing them into situations in which they taste the sweetness of kindliness, and the satisfaction of good sportsmanship, stirring their blood with examples of fine achievement, the game could be won."[68]

Clearly, Starbuck's efforts through the years in character education were attempts at implementing into the educational system the practical ends of this faith.

On numerous occasions Starbuck spoke of character education as the one great aim of education. Clearly, however, the educational world, during Starbuck's day, was not united in its approach to methods and principles of character education. It had, in fact, a general tradition of moralism and repression, completely contrary to Starbuck's view of character training. The nature of that difference is plainly revealed in the following statement, representative of Starbuck's position throughout his career.

> "At its best, character education is the refined sublimation of harshness translated into moral solicitude and the desire of parents and teachers that the children shall share their idealisms. At its worst, it is legal codes, verbalized virtues, self-righteous 'goodness,' and its attitudes are fraught with heaviness . . . Its methods are those of argumentation, rationalization, preachments, didacticism and moral surgery."[69]

The key issue in Starbuck's consideration of character education is one of methodology. It centers about the question as to whether the direct or indirect approach is the most desirable way to cultivate character development. From the very beginning of his involvement in this field, Starbuck, very much in the minority, advocates the indirect, or natural method; and this position does not change throughout his career. Repeatedly, he challenges participants in public and religious education, who are concerned about the moral development of their children, to abandon the didactic method of administering morals or inculcating "virtues." He was convinced that it was generally useless to attempt thoughtfully to persuade a child

217

into righteousness. One does not argue another into goodness. As Starbuck put it, "Goodness is contagious."[70] The real work of character education, that is, change in children's attitudes and behavior, is accomplished, according to Starbuck, by the example of the personalities they confront. He wrote:

> "It does not make so much difference that wise notions are expressed to these sensitive creatures; it makes all the difference the attitudes of mind and heart that suffuse the ideas. Indeed, talk about concepts and ideals of behavior may be entirely absent. The real work of influencing personality goes on just the same."[71]

Attempts to establish in children's minds "right" thinking about behavior, Starbuck believed, were doomed to failure. The key to character education was to be found in conduct. What a child experienced, then, was fundamental to the process of training character; and Starbuck, urged, whenever possible, that educational systems do their best to provide students with practice in confronting life situations.

Starbuck was incited with the vision of a better world. He was convinced that practical steps towards that dream could be implemented. Two of those steps, in particular, are noteworthy of our attention, his development of a model for methods in character education contained in the Iowa Plan, and as an outgrowth, his creation of an Institute for character research. These projects together formed the basis for the major efforts of his career from the 1920's on.

The Iowa Plan

The underlying principles of this project are stated in Chapter I of the study. A shortened version of this list includes: (1) having a goal; (2) measuring the progress being made and the final product; (3) viewing the end of education as personal,

218

social, and practical; (4) laying the foundations of character through conduct, both, in terms of the child's own practice of it, and in terms of making readily available to the child the imagery and symbols of good conduct; (5) quickening conduct naturally through the child's own sympathies; (6) developing the ethical consciousness in steps; (7) transforming "duty into beauty;" (8) acquainting the child with the values of his heritage; (9) engendering loyalty to a reachable cause; and (10) promoting an attitude of reverence for life.[72]   Such were the articles of the educational creed affirmed by Starbuck and his collaborators.

Related in general to these principles was a fundamental concept Starbuck developed in this chapter which he called the "Three-Fold Re-Centering" (see Figure 1). His picture of the child at birth is of basically an unorganized self full of potentiality. The two major factors determining the nature of his development toward mature selfhood are: (1) the natural evolution of his instinctive tendencies, and (2) broadly speaking, his educational experience, including the more direct approach of teachers and parents towards handling the instincts appropriately, and the more indirect approach of creating a certain environment. Since the dominant tendency of childhood is towards self-regard, the efforts of education, according to Starbuck, should be centered around the socialization of the child, encouraging him to participate in the life of others, and attempting to foster his interests in ideals. This process of "othering" Starbuck regards as the true aim of character education. The re-centering, if affected, is threefold as follows: (1) There is a transformation from a "lower," ingrown self with base instincts and desires into a "higher" self with refined tastes, insightful perspective, and worthy purpose. (2) There is a growing understanding and appreciation of the interests and ideals of others, as well as a concern for their welfare. (3) A respect for the values in a larger world of "Nature and Life" develops finally into the attitude of reverence.[73]

In the second chapter we are introduced to the

Figure 1. The Threefold Re-centering

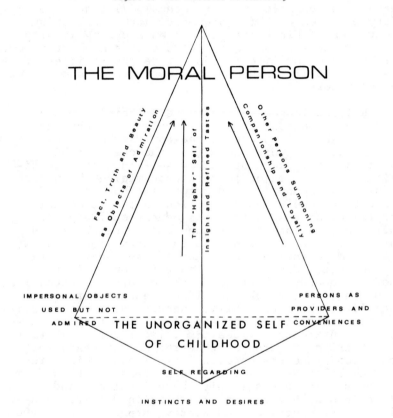

THE MORAL PERSON

Fact, Truth and Beauty as Objects of Admiration

The "Higher" Self of Insight and Refined Tastes

Other Persons Summoning Companionship and Loyalty

IMPERSONAL OBJECTS USED BUT NOT ADMIRED

PERSONS AS PROVIDERS AND CONVENIENCES

THE UNORGANIZED SELF OF CHILDHOOD

SELF REGARDING

INSTINCTS AND DESIRES

Source: <u>Character Education Methods</u>, Figure II, p. 4.

ideal characteristics of the type of person Starbuck conceives the school ought to be developing. Stated succinctly, his view is of the following product:

> "A person with powers proportionally developed, with mental discrimination, aesthetic appreciation, and moral determination; one aware of his social relationships and happily active in the discharge of all obligations; one capable of leisure, loving nature, revering human beings, their aspirations and achievements; one observant of fact, respectful of law and order, devoted to truth and justice; one who while loyal to the best traditions of his people, dreams and works towards better things; and one in whom is the allure of the ideal, and whose life will not be faithless thereto."[74]

Clearly, this is the aim; it certainly was not what Starbuck thought would be quickly and easily achieved.

One of the fundamental methodological procedures is discussed in Chapter III. It has to do with the organization of the school along the lines of democratic structure. Starbuck felt that organization of the school affected greatly the efforts in character education. Traditionally education had been authoritarian and repressive. For over a century, western school systems had borrowed notions of organization from Prussia where imperialistic methods had been dominant. Starbuck's call for the structuring of schools as democratic communities was a call for "freedom" and "initiative."

Starbuck's model did not eradicate every form of authority and leadership; but it did emphasize the central need for respect of pupil individuality and initiative. In fact, he believed that student participation should be encouraged in every way possible. Character is formed most naturally by parti-

221

cipation in the actual structures of the school community. Starbuck felt that the student who feels
accountable for his own school community likely will
begin to consider as more important the functions of
that community, and participate in its work with
pride. This evolvement sets the stage for ideal character training.[75]

A discussion of school governance and discipline
is included in this chapter also. While Starbuck and
his associates favored a set of well-defined regulations for behavior, they were convinced that moral
maturity was most readily achieved through expression
rather than repression. Pent up emotions usually resulted in misconduct, they believed. Regarding the
regulations, it was felt that conduct could be best
controlled by the will of the body. The teacher's
best disciplinary instrument was the power of suggestion, which included the more subtle influence of
well-placed images of art, literature, music, and
biography.[76]

In Chapter IV three methods are suggested which
are directed at the development of the child's integrity. (1) The "Noble Deeds" method has the teacher
select an especially inspiring quotation from literature, which is then discussed by the pupils, and illustrated in their own way in a notebook. (2) The
"Socialized Recitation" method capitalizes on the
cooperative group process. Here the pupils work as
a committee on some problem which duplicates to some
extent a real-life situation. (3) The "Project-
Problem" method involves dealing with a practical
problem in its natural setting, with the utilization
of authentic aids in the process of solution.[77]

The methodological approach of Chapter V is also
fundamental. Materials and methods of character education are not to be administered with disregard for
the child's development. Rather they are to be fitted
to the interests and needs of the child in line with
the particular stage or period of his growth through
which he is passing. Illustrative of the point, four
periods are briefly discussed: (1) The kindergarten
period, three years to six years, is characterized by

the impulses of drama, play, and imitation. This
period is considered ripe for quickening the feelings
of "trust, confidence, kindliness, and cooperation."
(2) The primary and intermediate periods, when considered inclusively, include the years six to eleven.
Three mental functions are developing very little:
imagination, the power to reason abstractly, and
moral responsibility. However, two things are coming
into full activity: thinking in terms of objects,
and memory for detail. (3) If the years nine to
eleven are viewed separately, the social impulse becomes evident, and the interest in hero-worship
emerges. (4) The high school period, including the
ages twelve through eighteen, is marked by the youth's
rapidly growing ability to think logically. Not only
is there an awakening of social impulses; there is
evidence of a whole new evolving selfhood.[78] It is
held that such factors at each level of growth must be
understood, appreciated, and incorporated into the
programming of character education of any sort.

Starbuck diagrammed this approach in the same
chapter (see Figure 2). It is designed to show the
fluctuation, according to grades and ages, of the predominant interests and appeals within the "stream of
consciousness" of childhood and youth, and attempts
to match these factors with corresponding orientations
towards ethical development. The most active enthusiasms are generally recorded by a word or phrase under
the grades or ages, while some which span a number of
years or grades are represented by the curved lines.

Chapter VI proposes a type of moral curriculum
for the schools, a classified bibliography of material,
which is to assume no more than a supplemental role to
the general curriculum (see Figure 3). It is believed
that all school subjects are conducive to moral considerations and can be aided in their objectives by the
proposed moral program. Propagation of moral "virtue"
would not be the aim of the supplemental moral curriculum; rather it would suggest projects, problems, and
situations appropriately matched to the child's age
level, and related to the characteristics of that
period, which would hopefully widen the child's awareness and appreciation of moral meaning and value in his
own real world.[79]

223

Figure 2. Showing the Nascencies of Development and the Centres of Ethical Emphasis.

Centres of Ethical Emphasis

- Furnishing the mind with imagery
- Free expression in the group
- Living together Confidence in Nature
- Mastery of tools of expression and of appreciation
- Knowledge of other times and peoples
- Mastery of the meaningful facts and events
- The clean, strong life, Chivalry
- Heroes of war, peace, science and invention
- "Noble deeds" Great movements of thought and history
- The building of a great nation
- Self-discipline through mastery of the tools of knowledge
- Discipline, Insight Discovery
- Moral thoughtfulness Specific lines of preparation for active life interests
- A man and a citizen

QUESTIONING AGE — FREE PLAY OF FANCY SYMBOLISM — MANIPULATION WITH OBJECTS — CONSTRUCTIVENESS WITH OBJECTS — HERO-WORSHIP — BLIND STRIVING SELF-ASSERTIVENESS — SELF-REALIZATION

THINKING IN TERMS OF OBJECTS — THINKING IN TERMS OF IDEAS

Age	3	4	5	6	7	8	9	10	11	12	13	14	15	16	17	18
Grade			Kg 1	Kg 2	I	II	III	IV	V	VI	VII	VIII	IX	X	XI	XII

Waves in the Stream of Consciousness or Nascencies in Development

PLAY OF FANCY — THINKING IN TERMS OF OBJECTS — THINKING IN TERMS OF IDEAS

- Objects in fanciful relations — Manipulation of objects — Constructiveness with objects
- Spontaneous play impulse — Individualization — Gang Spirit — Socialization — Apprenticeship in citizenship
- Dramatic impulse — Interest in detail — Hero-worship — Moral thoughtfulness
- Finer sentiments — Suggestibility — Passion to count as a person — Self-realization — Self-discovery
- Individualization — Self-centred — Adventure — Restless striving — Mental poise and stability
- Nature admirations — Unmoral — Competitive socialization — Pubescence — Organization of a new self-hood
- Symbolism — "Moral interregnum"

Subject Matter and Method

- Story telling / Dramatization
- Cutting
- Modeling — Memorizing — Heroes — Rationalized conduct — Moral thoughtfulness
- Projects — Projects — "Case methods" — Elementary Ethics
- Plays and games — "Cubs" — "Noble deeds" — Adventure — Vocation and group Ethics
- Make-believe—fairies and fables — Myth and legend — Scouting — Socialization — Idealization
- Free expression — Cooperative play and work — Stories of great men — Fiction — Call to life and action

Source: Character Education Methods, Chart I, between pp. 24 and 25.

Figure 3. Suggestions of Projects and Problems to Enrich A Character Training Curriculum

This outline presupposes that all subjects be taught in the light of their contribution to life

OBJECTIVES	KINDERGARTEN	GRADE ONE	GRADE TWO	GRADE THREE	GRADE FOUR	GRADE FIVE	GRADE SIX	GRADE SEVEN	GRADE EIGHT	GRADE NINE	GRADE TEN	GRADE ELEVEN	GRADE TWELVE
HEALTH	Making a bit of Fairyland Health Fairies Health chores Dramatize the day's health program	Games requiring group movements Making plans and specifications for something to be built by Grade VI	Prepare and act a scene which teaches neatness A Health Fairy Pageant	Clean-up clubs Plan isolation of case of infectious disease at home Pageant emphasizing proper eating and sleeping Sunshine club to promote happiness in own group	Garden Club Plan a surprise party for Grade V Report to Board of Health breeding places of flies and mosquitos	Campaign for extermination of flies Committees plan a week-end camp Make iceless refrigerator for care of milk	Form a mosquito brigade Blaze a trail to ______ without injuring trees Protection of body against disease germs (an exhibit or a play)	Mathematics of the sporting page Construct a miniature stage and act out a scene with paper figures Sculpture project	Write a school creed Hold a tournament Training table menus Manage measuring and weighing of school children Study physical excellence of Greeks	Entertainment of visiting team Compare Ideal plan for a day / Actual use of time in day Committee report on "Self Culture Through the Vacation." Griggs	Heroes of science Pasteur, and others Athletics Committee report on some martyrs and heroes of science	Athletics "Self Reliance" Emerson, Carlyle and others Overcoming obstacles - a group of examples Roosevelt etc.	Athletics "What Men Live By" Cabot. Work, play love, worship Use of Leisure Scott and other classics on same theme
LIFE IN THE GROUP	Games for getting acquainted Doll party acting out courtesies of a group	Winter feeding of birds Courtesy games showing customs in other lands Acting home and street scenes to show courtesy Proper distribution of pkg of varied kinds of confections	Making a bird restaurant and supporting it collectively Acting story to entertain other grades Two groups act out settlement of a quarrel Present story in scenes, tableaus	Playing teacher in settling a quarrel Plan a Thanksgiving dinner for newsboys	Class is a party of explorers e.g. De Soto's Organize to accomplish their purpose and to live together Class land as a colony - group solution of problems	Living with Indians as neighbors Solve their problem - avoid their mistake Form and Indian tribe and land an English colony and live together	Scouts or "Cubs" Building something for Grade I in accord with their specifications Journey Geography Christmas in other lands	Scout and Campfire Organize a Round Table for seeking "quests" Adopting a family for Christmas or Thanksgiving	Scout and campfire Plan and carry out a lesson for drill and review which will interest and help the class Publish a school paper	Scout and Campfire Act out the courtesies of a Roman and a Hebrew home	Rewrite several of Aesop's fables to fit present social conditions Forms of salutation in all countries	Dramatize "The Melting Pot" Junior-Senior banquet as model of social forms "The Cultivated Man" Eliot Class study Friendship, Emerson, Tennyson and others	Impersonate classes in American life When duties clash what? "Loyalty to Loyalty" Royce
CIVIC RELATIONS	Stories of Washington's and Lincoln's boyhood Songs and stories of American patriots	Rules for our new game Make badges to wear Feb 12 and 22	Child patriots of France Design decorations for the table for party Feb. 22	Make model of a plantation home	Make booklet of history of first settlers in your community Origin of the flag How do firemen save time	Form two Indian councils Unite into a federation for protection	"A Message to Garcia" Washington's journey to the Ohio Construct a class flag When Lincoln's humor saved the day	Establish a post-office Draw up an oath of allegiance Draw plans and make relief map of Valley Forge	Work out the story of the builders of your community or city Construct a government on a desert island, make laws, build a constitution, create courts, and establish social customs and rules of conduct	Select a delegate or officer by the election methods of 1789 Project a plan of student government	Dramatize "The Man Without a Country" Make a bibliography and card catalogue of the civics library Dramatize a session of Lincoln's cabinet	The vow of citizenship Catalogue the organizations in your neighborhood. "Americanization" Russell and Wade "The Soul of Democracy" Griggs Distinguish between a democracy and a republic	Draft a constitution for the family of nations "American Ideals yet to be Attained" Cabot
ECONOMIC RELATIONS AND VOCATION	Kindergarten store for learning value of coins Bird houses	Starting a group account Collection of seeds from the harvest Make an Indian Corn Husk doll Cooperative purchase of bird houses from Grade VII	Make candle to study by Starting a savings account Plan entertainment to raise money for group account Cooperative building of bird houses	How many people help bring the bread to the table Organized barter	Plan and earn money for dinner for adopted family A day properly divided for work and play	A stamp collection Estimate profits on home garden	Establish a school bank Plan a picnic or camp dinner to come within set price Insect enemies of trees, a collection	A school expenditure card to determine waste in school materials Compute waste in your district from weathering of machinery Estimate in detail the cost of some product - labor's share - capital's share	Plan and carry out a "cooperative store" for the school Conservation of trees Shop visitation Organize an employer's council and labor union and settle dispute Construct a scheme of tax for revenue	Who makes our currency? How many miles of turnpike will one dreadnaught build Individual invention (a) camp utensil (b) auto or agricultural appliance	Credit buying - how much interest does the debtor pay Get a merchant to help class estimate "overhead" in a store. Specific studies on value of system in business. The value of truth in advertising. The money value of courtesy	Visit and study bank Vocational self measurement - use a standard scale Forming vocation clubs. See Davis	Self Measurement See Hyde A display of vocations - See Muensterberg Visiting vocations and classifying them Partial apprenticeship in vocation as part of school work
FAMILY AND PARENTHOOD	Make a doll house Doll's tea party etc. Dramatize house, mother and helpful children	Mothering an orphan animal Observation trip to locate insect homes	Build an Eskimo house Booklet of animal families compiled by class Locate and observe animal houses	Estimate the work of a pair of birds in one day's feeding of young Make a winter home for pets How to set a table	Collect pictures of homes and children in other lands Estimate mother's work in home Book of bird families	Construct a model kitchen Flowers, winds, and bees, working together in fertilization	Observations on heredity in stock and poultry breeding Design a hall clock A study of Madonnas Indian Homes	Trace the evolution of homes, and make models of enough examples to form a series Dramatize King Arthur stories	Design from plastic materials a home and environment Service to humanity from plant breeding Burbank	Controlled experiment in cross fertilization Committee report on "The Meaning of Infancy" Fiske	"Improvement of the Human Plant" Burbank "Carrying on" the present race problem	"Mutation" de Vries "The Blood of the Nation" Jordan Committee report on race improvement "Call of the Twentieth Century" Jordan	Make several family budgets Collect descriptions of home life of great Americans "Genetics" Walter
APPRECIATION OF BEAUTY	Finding Nature's favorite colors and combinations of color Feeding birds Arranging flowers in a vase	Nature's color work a. Autumn - color combination - observation and collection of corresponding colors for permanent exhibit	Find the age of a tree Collection of seeds for spring planting Chart locating most beautiful shade trees in community	Find conditions of strength and weakness in plants Planting for the future, "Apple Tree John" Leaf forms and colors (a collection)	Carefully recorded observations of the building of one bird's nest Find a winter scene - rearrange scene to put in a road Make a model of a church interior	Make collections of shells and stones Herbarium Change a summer scene into a winter scene	Living for a week "in training" Collect pictures of Greek Heroes in sculpture	Create beautiful designs A pageant of Knighthood Collection of pictures of knights	A Golden Deeds Book emphasis upon service, invention etc. Make a plan for a park	Pick out and draw three best pieces of architecture in the neighborhood Devise, finance and carry out a plan for the yearly purchase of a work of art How to treat an enemy - collect examples	Origin and meaning of forms of civility Compare music, poetry and architecture A study of "The Art of Truth Speaking" Biographies of Great Americans	The "Oversoul" Emerson - collect similar sentiments. Write a companion piece to a winter poem Collect pieces of music and painting with theme of "Oversoul" Make a model or design observing laws of structure	"Through Nature to God" Fiske Devise plan for the art improvement of your schoolhouse Dramatize "The Christmas Carol
MASTERY OF TRADITION	Dramatization of Christmas stories etc.	Representation of Santa Claus and his home Flag ceremonies	Indian projects Make an Indian canoe etc Make furniture like that in Lincoln's home Book of Xmas songs	Devise a game to be played with choice sayings of Lincoln Collect stories about protecting the colors Plan and give a Xmas program for Grade I	Dramatize incidents in lives of Washington and Lincoln Pioneer life projects Make model of cabin showing the first Thanksgiving in face of hardships	Collect stories from Grand Army men Pilgrim pageants	Give an exhibition of Spartan gymnastic training Indian woodcraft	Living pictures of knights, Raleigh etc A book of Indian traditions of your state Journey geography	History of Christmas customs Pantomime of heroes of the Civil War Models and pictures of prairies schooners, stage coaches etc. Ranching and homesteading		Projects related to the tradition contained in various subjects	"The Soul of America" Stanton Coit	

Source: Character Education Methods, Chart III, between pp. 30 and 31.

In the remaining chapters the considerations can be summarized as follows: (1) There is limited discussion of the relationship and long range effect of school studies and experiences on civic responsibility and family life. (2) A brief study in character rating is made, with the notion that character valuation is even more important than the rating of intelligence. (3) The teacher's responsibility for moral training is discussed, as well as the nature of her preparation for this task. A teacher's personality and skills are acknowledged as central to any effort toward character education. (4) The place of cooperating agencies, in terms of character education, is considered. Agencies discussed are the home, a parent-teacher organization, the church, church school, and the community, as well as several less formal ones.[80]

Of these final considerations, all of which are dealt with summarily, the second, investigating the measurement or rating of character, is the most interesting and innovative. Although it is admitted that the norms had not been adequately established for such tests, their usefulness is still affirmed, and prediction of their improvement in reliability and validity is made.

The first of the character-rating scales presented, and the one upon which the most effort had been expended, was developed for high school students (see Figure 4). Thirty qualities, deemed essential to character development were rated. Eight gradations are described for each quality, with four on the right denoting desirable features progressively weighted from the center out, and with four gradations on the left signifying undesirable characteristics. Particularly noteworthy is the attempt to establish a more discriminative basis for judgment by allowing ten points to be distributed among the eight gradations for each quality. As it is likely that several gradations rather than one best portrays an individual's character, the use of points weighted appropriately to the nature of the gradation produced a more accurate picture, in terms of general strengths and weaknesses, and, thus, provided more useful information.

Figure 4. Self-Measurement Scale

−4	−3	−2	−1		1	2	3	4
Sickly ailing all the time ( )	Complaining most of the time ( )	Often incapacitated by illness ( )	Some slight physical weakness ( )	**GENERAL HEALTH**	Fairly free from bodily or organic weakness ( )	Good, need give little or no thought to health ( )	Strong, robust, never sick ( )	Joy in abounding health ( )
Helplessly inefficient, impassive ( )	Sluggish, languid, sleepy ( )	Listless, uninterested, halfhearted ( )	Drags, along through daily tasks ( )	**PHYSICAL VITALITY**	Does work in matter-of-fact way ( )	Interested, awake to opportunities ( )	Alert, enthusiastic ( )	Exuberant overflowing vitality "Full of pep" ( )
Slovenly, uncouth, utterly indifferent ( )	Slouchy, careless ( )	Ungainly cumbersome ( )	Listless, or affected, unnatural ( )	**BODILY CARRIAGE**	Fairly natural in bodily actions ( )	Pleasing bearing and tasteful in manners ( )	Graceful and easy ( )	At perfect ease and graceful under all circumstances ( )
A regular blunderer ( )	Unsteady, irregular, cannot depend on ( )	Awkward, often makes blunders ( )	Occasionally clumsy and bungling ( )	**MUSCULAR CONTROL**	Has normal use of muscles ( )	Has steady and regular bodily movements ( )	Able to control and direct accurately ( )	Specially gifted in muscular activity ( )
Lazy, resents work ( )	Shuns work and complains when asked to do anything ( )	Given to loafing ( )	Inclined to waste time ( )	**WORK**	Usually busy at some task ( )	Faithful in doing work ( )	Welcomes opportunity to work, resourceful in finding tasks ( )	Accomplishes most possible, makes most of opportunities ( )
Helpless in presence of difficulties ( )	"Loses head" in a pinch, easily confused ( )	Hard to see way around difficulties ( )	Impractical ( )	**FACILITY**	Meets difficulties half way ( )	Unravels difficulties with ease ( )	Has remedy for every trouble ( )	Always master of the situation ( )
A slave to appetite, gluttonous ( )	Often eats and drinks immoderately ( )	Hard to control desire for ( )	Craving appetite for ( )	**FOOD AND DRINK**	Able to curb appetite for that which is harmful ( )	Has a natural and healthy desire for ( )	Chooses that which is nutritious and beneficial ( )	Enjoyed and used properly ( )
Uncontrolled, sensuous ( )	Perverted use of ( )	Misdirected desires, acts, and thoughts, etc. ( )	Undue strength of ( )	**MATING INSTINCTS AND DESIRES**	Able to withstand undue impulses of ( )	Able to control ( )	Healthy minded attitude toward ( )	Able to direct towards "ideal love," home making, children, etc. ( )
Pessimistic, always sees and magnifies difficulties ( )	Grouchy, hard to please ( )	Has "the blues" often ( )	Gloomy, inclined to see worst things ( )	**DISPOSITION**	Inclined to look on bright side ( )	Cheerful, glad to be alive ( )	Good natured, easy to get along with, controls temper ( )	Optimistic, never willing to give up ( )
Easily satisfied, anything will do ( )	Slipshod and careless of how work is done ( )	Inclined to "let well enough alone" ( )	Indifferent as to quality of work done ( )	**THOROUGHNESS**	Usually careful in performance of work ( )	Methodical and orderly in work ( )	Takes special pride in doing good work ( )	Never content until work is correct ( )
"Muddlehead," wholly dependent on thought and others ( )	Works without definite plan or end in view ( )	Slow to make use of knowledge gained ( )	Slow to "catch on" ( )	**MENTAL ACTIVITY, APPREHENSION, ACUMEN**	Fairly quick in work and understanding ( )	Quick to "see the point" and make most of it ( )	Able to think through subject creatively ( )	Has real insight into ( )
Biased, warped, impractical, distorted ( )	Unreliable in choice and estimates ( )	Inclined to "jump at conclusions" ( )	Often make errors in ( )	**JUDGMENT**	Usually able to see things in right relations ( )	Able to make fitting and appropriate choices ( )	Steady and reliable ( )	Accurate, depend able, sound ( )
Forgetful, unreliable, mind a "leaky sieve" ( )	Hard to retain even essential facts ( )	Facts slip from mind easily ( )	Inclined to be forgetful ( )	**MEMORY**	Able to keep in mind reasonably well ( )	Memorizes fairly well ( )	Fixes essential facts easily ( )	Accurate, depend able, recall facts and events indefinitely ( )
Unable to originate or invent anything--even a thought ( )	Dull, never makes plans to or used to any advantage ( )	Ineffective, never stated in planned terms ( )	Hard to "see anything" not stated in plain-set terms ( )	**IMAGINATION**	Easy to supply detail from facts at hand ( )	Active and useful, formulates plans in life ( )	Productive of Poetic, inventive projects ( )	Poetic, inventive, original, creative ( )
"Pigheaded," arbitrary, "imperious", Kaiseristic ( )	Resentful toward those who disagree ( )	Will not listen to views of others ( )	Tries to impose views on others ( )	**TOLERANCE**	Not insistent on own ways and ideas ( )	Can see and appreciate good points in others ( )	Willing to adopt views of others if better ( )	Open minded, inclined to take best view from any source ( )
An egoist, no one else quite so good ( )	Inclined to be assertive, no room for improvement ( )	Conceited, overestimates own powers and influence ( )	Has "too good an opinion" of self ( )	**SELF-ESTIMATION**	Realizes own powers and shortcomings ( )	Recognizes possibilities of growth and development ( )	Considers self as created for higher and best things ( )	Realizes highest for self, better self predominates ( )
A mental "shut in", gets it blindly ( )	Has a small circumscribed horizon ( )	Takes narrow view of life and of events ( )	Cannot see relationships easily ( )	**VISION, GRASP**	Able to see connection in things and events ( )	Can see cause and effect in science ( )	Able to think things out in wide relations ( )	Able to take a world wide view of things ( )
Cowardly will "show white feather" in a pinch ( )	Will compromise on any subject ( )	Will "give up" rather than pay price of success ( )	Inclined to magnify difficulties ( )	**COURAGE**	Does not complain at hard tasks and hardships ( )	Expends energy freely in performance of duty ( )	Loyal to convictions, reverences in spite of failure ( )	Heroic in support of judgments and conviction ( )
Irresolute, vacillating, never know where you stand ( )	Wavering, doubleminded in matters of principle ( )	Inclined to side with the crowd ( )	Uncertain changes mind easily ( )	**STABILITY**	Takes definite stand when issue is understood ( )	Retains convictions even when alone ( )	Stands firm in matters of principle ( )	Determined, unyielding in stand for truth and right ( )
Perverted, lacks power to appreciate beauty ( )	Indulges in cheap and sensuous in art and life ( )	Does not resent cheap, ugly and uncomely ( )	Indifferent how "things look" ( )	**TASTES**	Fairly tasteful in dress, home, the arts nature, appreciation ( )	Enjoys the artistic and beautiful ( )	Able to choose and appreciate beautiful in art and life ( )	Devoted to and productive of most beautiful in art and life ( )
Unscrupulous and ungracious in word and deed ( )	Dishonest, will cheat, steal or defraud ( )	Tricky, cannot be relied on ( )	Not conscientious, not always "on the square" ( )	**HONOR**	Has fairly clear convictions of right and wrong ( )	Honest and upright in dealing with others ( )	Fair and just, scrupulous in keeping promises ( )	Your word as good as your bond, faithful and true ( )
Insubordinate, quarrelsome, overbearing, mean ( )	Disagreeable and boorish towards ( )	Neglectful, indifferent towards ( )	Inclined to be disrespectful, wilful ( )	**ATTITUDE TOWARD FAMILY**	Generally pleasant and agreeable ( )	Respectful, helpful ( )	Has due regard for, glad to yield to their wishes ( )	Devoted to, finds greatest satisfaction in serving ( )
Vulgar and surly, insulting ( )	Impolite, boorish, rude ( )	Ill-mannered, discourteous ( )	Indifferent, careless in treatment of others ( )	**ATTITUDE TOWARD OTHERS**	Usually well-behaved, mannerly ( )	Obliging, polite ( )	Winning, affable, gracious ( )	Courteous, respectful, considerate ( )
Resists social measures, tears down when possible ( )	Opposes plans for community betterment ( )	Places own welfare above that of others ( )	Indifferent to social demands ( )	**ATTITUDE TOWARD SOCIETY**	Will forego plans and desires for benefit of ( )	Gives time willingly to demands of ( )	Thinks and plans for community as well as self ( )	Devoted to welfare of ( )
Defiant, rebellious belligerent, "Red" ( )	Unruly, impatient of control ( )	Pin, la their laws and, rules irksome ( )	Inclined to slight and ignore more them ( )	**ATTITUDE TOWARD OFFICIALS**	Willing to submit to, but not unreasonable ( )	Loyal and helpful, treats with respect ( )	Devoted to, responsive to wishes of ( )	Enthusiastic supporter, not a blind follower ( )
Profane, ungodly, atheistic, a reviler ( )	An unbeliever, irreligious ( )	Skeptical, belittles religious teachings ( )	Inclined to disregard and slight ( )	**ATTITUDE TOWARD RELIGION**	Usually tolerant and respectful ( )	Reverent and worshipful ( )	Believes and practices teachings of ( )	Devoted to and principles of ( )
A dependent, does not know value of money ( )	Always "broke" and in debt, a spendthrift ( )	A squanderer, spends freely as of, often spends long as have foolishly ( )	Wasteful in use ( )	**ATTITUDE TOWARD MONEY**	Plans to make "both ends meet", objects to going in debt ( )	Thrifty, has savings account and tries to add to it ( )	Earns as much as possible and cares to beat advantage ( )	Realizes value and responsibility in use of ( )
An idler, enjoys the company of idlers and loafers ( )	Procrastinates, never ready for tasks ( )	Always tardy, never enough time ( )	Does not know how to use time ( )	**ATTITUDE TOWARD TIME**	Realizes value of proper use of time ( )	Uses time profitably ( )	Punctual, "on time" ( )	Uses conscientiously to best advantage ( )
Uses profanity, enjoys coarse and vulgar language ( )	Not consistently cautious about use of profanity ( )	Careless and ungratful in use of language ( )	Uses slang and by-words frequently ( )	**LANGUAGE**	Careful in choice of language ( )	Chaste and pure in speech, master of language daily ( )	Uses good language habitually ( )	Rejoices and encourages pure speech and good literature ( )
Uses to dissipate time and energy or in sensuous enjoyment ( )	Uses harmfully ( )	Uses wastefully ( )	Uses to satisfy the whim of the moment ( )	**PASTIME AND LEISURE**	Uses for relaxation ( )	Uses for healthful recreation ( )	Uses so as to strengthen the higher impulses and desires ( )	Uses for self improvement, study, research, social well being ( )
Total ( )	Total ( )	Total ( )	Total ( )		Total ( )	Total ( )	Total ( )	Total ( )

Source: _Character Education Methods_, between pp. 38 and 39.

A representative Self-Measurement Scale for children in grades five through eight is also included (see Figure 5). This scale is patterned after the one just previously discussed, although it is modified appropriately for the sake of younger students using it. There are less qualities to grade, only twenty-two, and the number of gradations has been decreased to six.

Two other tests, altogether different in structure than the two scales preceding are also presented. One is for use with kindergarten and primary children (see Figure 6), and the second is for children in grades three and four (see Figure 7). These two tests provide no means for quantitative gradation; they merely focus the child's attention upon desirable attitudes and activities. The process of answering the questions turns out to be indirectly suggestive of such behavior.

Although there is no standardized criterion to be used, with the first two self-measurement scales, as a means of interpreting the numbers totalled with respect to the gradations of the qualities, the collaborators contend that the data provided by the scales will prove to be useful to both the pupil and teacher. If nothing else, the act of examining oneself honestly in light of qualities of given worth is thought to be productive, in spite of the fact that such analysis may not always represent the highest degree of objectivity, and the data is capable of divergent evaluation. Clearly, however, the lack of norms and guidelines for the interpretation of these scales likely deterred rather extensively their use in the public schools.

It is clear that the methodological insights of Starbuck and his collaborators were progressive. Their indirect approach to the development of character revealed an understanding of the ultimate ineffectiveness of rigid, direct ethical systems and curriculums. And they had promulgated their methodological position when such a stand was unpopular among the public and even among a majority of American educators. It does not appear, however, that these were the main factors standing in the way of adopting the precise program for

Figure 5. A Self-Measurement Scale for Children, Grades V to VIII

Lazy, gets out of work when possible ( )	Doesn't like to work, complains ( )	Works only when teacher is watching ( )	**WORK IN SCHOOL**	Does work assigned willingly ( )	Works willingly and cheerfully ( )	Finds work whether assigned or not ( )
Lazy, never wants to do anything ( )	Complains, grumbles when asked to do anything ( )	Does not do anything without being told ( )	**WORK AT HOME**	Does what asked to do willingly ( )	Ready and willing to help ( )	Seeks opportunity and offers to help ( )
Slip-shod, slovenly in work, anything will do ( )	Does work any way just to get through ( )	Neglects and slights work ( )	**THOROUGHNESS**	Does work well most of the time ( )	Careful that work is correct and neat ( )	Never satisfied until work is done best possible ( )
Always puts off work as long as possible ( )	Doesn't care whether is on time or late ( )	Often tardy, slow to begin work ( )	**PROMPTNESS**	Tries to be on time and have work done on time ( )	Seldom tardy, nearly always ready when time to begin ( )	Always prompt to begin and finish work ( )
Never thinks out or plans work, depends on others ( )	Doesn't like to correct own mistakes ( )	Does not think out lessons without help ( )	**INITIATIVE**	Thinks out lessons alone sometimes ( )	Uses head, finds the best way to work ( )	Thinks, sees what is to be done and does it ( )
Face and hands usually dirty, clothes untidy ( )	Careless in care of body and of clothes ( )	Doesn't like to take exercise or try to keep clean ( )	**HEALTH**	Takes exercise, washes and keeps clean when reminded ( )	Takes exercise and keeps clean of own accord ( )	Health habits well established, keeps clothes tidy ( )
Careless, eats too much and too often ( )	Eats rapidly without chewing properly ( )	Eats what likes whether healthful food or not ( )	**EATING**	Careful what and when eats ( )	Eats slowly and chews food well ( )	Eats only good food, never too much rich food or sweets ( )
Cross, hard to get along with, loses temper easily ( )	Gets angry, and sulks when can't have own way ( )	Quarrels with playmates over trifles ( )	**DISPOSITION**	Is pleasant and agreeable most of the time ( )	Does not quarrel even if others do ( )	Cheerful and keeps temper even when things go wrong ( )
Cannot arrange room, dress or anything to look well ( )	Does not care for flowers, birds, pictures, etc. ( )	Often makes poor choices ( )	**TASTES**	Can tell when things are arranged tastefully ( )	Notices and enjoys the beautiful—birds, flowers, sunsets, pictures, etc. ( )	Able to choose tasteful clothes, good books, entertainment, companions ( )
Cruel to playmates and pets ( )	Teases and hurts playmates and pets just for fun ( )	Rough and thoughtless in play ( )	**KINDNESS**	Careful not to hurt playmates or pets ( )	Gentle and sympathetic in treatment of others and of pets ( )	Would rather suffer pain than cause pain to others or to pets ( )
Wastes money, never tries to save any ( )	Spends money foolishly for candy, movies, gum, etc. ( )	Does not try to earn money ( )	**MONEY**	Earns money when has a chance ( )	Has a savings account and earns and saves when has a chance ( )	Spends money only for what is useful and helpful ( )
An idler, wastes time when ought to be at work ( )	Loafs and careless in use of time ( )	Inclined to waste time ( )	**TIME**	Busy at some task most of time ( )	Tries to use time profitably ( )	Plans to use time to get most possible work done ( )
Unreliable, makes errors in judgment ( )	"Jumps at conclusions," doesn't take time to think ( )	As likely to make a bad judgment as a good one ( )	**JUDGMENT**	Able to judge right most of the time ( )	Thinks out problems and decides accordingly ( )	Reliable, can always be depended on to make wise choice ( )
Tells lies, can't be depended on at all ( )	Tricky, deceitful, can't be trusted ( )	"Stretches the truth" sometimes ( )	**TRUTHFULNESS**	Tells the truth most of the time ( )	Can be depended on to tell the truth ( )	Tells the truth even when it hurts ( )
A slouch, never puts things away ( )	Neglectful, does not care how things look ( )	Does not try to have clothes and work look neat ( )	**NEATNESS**	Fairly neat in dress and in work ( )	Keeps clothes, desk and room in good order most of the time ( )	Orderly, keeps things in proper place ( )
Quarrels over games, thinks only of self ( )	Wants to have own way in all the games ( )	Wants to be first or have best place in games ( )	**PLAY**	Doesn't get mad if not given best place in games ( )	Willing to give up to please others ( )	Tries to help others enjoy play as well as self ( )
Rude, noisy, annoys others ( )	Pushes past others when going indoors, passes in front of others ( )	Speaks while others are speaking ( )	**MANNERS AT SCHOOL**	Listens when others are speaking ( )	Lets others pass indoors first, does not pass in front of others ( )	Greets others pleasantly, steps aside to let others pass ( )
Discourteous, noisy, impolite ( )	Never stops to think if actions annoy others ( )	Cross and stubborn ( )	**MANNERS AT HOME**	Kind and gentle towards rest of the family ( )	Quiet when likely to annoy others ( )	Courteous, thoughtful of the welfare of others ( )
Steals, can't be trusted out of sight ( )	Cheats in work and in play ( )	Uses what belongs to others without asking ( )	**HONESTY**	Doesn't take what belongs to others without asking ( )	Square in work and in play ( )	Always honest, can be trusted anywhere ( )
Does what wants to, right or wrong ( )	Will break a promise if to own advantage to do so ( )	Careless in living up to promises and agreements ( )	**TRUST-WORTHINESS**	Careful in making promises ( )	Tries hard to keep promises and agreements ( )	Can be depended on to do what promises or agrees to do ( )
When guilty tries to sneak out or lay on others ( )	Quits when fails or finds task difficult ( )	Babyish, won't try anything that looks hard ( )	**COURAGE**	Will try task even if it looks hard ( )	Keeps on even if task is made fun of ( )	If does wrong owns up and tries to make it right ( )
Gets angry when joked or teased by others ( )	Likes to tease others but not to be teased ( )	Doesn't care for jokes or humor ( )	**HUMOR**	Can see and appreciate good jokes ( )	Enjoys joking with fellow-students ( )	Witty, "cracks jokes" and takes jokes good naturedly ( )

Source: _Character Education Methods_, between pp. 38 and 39.

229

Figure 6.   A Character Test for Primary Children

	Mon.	Tues.	Wed.	Thurs.	Fri.	Mon.	Tues.	Wed.	Thurs.	Fri.
1. Did you sleep 10 hours or more last night?....										
2. Did you take ten or more long, deep breaths yesterday?										
3. Did you wash your hands before each meal yesterday?										
4. Did you wash your teeth yesterday?...........										
5. Did you spend 30 minutes or more in the open air yesterday?										
6. Did you put away your wraps when you came home from school yesterday?..................										
7. Did you arrange your clothes last night so that they would be easy to find and put on this morning?										
8. Did you take a bath yesterday?...............										
9. Did you go straight home from school yesterday?										
10. Did you try to keep from soiling or tearing your clothes yesterday?										
11. Did you step aside to let anyone pass you yesterday, on the sidewalks, in the halls, or at doors?										
12. Do you have a savings account or bank?.......										
13. Did you earn and save anything yesterday?										
14. Did you do anything yesterday that you ought not to have done? ....,.....										
16. Did you share anything (apple, candy, nuts, cake, etc.) with brothers, sisters, or playmates yesterday?										
17. Did you cry yesterday?........................										
18. Did you complain when asked to do anything yesterday										
19. Did you quit playing or pout yesterday when you could not have your own way?...........										
20. Did you quarrel with anyone yesterday?......										
21. Did you go away from home yesterday without telling anyone where you went?.............										
22. Did you bite your finger nails or put pencil in your mouth yesterday?										

Source: Character Education Methods, between pp. 40 and 41.

230

Figure 7. A Character Test for Children, Grades III and IV

1. Did you do your health chores yesterday?
   a. Wash your teeth?...
   b. Wash your hands before each meal?........................
   c. Take a bath?...
   d. Spend 30 minutes or more in the open air?.................
   e. Take some special exercises?..............................
2. Did you waste any time yesterday when you ought to have been
   at work? ....
3. What did you do yesterday to help someone at home?..........
   ....
4. What did you do yesterday to help someone without being asked?
   ....
5. Were you tardy at school or late at meals yesterday?............
   ....
6. What did you see yesterday that was really beautiful?..........
   ....
7. What good music did you hear yesterday?......................
   ....
8. Did you hurt anyone or make anyone cry yesterday?............
   ....
9. How much did you earn yesterday?.............................
10. Did you quit playing or pout yesterday when you could not have
    your own way? ....
11. What did you have to hunt yesterday because it was not put
    away in its proper place?.....................................
12. Did you step aside to let someone pass you yesterday on the side-
    walks, in the halls, or at doors?..............................
    ....
13. Did you plan last night something to do today?.................
    ....
14. Did you do anything wrong yesterday...........................
    Did you own up to it?.......Did you try to make it right?.........
15. Did you promise to do anything yesterday that you did not do?
    ....
16. What did you read yesterday just because you wanted to?......
    ....
17. What did you hear or see yesterday that was funny?...........
    ....
18. Did you refuse to do anything yesterday that someone wanted
    you to because you thought it was wrong?......................
    ....
19. Did you quarrel with anyone yesterday?........................
20. What did any of your playmates do yesterday that you thought
    was wrong? ....
21. Why did you think it was wrong?...............................
22. Are there any of your playmates that do not like you?...........
    ....
23. Why don't they like you?......................................
24. What did you do after school yesterday?........................
    ....
25. Did you try to keep cheerful yesterday?........................

Source: <u>Character Education Methods</u>, between pp. 40 and 41.

231

character education being promoted in the Iowa Plan.
Rather, it is our contention that the fundamental
drawback was that, in effect, it was only an introduction to the plan, not a finished product, and that
few educators were willing to experiment with limited
materials. If all the grades had been charted and a
full range of bibliographical supplements prepared,
such a package program very well may have received
national prominence in the educational system. As it
was, in spite of Starbuck's tireless efforts, such
supplement materials were never fully completed, and
those that were produced were consequently not widely
used. Notwithstanding, the foundational principles
of the Iowa Plan, as delineated specifically in
Chapter I, and which formed the basis of Starbuck's
methodological approach to character education, penetrated in time deeply and extensively the American
public school system.

Institute for Research in Character

The major projects of Starbuck's career were
primarily the results of his work in the character
research institutes he established at the universities
of Iowa and Southern California. The first project,
begun early in the life of the Institute, in fact,
emerging out of the Iowa Plan, was the attempt to objectively assess children's literature for the purpose
of character training. Starbuck, and every member of
the committee who assisted him in producing the Iowa
Plan, had unwavering convictions about the approach to
personality and character development. They rejected
the notion that the way of direct moral preachments
was desirable and productive of improved behavior.
Instead, they insisted that moral education should be
indirect and proceeded to do their work on this basis.
Convinced that choice literature serves to inspire the
reader and that selected pieces can function to foster
growth in character, the committee worked toward scientifically assembling, judging and classifying the best
selections from the world of children's literature.
They sought to chart the best character training materials by preparing a classified bibliography for
each grade in the public schools which would supplement the teachers' efforts along this line. It was

232

felt that if such a bibliography were easily accessible to every teacher interested in enriching her own school preparation and activities, she could find no excuse for failing to use available aids.

The committee's work was extensive. It involved:

> "(a) an inquiry into all the essential types of courses of study to learn what shall be the subject matter each year that needs enriching in a character education program (b) to discover such projects and materials as are consistent, both with the prevailing curricula and with the objectives of character training (c) to accumulate and judge as to its worth essentially all of the available publications that promise assistance (d) to set up an inquiry among thousands of school people into the materials and aids that have practically proven useful in such concrete instances that the result of its use can be specifically described (e) to classify the tested and tried materials and place them in a form for convenient reference for the use of teachers."81

The last item alone was a tremendous undertaking, but the collaborators approached the task with less than a reserved degree of optimism. They made significant progress toward the building of a detailed bibliography for classroom use, but did not finish the project. In the pages of the Iowa Plan, submitted in 1921, is revealed how little even the members of the committee understood the extent of the work which would be required to develop a practical reference work for the schools. They wrote, "The necessary research and the accumulation of bodies of material have grown to such proportion . . . that it must take weeks, if not months, with skilled readers and assistants to complete the project." Not only was this project not completed for the report, but the project was carried

on for several years, being assumed eventually by the
staff members of the Institute, under Starbuck's direction. Starbuck recalls:

> "My students and I set out to take
> over that project of salvation
> through literature, as a regular
> part of the college and university
> work. The University of Iowa was
> hospitable to the idea."[82]

When subsidization was secured from a couple of
foundations, Starbuck was able to select a staff of
experts who served as literary critics, and several
secretarial assistants. Supported by grants from
foundations, and eventually, in part, by the university itself, the Institute published two volumes
which served as guides to children's literature for
the purpose of character education. These volumes,
A Guide to Literature for Character Training: Vol. I
Fairy Tale, Myth and Legend, and A Guide to Books for
Character: Vol. II Fiction, were not finally published
until 1928 and 1930 respectively. Even then, they were
the only two volumes produced out of about eight volumes of this Guide envisioned.[83]

One of the characteristics of the Institute was
that it proceeded on the basis of a highly disciplined,
empirical methodology for its day. From the very beginning of his professional career, Starbuck upheld the
rigid demands of the scientific approach. These two
volumes for instance, represent the first application
of the scientific method to the selection of children's
books for character development. The literature for
children was judged under scientific discipline. One
evaluation, in comparing this project, under Starbuck's
leadership, with other efforts along the same line,
concludes that Starbuck's efforts differ in the following three ways, all of which point to a more exacting
science:

> "(a) it is more inclusive--
> world-wide in the sources from which
> it draws; (b) it is more objective--
> each item evaluated according to a

> graduated scale as to literary
> excellence, educational fitness,
> and character value; (c) it is
> more critical--each entry must
> be approved independently by
> three trained critics."[84]

Both the reliability and validity of the selection
and judgment of literature listed in these two volumes
of the Guide were evidenced not only by the statistical data obtained in the procedure itself, but by the
methods used in preparing the volumes as well. Nine
major steps were taken to assure general trustworthiness of the Guide. The steps listed are virtually
the same for both volumes. Volume I lists the following:

> "first, the establishing of an am-
> ple workshop in which presumably
> appropriate literature could be
> studied on a comparative basis;
> second the assembling of all offer-
> ings published in English that
> seemed to be fitting candidates for
> inclusion in the Guide; third, the
> employment on full time schedule of
> a staff of readers trained in liter-
> ary criticism; fourth, the clear
> definition of a set of standards of
> excellence; fifth, the insistence
> that all materials before being in-
> cluded in the Guide should have the
> independent judgment of four readers;
> sixth, the recording of all judgments
> on a quantitative scale; seventh, a
> bi-monthly statistical check on the
> judgments of all readers to determine
> the extent of agreements; eighth, the
> prompt rereading of all materials
> showing wide disagreements; and ninth,
> a careful comparative editing of all
> materials by a committee having in
> mind the full field of selections and
> the entire range of judgments."[85]

Another feature of the volumes, which portrays one other characteristic of Starbuck and his work, is their practical usefulness. Although over one thousand of the world's best books for children are listed, extremely helpful lists and indexes have been compiled to foster easy and simple selection of desirable reading materials. One list insures the selection of a suitable book for a particular age. This list includes the choice books for children of each age group according to grades. It provides a brief description of each book and grades them according to their excellence. Another list classifies the books in terms of situations as well as by age. Books may be selected with respect to the specific qualities they exemplify. One index lists desirable attitudes and the particular books which best cultivate them. Another index classifies books on the basis of subject matter, allowing for the selection of certain subjects and particular kinds of stories which would likely interest the child.

Although it is difficult to assess the extent of its actual usage in the schools, the response of educators indicates that it was well accepted. A promotional monograph, quoting the early reactions of educators throughout the country, reveals how complementary they were about the project.[86] First, its dependability and thoroughness is noted. Joseph Kennedy, Dean of the College of Education, at the University of North Dakota, comments:

> "These volumes are a boon to those seeking proper literature in the fields covered. Your index of titles and authors is excellent and enables a person to find just what he needs and is looking for. Indeed, both volumes are real Baedekers in character literature. Without your volumes it would be kind of a 'hit and miss' process to find applicable material; but now the whole field is open and before us--and what is better, is systematized so that one can find appropriate literature for the asking."

236

Goodwin B. Watson, Associate Professor of Education, Teachers College, Columbia University, says, "You have integrated in very able fashion valid criteria from the standpoint of literary appreciation and similar criteria from the standpoint of educational principles." Commending Starbuck directly, M. E. Haggerty, Dean of the College of Education at the University of Minnesota, writes:

> "You and your collaborators have rendered a service not merely to the field of literature but to the whole area of education. One rarely finds so much that can be made of direct use in the education of children within the space of a single volume such as yours. With such a Guide teachers everywhere will find it easier to introduce children to genuine literature."

Regarding the selection of character-building material, Karl R. Stolz, Dean of Hartford School of Religious Education, comments on Volume II:

> "I read your recently published Volume II of A Guide to Books for Character with a growing sense of its worth and quality. It is not just another book in the field of education, for it is unique in plan, purpose, and execution. You and your associates have most successfully realized your purpose to disengage books of first quality from the mass of children's fiction with which we have been deluged."

George A. Coe, a pioneer in religious and character education, himself, writes to Starbuck:

> "After examining it carefully, applying several informal tests, and discussing it with a high-school student advisor, I am convinced that

237

you have produced an indispensable
book for character education. The
labor that it represents is amaz-
ing, but more noteworthy is the
educational judgment that has pre-
sided over and shaped the whole."

A commendation, as well as a personal note about the
use of the volume, is made by the Director of Psychological Laboratory at Colgate University, D. A. Laird.
He states:

"Both of these books are noteworthy and should be indispensable
to all persons interested in the
training of children. The work
back of them is little short of
heroic. Some idea of how seriously
I take the guides is shown by our
using this in selecting the book a
week to be read by our ten-year-old
boy."

A number of comments also attest to their psychological soundness and scientific thoroughness. Mark
A. May, of Yale University, notes:

"It is by all odds the most
scientific and therefore the most
trustworthy thing that has ever
been done in this field. It is a
book that should not only be in the
hands of every librarian, but also
in the library of every public
school in the country."

And Clarence Marsh Case, of the University of Southern
California, expresses:

"The scientific and logical
thoroughness with which this vast
undertaking has been conducted and
tested as to its results elicits my
great admiration. It seems to me
that three good fellows have met

238

together in this work, namely good
esthetics, good ethics, and good
scientific procedure. The result
well repays their meeting."

One of the highest acclaims for this work is rendered in the final quotation. Roger W. Babson, an
economist and business educator, and who served in
World War I as director general of information and education, had this to say about the project:

"I believe the work that you
are doing is of the greatest importance;--in fact perhaps the most
important of any work being done in
the country today. I have enjoyed
reading Volumes I and II and think
that they are very valuable and
should be in the hands of every educator and preacher in the United
States."

Naturally, the purpose of such a monograph is to
promote the particular publication being reviewed.
Consequently, the information used is included for the
sake of acclaiming its value. The monograph, from
which the preceeding quotes were taken, undoubtedly
has a similar aim. For this reason the responses
quoted are not as objectively critical as would be
expected from an independent reviewer. Still, it is
clear that the quotes were highly complementary, and
that the responses were made by respectable educators
of renown. Such praise, though weighted cannot be
ignored in analyzing the value of this work.

Not all educators were sympathetic to the act of
judging the relative worth of children's literature in
order to establish by selection the world's best literature for children. Starbuck claimed to accomplish
this through a more scientific method than had ever
been used before. In 1932, Ernest A. Baker, the Director of the School of Librarianship at the University
of London, and James Packman, published A Guide to the
Best Fiction, in which they were highly critical of
such an approach. While not mentioning Starbuck direct-

ly, they do refer negatively to such work as might encompass his volumes. An introduction of their publication, and an obvious negation of the "best books" approach, such as Starbuck used, is included in the preface:

> "It is a guide, not an autocratic proclamation that such and such are the world's best novels, and that all the rest are inferior. A proclamation of that sort would instantly meet with the same fate as sooner or later has befallen certain too authoritative pronouncements, whose authors have singled out what they considered the best books without reflecting that "best" is a relative term, relative, that is to say, not only to the other things with which there is a comparison, but also to the purposes of the books and the needs of the readers."[87]

Starbuck would concede that the judgment or valuation of literature is a relative procedure; but he still would contend that such a procedure can be objectivized to the point of preparing, as he did, a much more scientific and thus authoritative guide than any random selection along individual whims or persuasion.

Whatever acclaim this project had at the beginning does not appear to have been matched by its incorporation, in terms of any significant duration, into the public school programs. It is clear that to be permanently useful, the bibliographies would have to have been revised every few years for the purpose of including new material. With no new revisions forthcoming, the demand for current materials probably impaired, in a relatively short time, the volumes' usefullness.

Each volume contains several chapters, written by Starbuck which are fundamental both to an understanding of the proper use of the Guide, and to an appreciation of the underlying principles prefacing such an effort. The first two chapters in Volume I deal with

240

this latter element, in terms of the relationship of literature to character education. In the first chapter, Starbuck not only affirms the significance of fairy-tales and other such stories, but also attempts to establish the importance of story-telling as an art. He speaks of it as involving the "interplay of life upon life," as the artist and reader or listener are linked together by the living imagery of the tale. Its ability to enable its reader to live the life of another, or to share another's experiences, is a form of socialization, which ultimately carries with it moral implications. In terms of this "othering" process, the story has potentially powerful moral significance.[88]

Chapter II deals with the question of judging literature. Starbuck is aware of the problems involved in labeling the worth of literature, but he considers that this Guide differs from other attempts in its scientific approach to the definition and measurement of the literature examined. With the use of qualified literary assistants on his staff, approaching the appraisal under controlled conditions, Starbuck considered that this book clearly attested to the validity of grading literature comparatively according to its excellence. Early in the midst of their work, Starbuck and his staff of critics were able to agree upon such interpretation of children's literature in terms of eight general standards of judgment. These criteria were "unity, right craftsmanship, agreeable emotional tone, effectiveness, artistry in appeal, truthfulness, refinement of the fundamental human attitudes, and proper orientation."

At this point, perhaps a word about the trustworthiness of the two volumes would be in order. Even apart from any statistical evidence, the general procedure used to produce the Guides indicates a genuine concern for objectivity. A statistical analysis, however, provides sounder evidence of the trustworthiness of the two volumes. In the first volume, for instance, a review of tests made on the three classifications to measure their accuracy, reveals high reliability. Classification in terms of the thirty-two ethical situations developed proved to be appro-

priate and workable. Classification in terms of quality, judged by degrees of merit, was tested by two
procedures. The first compared the judgments of the
readers themselves. One reader was correlated against
the judgments of three others, and then two against
two were compared. The correlations were high, ranging from .55 to .85. The second procedure, considered
even more significant, compared the judgments of the
readers with the rankings of outside groups. Sixteen
separate investigations revealed significant positive
correlations. Testing the accuracy of classification
according to the school grade revealed similar results.
Comparing the judgments of the Guide with outside ranks
of various sorts indicated that about seventy per cent
of the material was accurately placed in terms of the
appropriate school grade with only four to five per
cent misplaced by two or more grades.[90]

The second volume, on fiction, when analyzed, produced similar results. A statistical treatment of the
same three features as tested in Volume I was made,
and the following assessment of trustworthiness established:

> "Summarizing these findings
> briefly: nonstatistical evidence
> of trustworthiness is provided by
> the varying viewpoints, experience,
> and special training of the mem-
> bers of the staff and by the extent
> and manner of sampling the field of
> fiction. Statistical findings show
> that the readers' standards through-
> out the process were kept level,
> the readers' judgments were equal-
> ized throughout, and classification
> according to situations, level of
> merit, and grade placement was
> found to be highly reliable."[91]

In the first chapter of the second volume of this
series, Starbuck discusses the place of fiction in the
development of character. At the beginning he notes
the growing popularity of fiction, citing an estimation that nine-tenths of the books children withdraw
from public libraries are fictional. Starbuck considers it highly unfortunate if this interest is not
satisfied with good literature, in this case, fiction.[92]

242

To Starbuck, the value of the arts in the character developing process is practically inestimable. The arts, including literature, are revealers of the "deeps of character," and fiction is one of the most potent of the arts for it can so capably picture the labyrinth of personality. This capacity is akin to character development, according to Starbuck. He states:

> "Since the flow of humanity's life is through selves, it follows as a truism that to influence the tastes of children for fiction is identical with shaping vitally the course of human culture."[93]

Elsewhere, Starbuck summarizes his view of this relationship:

> "The net result of philosophical quest up to this point is that art including fiction is an expression through personalities of the creative life of the world. Art and morality are at one; for both function in terms of self-realization, the othering of the self and the recentering of life in a world of ideal values."[94]

It is clear why Starbuck approached so seriously the work of these two volumes. As he saw it, so much was at stake for humanity.

During the years 1927 through 1931, another project, not unrelated to the first, demanded Starbuck's attention also. With some help from members of the Institute, Starbuck edited four volumes of the University of Iowa Studies in Character.[95]

The intention and substance of these studies is revealed in the Forward of Volume I. Starbuck states:

> "This is the first of a series of monographs to be issued from time to time by the Institute of Character

243

> Research at the University of
> Iowa. The studies will have ref-
> erence to problems of character
> and personality, methods of charac-
> ter training, and the content of
> the curriculum."[96]

One of the characteristics common to the various contributions to this series is that, for the most part, they are the result of scientific research. In almost every instance the studies are based primarily upon objectively controlled data, and the conclusions are capable of validation. Even in one of the less technical studies this is true. For example, Dr. James C. Manry studies the effect of certain kinds of education and experience upon an individual's "international mindedness." In introducing this study, Dr. Starbuck states:

> "While Dr. Manry's research is
> significant from the practical stand-
> point, its real value, perhaps is its
> contribution to methodology in the
> field of Education. It represents a
> victory in scientific procedure. It
> applies well controlled, objective
> methods to the solution of an intri-
> cate, involved, and relatively inac-
> cessible problem of Ethics and Educa-
> tion. It substitutes proof for im-
> pression, employs quantitative mea-
> surement rather than intuitive convic-
> tion, and validates its conclusions
> instead of logically deriving them."

In the view of Starbuck, Dr. Manry's study of "World Citizenship" yielded data which was useful to the continuing growth of man's understanding of the science of character education or training. Starbuck is critical of the acceptance of any unsophisticated approach to attitudinal and behavioral change. Consistent in his concern for objective methodology, Starbuck states at the time of the publication of the first volume of this series:

> "There has been always a naive

244

assumption that whatever devices
for character training have been
thought out by earnest minds must
of necessity produce beneficient
results in moral attitudes and
conduct. In the new time all such
claims must subject themselves to
rigorous scientific discipline and
prove by objective tests and measurements their validity . . . The
Time is quite ripe for taking most
problems of methodology out of the
range of fancy and speculation
over into the sphere of fact and
proof."[97]

In harmony with this plea for disciplined research, the Institute concerned itself with the development of techniques for the scientific study of
character. Several studies dealt with the mental and
social characteristics or factors involved in character and personality. Among the more sophisticated
works are those by Frank K. Shuttleworth and W. E.
Slaght, included with Manry's study in Volume I of
the series.[98] Challenged by the general low correlation between intellectual ability and academic achievement, Dr. Shuttleworth sought to explore elements,
other than cognitive ones, possibly involved in scholastic success. Shuttleworth developed three techniques for measuring these character and environmental
factors. Predictions of success from his tests compared favorably with the better mental measurements
available. It was hoped that these tests would prove
useful to personnel departments in colleges and universities. The investigation of Dr. Slaght is considered the first successful study to apply laboratory
methods to an ethical problem. He was able to isolate
the major factors contributing to truthfulness, dis-
covering that intelligence does not appear to be a
significant determinant of this trait. This research
was thought to have laid a groundwork for other controlled studies dealing with methods of training for
honesty.

Two futher studies of the series, possibly repre-
senting the first attempts to study a religious pro-

blem through the use of rigid empirical methods, including experimentation and factors of strict control, are those by Thomas H. Howells and Robert Daniel Sinclair in Volume II.[99] Dr. Howells' study dealt with the comparison of conservatives and radicals in religion. He managed to isolate and analyze a number of personality characteristics associated with these two types, and several of the social factors conditioning their attitudes. In a similar study, Dr. Sinclair compared the mystically minded with those who are not so inclined. Here, as in Howells' investigation, the mental and social factors were studied. The mystics versus the "tougher-minded" type were compared.

Some other interesting religious studies, performed in light of the demands of objective standards of measurement, were also conducted. Samuel P. Franklin investigated the comprehension ability of children of various ages to understand the sayings and parables of Jesus.[100] Dr. Franklin's work had special relevance to the development of religious education curricula. Related was the study of Ralph Thomas Case, who sought to measure the capacity of differing aged children to understand the teachings of the Old Testament prophets.[101] Also dealing with the study of religion, specifically focused in on the relation of the Bible and character development, were the studies by Pleasant Roscoe Hightower, and George W. Beiswanger.[102] Finally, Dr. Herbert L. Searles, in an interesting pioneering work, studied, from the points of history and legality, the place of religion in state universities.[103]

Even a casual scan of these studies reveals the central part Starbuck played in their formation and development. The high measure of indebtedness Starbuck's students had to him, with respect to his contribution to their studies, is evidenced in every instance. Typical of the acknowledgments given to Starbuck for his assistance and inspiration are those expressed by Samuel Franklin. He states:

> "He /the writer/ is especially indebted for guidance and kindly criticism in the selection of the subject and in the method of securing data to Professor Edwin D.

Starbuck, who gave much assistance
in defining clearly, the problem
and in guiding its development,
and whose continued interest and
generous spirit was ever an inspiration."[104]

Thomas Howells expressed not only gratitude for such
help, but also recognizes Starbuck as the originator
of the study. He acknowledges:

"The writer is chiefly indebted to
Dr. Edwin D. Starbuck, who origina-
ted the idea of making an empirical
study of types of religious persons.
His courage in undertaking difficult
tasks, if thereby he might get at
the heart of things has been a constant source of inspiration."[105]

The extent of Starbuck's association with his graduate
students in their work is further disclosed by the
acknowledgement of Ralph Case. He writes:

"In special degree Dr. Edwin D.
Starbuck has contributed to the
undertaking, in initial suggestion
of the study, in clear-sighted
guidance and helpful criticism, and
in wise counsel as to practical details of the project. Upon his
wisdom and insight there was constant dependence."[106]

Finally, the acknowledgement of George Beiswanger, who
was a Ph.D. candidate under Starbuck, and incidently
his son-in-law, typifies the gratitude Starbuck's
students had for his close supervision. Beiswanger in
reference to his particular topic, "The character Value
of the Old Testament Stories," states:

"The problem was suggested by
Dr. Edwin D. Starbuck, director of
the Institute of Character Research,
as one item in an extensive investigation, the discovery and evaluation

of the best literature for children,
and took shape under his counsel and
direction. Only those who know the
unfailing fertility of insight and
the richness of experience which are
his, and the gracious liberality with
which he gives his best to his students, can appreciate how inadequately
these words indicate the measure of
the author's indebtedness."107

Starbuck's work and association with his graduate
students and their research appears to be unusually
prodigious. Such evidence as has been presented only
serves to further reveal the nature of his life's investment in the lives of individuals, as opposed to
personal research and publication.

The remaining projects to be considered were not
only related to, but fundamentally the product of the
original project of literature assessment for character education. Under Starbuck's supervision two sets
of readers for children were finally completed. These
were only a small part, however, of the publications
Starbuck had projected from the work he and his associates of the Institute were conducting. The first
three volume set, The Wonder Road, was published in
1930 just prior to Starbuck's departure from the University of Iowa.108 These volumes contained what
Starbuck and his staff assessed as the sixty-one best
fairy tales, fables and myths for children in existence. They were far more than a collection indis-
criminately gathered together. This particular collection reaped the benefits of the research of the Institute. Thousands of stories over the years had been
tested and evaluated; and a compilation of the best
pieces was made. Therefore, the selections for this
series represented the results of competent, tried
literary judgment. The stories were considered the
best not only in terms of their appeal to children;
they were selected, also, from the standpoint of character education. Only those stories were chosen which
were judged to best motivate desirable conduct.

In harmony with the philosophy of the Iowa Plan

and the approach that Starbuck had always taken to character education, this series did not succumb to the artless approach of directly promulgating ethical principles, or in other words, moralization. Rather, Starbuck and the others responsible for this series, confidently believed that to surround children with such literature would assist the more natural process of developing patterns of positive habits of character. A student of Starbuck's substantiates this interpretation, and adds a note of personal support to this philosophy. Referring to Starbuck, the student states:

> "He was dedicated to a religion of good conduct--and his monumental, life-time work was devoted to character education. He liked to repeat that 'Ethics is caught, not taught.' His series of volumes in character education pursued this process . . . I think he was correct in illustrating the positive virtues of human kind as an incentive to good conduct. Certainly our value system is acquired very much by the unconscious process of conditioned learning."[109]

Such a project as this was important to Starbuck. Its relationship to the Institute was significant for it represented the practical realization of the results of the vast amount of tedious research in character conducted by members of the Institute. It is extremely unfortunate, not only in terms of Starbuck's reputation, but even more importantly, to the generation of potential young readers in Starbuck's day, that the overall scheme for publications did not materialize.

The second set of readers, also three volumes, was not published until 1936.[110] This series, Living Through Biography, consisted of a highly select group of biographies designed to appeal particularly to children in grades seven through nine, but suitable also to other grades in that general vicinity. Again, the intent was that this series be used in a supplementary way within the context of the programmed curriculum being offered in the schools. Besides the select biographies reproduced for reading, at the end of each volume a selected bibliography of biography listed numbers of other studies which might interest the reader also.

The method of selection had been time consuming, actually a matter of years, and as a result unusually thorough. Trained literary critics examined approximately 5000 volumes from which 1590 were excluded because of inferiority or predicted failure to interest children. Out of the remaining volumes, through an objective process of judgment, 700 volumes were selected which met specific standards of excellence. From these volumes, after evaluation by groups of students, the final selections were made, thirty-one of which were included in the three volumes published.[111]

Conclusion

Neither project endured in terms of its initial structuring. There is no "Iowa Plan" as such for character education being used in the public schools today. Shortly after his departure from Iowa in 1930, Starbuck's Institute of Character Research was extinct; and with his death in 1947 a similar Institute he had established at the University of Southern California, for all practical purposes, folded. Nevertheless, these projects were significant contributions in the unending flow of educational reform. What Starbuck envisioned early in the Iowa Plan, the utilization of the regular studies and experiences of the school as a natural indirect setting for character education, surrounding the students with the kind of literature which subtly exposes them to examples of good conduct, and organizing the school into a community that is shaped by the decisions of its own members, including students, who learn something about responsibility as they assume it, later became commonplace in progressive public education. His voice, along with others like John Dewey, served to penetrate the inroads of traditional and authoritarian educational processes. And while his efforts, through his Institutes for character research, to develop readers which would supplement the regular school curriculum in character training, were never fully realized; still, Starbuck's promotion of research in character towards practical means, particularly in the educational institution, did not go unheeded in the following decades, as evidenced by the amount of research in character and personality undertaken especially in the fields of education and psychology.

NOTES

1. A tabulation of these sources reveals that
Starbuck wrote seventy-three articles, had two books
published, wrote single chapters for six books, nine
chapters in books he edited, and two book reviews.
He co-authored one article and was involved in the
multiple authorship of two articles and one book, the
latter being largely Starbuck's product. In addition,
Starbuck edited twelve volumes. Of the seventy-three
articles published, thirty-one of these, or parts
thereof, are to be found in a collection of his works,
entitled, Look To This Day, produced, just two years
before his death, in 1945, by the staff of the Institute of Character Research, at The University of
Southern California.

2. It should be noted that, to the present, the
bibliography found in the appendix of Look To This
Day, pp. 425-427, has served as the most complete
listing of Starbuck's published works available.
Fifty-four items are listed in the bibliography itself, and ten additional items, not listed in the
bibliography are to be found either in the contents
page or in another part of the appendix section. A
careful search in various periodical, educational,
psychological, and religious indexes, and a perusal
of the index listings of major journals in the areas
of Starbuck's interests, covering the years of his
career, has enabled the present writer to prepare an
expanded listing of Starbuck's writings, one hundred
and eight items in all. See Starbuck's Works at the
end of the book.

3. Starbuck, "A Study of Conversion," pp. 268-308,
and "Some Aspects of Religious Growth," pp. 70-124.

4. Edwin D. Starbuck, "Religious Education as a
part of General Education," Religious Education Association, Proceedings of the First Annual Convention
(Chicago, February 10-12, 1903), pp. 52-59.

5. Ibid., p. 53.

6. Edwin D. Starbuck, "The Feelings and Their Place
in Religion," American Journal of Religious Psychology
and Education, I, No. 2 (November 1904), pp. 168-186.

7. The two articles by Starbuck found in the
Religious Education Association, The Proceedings of the
Third Annual Convention (Boston, February 12-16, 1905),
are: "The Foundations of Religion and Morality: How

Far, and How Can the Foundations of Religion be Laid
in the Common Schools?", pp. 245-250; and "The Growth
of the Larger Sense of Social and Civic Responsibility
in Youth," pp. 339-343. The first article is the one
to which we refer as particularly important and from
which we shall quote.
8. Ibid., p. 250.
9. Chapter III in Moral Training in the Public
Schools (Boston: Ginn and Company, 1907) pp. 89-121.
10. Starbuck, Character Education Methods: The
Iowa Plan.
11. Moral Training in the Public Schools, pp. 91-92.
12. Ibid., p. 121.
13. Edwin Diller Starbuck, "The Child-Mind and
Child-Religion," The Biblical World (Chicago: University of Chicago Press). Part I: "The Child-
Consciousness and Human Progress," XXX, No. 1 (July,
1907), pp. 30-38; Part II: "The Nature of Child Consciousness," XXX, No. 2 (August, 1907), pp. 101-110;
Part III: "The Method of Evolution of Consciousness
and of Religion," XXX, No. 3 (September, 1907), pp. 191-
201; Part IV: "The Development of Spirituality," XXX,
No. 5 (November, 1907), pp. 352-360; Part V: "Stages
in Religious Growth," XXXI, No. 2 (February, 1908),
pp. 101-112.
14. Part II, pp. 101-102.
15. Part III, pp. 192-193.
16. Ibid., p. 193.
17. Ibid., p. 201.
18. Part V, p. 112.
19. Edwin D. Starbuck, Volume II: "Backsliding,"
1910, pp. 319-321; Volume III: "Climate," 1911,
pp. 693-694; Volume IV: "Double-Mindedness," and
"Doubt," 1912, pp. 860-862, and 862-865, respectively;
Volume V: "Female Principle," 1913, pp. 827-833:
Volume VIII: "Institutionalism," 1915, pp. 397-400;
Volume IX: "Old Age," 1917, pp. 458-462; Volume XI:
"Self-Expression," 1919, pp. 357-359, Encyclopedia
of Religion and Ethics, James Hastings, ed. (New York:
Charles Scribner's Sons).
20. Edwin D. Starbuck, "Hopeful Lines of Development
of the Psychology of Religion," Religious Education,
VIII, No. 5 (December, 1913), pp. 426-429.
21. Edwin D. Starbuck, "The Intimate Senses As
Sources of Wisdom," Journal of Religion, I, No. 2
(March, 1921), pp. 129-145.

22. Ibid., p. 134.

23. Edwin D. Starbuck, "What Can Religious Education Do With Human Nature?", Religious Education,
XVIII, No. 2 (April, 1923), pp. 72-77.

24. Edwin D. Starbuck, "Fundamentals of Character
Training," National Education Association, Addresses
and Proceedings of the Sixty-Second Annual Meeting
(Washington, D. C., June 29-July 4, 1924), LXII (1924),
pp. 159-165. This address was reprinted as an article
in School and Society, XX, No. 500 (July 26, 1924),
pp. 97-101. Page references are to this latter article.

25. School and Society, p. 97.

26. Ibid., pp. 97-101.

27. Edwin D. Starbuck, "Tests and Measurements of
Character," National Education Association, Addresses
and Proceedings of the Sixty-Second Annual Meeting
(Washington, D.C., June 29-July 4, 1924), LXII, (1924),
pp. 357-361. This is later reproduced as an article
by Starbuck: "Methods of A Science of Character,"
Religious Education, XXII, No. 7 (September, 1927),
pp. 715-719. Starbuck had delivered this, also, as an
address on January 20, 1927 before the Third Annual
Conference on Character Education at Indianapolis.

28. Edwin D. Starbuck, "Character Training in the
Public Schools," Washington Education Journal, IV,
No. 5 (January, 1925), pp. 141-143, 157.

29. Edwin D. Starbuck, "Some Fundamental Principles
Underlying Religious Education," Proceedings of the
Sixth Annual Session of the Ohio State Educational Con-
ference, (April, 1926), pp. 417-425.

30. "The Challenging in the Life of A Child--
Abridged," National Education Association, Proceedings
of the Sixty-fourth Annual Meeting, LXIV (Philadelphia,
Penn., June 27-July 2, 1926), pp. 147-152.

31. Ibid., pp. 147-148.

32. Starbuck, ed., University of Iowa Studies in
Character. For a complete listing of the monographs
in each volume, as well as a general discussion of the
contents, see Chapter III.

33. Edwin D. Starbuck, assisted by Frank K. Shuttle-
worth, et al., A Guide to Literature for Training: Vol.
I Fairy Tale, Myth, and Legend (New York: Macmillan
Co., 1928).

34. Edwin D. Starbuck, et al., A Guide to Books for
Character: Volume II Fiction (New York: Macmillan
Co., 1930).

35. The Wonder Road: Book I: Familiar Haunts, Fairy Tales Selected by Edwin Diller Starbuck, and assistants; Book II: Enchanted Paths, Fairy Tales Selected by Edwin Diller Starbuck and Frank K. Shuttleworth, and assistants; Book III: Far Horizons, Fairy Tales Selected by Edwin Diller Starbuck and Frank K. Shuttleworth, and assistants (3 vols.; New York: Macmillan Co., 1930). See Chapter III for further discussion of this series.

36. Living Through Biography, selected and edited by Edwin Diller Starbuck and Staff, Volume I: The High Trail; Volume II: Actions Speak; Volume III: Real Persons. (3 vols.; Yonkers-On-Hudson, New York: World Book Co., 1936). See Chapter III for further discussion of this series.

37. Four of the more significant pieces, which represent most broadly Starbuck's thinking at this time, are to be especially noted. They are: Edwin D. Starbuck, "Character Rating," Child Study, IX, No. 1 (September, 1931), pp. 12-14; Edwin D. Starbuck, "Symbols in the Development of Personality," Chap. I in Life-A Symbol, by Maurice H. Farbridge (Manchester: Sherratt and Hughes, 1931). Edwin D. Starbuck, "The Human Animal That Thinks It Thinks," College of the Pacific Publications in Philosophy, Paul Arthur Schlipp, ed. I (Stockton, Calif.: College of the Pacific, 1932); Edwin D. Starbuck, "The Deeper-Lying Centers of Personality," (An address given December 14, 1934, before the Tenth Annual Indiana State Conference on Supervised Student Teaching - Central Normal College, Danville, Indiana), in Look To This Day, 1945, pp. 61-84.

38. Edwin D. Starbuck, "Psychology of Religion," Encyclopedia of Educational Research, Walter S. Monroe, ed. (New York: Macmillan Co., 1941), pp. 865-869.

39. Look To This Day: Selected Writings by Edwin Diller Starbuck, Assembled and Edited by the Staff of the Institute of Character Research (The University of Southern California Press, 1945).

40. Starbuck, The Psychology of Religion, p. 11.

41. Ibid., p. 10.

42. Edwin D. Starbuck, "Professor Starbuck's Summary," Religious Education, XXII, No. 5 (May, 1927), p. 451.

43. See Chapter V "Character Tests and Measurements," Bureau of Education Bulletin, Report of the Committee on Character Education of the National Edu-

cation Association, No. 7 (Washington, D. C., 1926), pp. 35-48, for an example of Starbuck's involvement. He chaired the committee and submitted the Report of the subcommittee on Character Tests and Measurements, which described the progress made to the end of the first quarter of the century in the scientific study of character and character education, and also introduced selectively the literature in the field.

44. Edwin D. Starbuck, "Methods of a Science of Character," Religious Education, XXII, No. 7 (September, 1927), p. 719.

45. Edwin D. Starbuck, "The Forward Look in Philosophy," (An address before the Free Religious Association of America, at its Forty-Sixth Annual Convention and Festival, Boston, May 23, 1913), in Look To This Day, p. 46.

46. Starbuck, "The Forward Look in Philosophy," p. 48.

47. Edwin D. Starbuck, "The Sources of Aesthetic Appreciation," in Look To This Day, 1945, p. 306.

48. Starbuck, "The Deeper Lying Centers of Personality," p. 63.

49. Edwin D. Starbuck, Chapter XVII, "Summary," in Interpretation of Physical Education: Volume III Character Education Through Physical Education, J. B. Nash, ed: (New York: A. S. Barnes & Co., Inc., 1932), p. 92.

50. Edwin D. Starbuck, "New Techniques for Judging Literature," The English Journal, College Edition, XXIV, No. 5 (May, 1935), p. 402. The official organ of the National Council of Teachers of English.

51. Starbuck, "Intuitionalism," Encyclopedia of Religion and Ethics, p. 397.

52. Starbuck, "The Forward Look in Philosophy," p. 50.

53. Starbuck, "Intuitionalism," p. 399.

54. Starbuck, "The Feelings and Their Place in Religion," p. 172.

55. Edwin Diller Starbuck, "Reinforcement to the Pulpit from Modern Psychology, Part I. Psychological Predestination," The Homiletic Review, Volume LII, No. 3 (September, 1906), p. 169.

56. Starbuck, "The Feelings and Their Place in Religion," p. 185.

57. Ibid., p. 186.

58. Ibid., p. 185.

59. Starbuck, "The Foundations of Religion and Morality," p. 249.

60. Edwin D. Starbuck, "A New World and Its Values," College Bulletin, V, No. 3 (September, 1912), in Look To This Day, p. 381. Quoted from the latter reference. A commencement address delivered at the Florida State College for Women, Tallahassee, Florida, May 30, 1912.

61. Ibid., p. 380.

62. Edwin D. Starbuck, "Religious Education in the New World-View," Bulletin of the Department of Religious Education, No. 2 (Boston: Beacon Press, 1913), p. 1.

63. Ibid., pp. 7-8.

64. Edwin D. Starbuck, "The Cultural Equivalent of Religion in the Secondary School Program," State of California Department of Education Bulletin, Proceedings of the Annual Convention of Secondary School Principles of California, No. 12 (June 15, 1932), pp. 36-39.

65. Ibid., pp. 35-36.

66. Starbuck, "The Foundations of Religion and Morality," pp. 247 and 246; cf. Moral Training in the Public Schools, pp. 103 and 94, respectively.

67. See Appendix C for a list of the questions asked in this main form. It should be added that Starbuck used 1265 cases in studying the age of conversion. See Appendix D for the question list sent to these persons.

68. Edwin D. Starbuck, "An Untried Way of Human Improvement," Look To This Day, 1945, p. 197.

69. Edwin D. Starbuck, "Medicated Morals," Look To This Day, p. 125.

70. Edwin D. Starbuck, "Home Influences in the Development of Character," Bulletin Ohio State Educational Conference, XXXI, No. 2 (August 15, 1926), p. 388.

71. Ibid., p. 382.

72. Starbuck, Character Education Methods, pp. 1-3.

73. Ibid., pp. 4-5.

74. Ibid., p. 6.

75. Ibid., pp. 9-12.

76. Ibid., pp. 14-16.

77. Ibid., pp. 17-23.

78. Ibid., pp. 25-27.

79. Ibid., pp. 29-32. It should be noted that only a moral curriculum for grade four was charted in this project as a type; however, the intention of the colla-borators was to eventually finish charts for all the grades. This effort was never completed.

80. Ibid., Chapters VII, IX, X, and XI.

81. Starbuck, Character Education Methods, p. 36.

82. Starbuck, "New Techniques for Judging Litera-ture," p. 397.

83. Starbuck, Childhood and Character, p. 7.

84. University of Iowa Service Bulletin, X, No. 20, (May 15, 1926), p. 5.

85. Starbuck, A Guide to Literature for Character Training, pp. 29-30. For a detailed analysis of the trustworthiness of the Guide, see Chapter IV, pp. 29-36, in Volume I, and Chapter V, pp. 41-46, in Volume II.

86. A Guide To Books for Character, An informa-tional monograph promoting the use of Volume I: Fairy Tale, Myth, and Legend, and Volume II: Fiction. In-cluded are quotes of educators throughout the country who are responding to the volumes. This monograph is in the possession of the present writer.

87. Ernest A. Baker and James Packman, A Guide to the Best Fiction (New York: Macmillan Co., 1932), p. V.

88. Starbuck, A Guide to Literature for Character Training, pp. 5-7.

89. Ibid., p. 13.

90. Ibid., pp. 30-36.

91. Starbuck, A Guide to Books for Character, p. 46.

92. Ibid., p. 3.

93. Ibid., p. 9.

94. Ibid., p. 11.

95. Edwin D. Starbuck, Ed., University of Iowa Studies in Character, (4 Volumes; Iowa City: University of Iowa, 1927-31).

96. Ibid., Volume I., p. 3.

97. University of Iowa Service Bulletin, XIII, No. 6 (February 11, 1928), p. 4.

98. Studies in Character, Volume I; Nos. 2 and 4 respectively.

99. Studies of Character, Volume II: Nos. 2 and 3 respectively.

100. Ibid., No. 1.

101. Ibid., No. 4.

102. <u>Studies in Character</u>, Volume III, Nos. 2 and 3 respectively.
103. <u>Studies in Character</u>, Volume I; No. 3.
104. <u>Studies in Character</u>, Volume II; No. 1, p. 4.
105. <u>Ibid</u>., No. 2, p. 3.
106. <u>Ibid</u>., No. 4, p. 3.
107. <u>Studies in Character</u>, Volume III: No. 3, p. 3.
108. <u>The Wonder Road</u>: Book I: <u>Familiar Haunts</u>; Book II: <u>Enchanted Paths</u>; Book III: <u>Far Horizons</u>.
109. Letter received from Dr. Lonzo Jones, March 3, 1969.
110. <u>Living Through Biography</u>, Volume I: <u>The High Trail</u>; selected and edited by Edwin Diller Starbuck and staff, World Book Company: Yonkers-On-Hudson, New York, 1936: Volume I: <u>The High Trail</u>; Volume II: <u>Actions Speak</u>; Volume III: <u>Real Persons</u>.
111. Promotional brochure put out by the World Book Company, entitled <u>Living Through Biography</u>. This is in the possession of the present author.

CHAPTER V

SUMMARY AND CONCLUSION

This study of Edwin Diller Starbuck's life and career has demonstrated the general nature of his pioneering efforts in the psychology of religion, and his contribution to the related fields of religious education and character education. Every effort has been made to treat, as objectively as possible, his life and work for the sake of portraying Starbuck, the man, whose failures, along with his accomplishments, cannot be ignored. It is clear that several of the major projects to which Starbuck devoted so much of his time were never fully realized. In Starbuck there fused the hopes of Idealism and the realities of Pragmatism. Thus, he faced squarely the practical problems in particular, of his involvement in education, but always with a dream in mind, a vision of creating a new generation of free but responsible citizens of the world. And, along the way, in spite of his failure to perpetuate many of the practical programs with which he was associated, his influence was keenly felt, as a teacher in the classroom, as a scholarly author and editor, as a widely traveled educator and lecturer, as a consultant in the religious education field, as the director of two research centers in character education, and throughout his career, as a psychologist/philosopher passionately interested in the study of religion, or the concomitant field of character development, and the application of the data to the ends of sound education.

In Chapter I various approaches to the psychology of religion were discussed, including Starbuck's own definition of the psychology of religion, thus setting it apart from more inclusive views which would implicate the beginnings of the field to be much earlier than the latter part of the nineteenth century. It is evident that the psychology of religion, as Starbuck defined it, approaching inductively the phenomena of religion in individual experience, thus ascertaining with some sense of prediction the laws operating in religious growth, has not emerged prior to Starbuck's own day. He is to be numbered among the few early pioneers who brought this field, as so defined, into

261

existence. It is made clear, too, that Starbuck's approach to the psychology of religion is not to be isolated from his interests in religious education and moral culture, thus indicating, as had been suspected, a direct relationship between his early work in the psychology of religion and his later work in character education.

For the sake of analysis, Starbuck's place and general involvement in the field was divided into three areas: (1) the psychology of religion, (2) religious education, and, (3) character education. The fact that Starbuck's early work, The Psychology of Religion, was almost universally cited in major pioneering works in the field indicates something of the impact his work had in this area. Important, too, was the fact that Starbuck had been the first to initiate an empirical study of individual religious consciousness, whose content and general form or methodology was repeated later by other leading pioneers in the field. Although James Leuba's article on "Studies in the Psychology of Religious Phenomena-Conversion" had pre-dated, by one year, the 1897 publication of Starbuck's two articles which were the foundational core for his 1899 classic, it was established that Starbuck's research began earlier than Leuba's. In fact, Starbuck's work had been initiated at Harvard prior to his move to Clark University where Leuba was a fellow graduate student who had been influenced, as were other students at Clark, by Starbuck's unique research. In keeping with the pioneering spirit of this important work, Starbuck offered for the first time, in 1897, a college course in the psychology of religion. Within a decade and a half over fifty colleges and universities were offering a similar course. Today, there is unlikely a single theological institution which does not offer some type of course in this field.

Starbuck's contribution to the related area of religious education is also notable. His participation, as a speaker, in the early national conventions of the Religious Education Association indicates his reputation as an innovative voice in the field. He lectured widely, responding to numerous invitations to speak at various conferences, throughout the country, dealing with the problems of religious education. The impact of his thought, as expressed in rather frequent articles in some of the key journals of the field, also, cannot go unnoticed. Finally, Starbuck's work with the Unitarian Association as a consulting psychologist and director of the development of a new, and one of the first graded, curriculums in religious education, during a sabbatical leave from the University of Iowa, marks the practical interests he had in the implications of his study of religion for education. The fact that his approach to this curriculum revision was largely child-centered, or oriented to life situations rather than doctrine, a relatively new idea in the field, supplies partial understanding as to why the work was never completed for a religious association, which though liberal as compared to other denominations, was still governed by members with a more traditional outlook. Still, some of the basic principles of religious education, for which Starbuck stood so early, such as the idea that the curriculum must be geared to the needs and interests of the various age levels, and that religious education has for its main objective the development of the individual, rather than the promulgation of a particular dogma, have been adopted in the work of religious education today, though, in some instances, not without extended battle.

Finally, Starbuck's affiliation with the movement of character education must also be underscored. It is evident that his work in this area was not foreign to his interests in the psychology of religion. Within the first decade of his professorial career Starbuck produced an essay on "Moral Training in the Public Schools," which won third place in a national contest, and was published in a book by the same title, designed, particularly, to provide direction for the programs of moral education in the public school system, as well as general guidance for parents, clergy, and others interested in the subject.

Not until the twenties, however, were Starbuck's major contributions in the field made. Most notable was his chairmanship of the Iowa Committee which won a nation-wide contest in 1921 for submitting the best judged plan in methods of character education for the public schools. With this event a national reputation was established for Starbuck in this field. Also, as a result of this event, Starbuck was moved to create a Research Station, later called an Institute in Character Education, at Iowa, the first and only one of its kind officially connected with a state university. With a competent staff, Starbuck used the facilities of the Institute, while at Iowa, to develop two volumes, A Guide to Literature for Character Training, and A Guide to Books for Character, reading lists for children, the first of their kind, and the most exhaustive attempt, to this day, to take into consideration the role of literature in character education. During this decade Starbuck also edited a significant series of four volumes, Studies in Character, the product of graduate studies in the field under Starbuck's direct supervision. Starbuck carried on his work in character education after his move to the University of Southern California in 1930, though, now at retirement age, with considerably less vigor.

Aside from Starbuck's own autobiographical sketch in Vergilius Ferm's Religion in Transition, no systematic assessment of Starbuck's life and career had been made until this study. Chapters II and III attempt to provide an informative biographical perspective. In Chapter II his personal life has been approached by way of examining his family background, education background, religious orientation, and personal background. Starbuck's ancestry, in this country, was traced to one of the "First Purchasers" of Nantucket Island, an island of hearty whalers and devout religionists. Starbuck's own parents were Quakers, who raised their family in the gentle and sincere manner of that tradition. Starbuck's own values, both ethically and religiously, were subtly shaped by this heritage, the vestiges of which remained with him the rest of his life.

Against this pietistic backdrop of Starbuck's earlier life, the ensuing years of his educational pursuit stand out in stark contrast. At the University of Indiana, where he earned his undergraduate degree, Starbuck found a "storm-centre" of what he called "New Thinking." During these years, a reconstruction occurred, which would point Starbuck in more liberal directions academically and religiously.

After graduating, with a major in philosophy, Starbuck was introduced to the teaching profession, taking positions first at Spiceland Academy and then at Vincennes University. Shortly, though, Starbuck returned to the ranks of student life, in graduate work, earning an M.A. degree at Harvard and his Ph.D. at Clark University. Starbuck chose Harvard because of its unique program for those interested in the integrated study of religion, philosophy, and psychology. At Harvard he began his classical study of conversion. When he learned of a particularly open program at Clark University, geared specifically to the pursuit of the psychology of religion, Starbuck, upon receiving a fellowship, moved to Clark University, where he completed his study and received the Ph.D. in 1897.

The nature of Starbuck's religious orientation was uncommonly broad, ranging from his "birthright" membership in the Society of Friends to his official position in the American Unitarian Association. Although his passion for religious study, and his interests in the cultivation of the religious life, never waned; in time, his disillusionment with the institutional church emerged. Still, his view of religion as man's entire response to reality, and the subsequent shaping of values it gives to all of life, continued to form, throughout his lifetime, the foundation for his personal and vocational striving. The direct influence of his religious background upon so many of his basic convictions and commitments has been made quite clearly evident in this study. Finally, primarily through the use of information supplied by interviews or correspondence with Starbuck's relatives, colleagues, students, friends and, in some cases, critics, an additional, and hopefully valuable, image of Starbuck's personal life and professional career has been presented. This included consideration of his physical, intellectual and psychological characteristics, as well as an assessment of his worth as a scholar and professor, and an intimate description of his own marriage and family life.

Chapter III has pursued chronologically the continuity of Starbuck's career, establishing the extent of his pioneering efforts, and analyzing the successes and failures involved. The details of his career have been divided into three basic blocks of time: the beginning of his career, from his first appointment in 1897 as Assistant Professor of Education at Leland Stanford Junior University to the end of his two year directorship of a new school of education at Earlham College in 1906; his career while at the University of Iowa, from 1906 to 1930; and his career while at the University of Southern California from 1930 until his retirement in 1943. A description of the general flow of his career during these periods has been presented, as well as an analysis of the major projects to which he devoted himself.

It is clear that Starbuck did not initiate the psychology of religion, as it has been defined in this study, alone. But his work, particularly the study of conversion and religious growth, can be numbered among the few most influential inducements towards the birth of other studies in the developing field. And he was the first to offer an official course in the psychology of religion at the college level.

Starbuck's pioneering efforts in the related area of character education were also demonstrated. Although Starbuck was the first to offer a college course in character education, his most concerted efforts in the field did not occur until the twenties. It was shown that winning the award, in 1921, for the best plan in character education methods submitted throughout the country, was a dividing point in Starbuck's career. From that time on, Starbuck's commitments were largely related to the problems of character education and development. His research centers, or Institutes, in character education, and his ambitious program for objectively judging the worth of literature for character training, were two of the major projects most indicative of the products of his vision. Unfortunately, his plans, in particular, for supplemental reading lists and readers, oriented to the development of character in the public schools, were never fully realized. An interpretation was made of the evidence accrued which offers several probable explanations for this latter failure.

In Chapter IV Starbuck's significant contributions were examined. His writings have been analyzed both from a chronological and thematic perspective, bearing in mind the extent to which certain items could be judged as pioneering contributions. The chronological survey has been divided into three phases: 1897-1906, 1907-1921, and 1922-1945. In each case, it has been possible to cite a specific publication of Starbuck's which initiates the phase by symbolizing the general direction subsequent publications would take during that period. The first phase was characterized primarily by Starbuck's initial pioneering endeavors and interests in the psychology of religion. The second phase was marked by Starbuck's growing interests in both religious education and character education. In the final phase, Starbuck's interests are restricted almost completely to the problems of character development and education. It has been possible to obtain an overview of the general movement of his thought and interests through the years by surveying, as we have, in chronological order, the content of his major publications.

Fundamental to a major portion of Starbuck's work were three broad recurring themes: (1) his unwavering interest in the empirical approach to the study of religion and character, (2) his recitation of the affection/cognition equation, and (3) his identification of religion and morality. From the very beginning Starbuck has been interested in the science of religion. He attempted to hold the rational and emotional dimensions of religion together through a scientific analysis of religious experience. His classical study which incorporated the tools of empirical methodology, set the stage for recommending the application of the scientific approach to other studies in religion. He was equally concerned that there be an adoption of disciplined research in the areas of religious education and character education, as was indicated, particularly, in the latter area, by his direction of several empirically oriented projects.

This first underlying theme of the splendor of science, however, was held in balance by his second basic theme regarding the relation of reason and emotion. Starbuck's contention was that the rational elements of man's life had been judged more worthy than the emotional factors. Consequently, he sought to raise, in particular, the place of affection in the

267

equation. His stress on the importance of feelings affected directly his approach to religion and education.

What today many contemporary educators and scholars are heralding with a sense of new insight and discovery, Starbuck sought to implement, though often with little wide-range success, over fifty years ago. Starbuck's commitment to the education of persons who must learn to feel and act as well as think has recently experienced rebirth. Charles E. Silberman, for example, in speaking of the purpose of education, declared himself wrong in considering, until recently, the aim of education to be intellectual development. He wrote, "What tomorrow needs is not masses of intellectuals, but masses of educated men--men educated to feel and to act as well as to think."[1] The words, let alone the idea, only seem to echo Starbuck's own philosophy of education.

In Starbuck, one discovers a blending of the mystic and the scientist, or perhaps, it might be said, the delicate integration of pietism and rationalism. His seeming paradoxical approach to so many issues, as illustrated by his promotion of intellectual objectivity through the application of empirical research to such a discipline as religion, while simultaneously challenging the dominance of cognition over affection in human living, can be most fully appreciated only when the nature of his background, as has been presented, is understood.

The third central theme demonstrated Starbuck's conception of the interrelationship of religion and morality, and consequently supported, as valid, our assertion of the continuity between Starbuck's early work in the psychology of religion, proper, and his later work in character education. It is evident that Starbuck meant essentially the same thing by religion and morality, or religious education and character education. Thus, in essense, Starbuck's pioneering work in the psychology of religion cannot finally be disassociated from his extended work in religious education and character education.

Clearly, Starbuck's contributions, in both written

and project form, reveal a passionate exploration into the jungle of religious and educational philosophy. But the questions regarding the nature and purpose of religion and education were not merely academic to him. He searched for concrete answers, and when he discovered them, as tentative and imperfect as he may have realized they were, he moved to establish their practical significance for the educational enterprise.

Had Starbuck been blessed with unlimited funds, enabling him to carry his dream of a supplemental moral curriculum for the public schools to completion, perhaps his work might have been more widely used. As it was, with limited funds, and minimal staff assistance, the laborious work of assessing literature for that purpose never produced enough of the curriculum to reveal a comprehensive picture of its benefits.

Starbuck cannot be considered a pioneer, in the sense of being the first and only forerunner in a particular field; but his pioneering efforts can, without question, be numbered among the few earliest enterprises in the development of the psychology of religion, specifically as they pertain to the study of religious experience, religious education, and character research and education. In this sense, he was a pioneer, ever moving in untried ways to discover truths that would be beneficial to the development of a better society, which was his dream.

NOTES

1. Charles E. Silberman, <u>Crisis in the Classroom:
The Remaking of American Education</u> (New York: Vintage
Books, 1970), p. 7.

APPENDIX A

SELECTED SURVEYS OF THE LITERATURE

For the best general surveys, see: David Henry Bremer, George Albert Coe's Contribution to the Psychology of Religion, 1949, (Unpublished Ph.D. Thesis, Boston University). Provides the most thorough survey and extensive bibliography in the field up to 1949. One of Bremer's major contributions is his discussion of the work of Coe's contemporaries in the psychology of religion, which in turn are contemporaries of Starbuck; James Bissett Pratt, "The Psychology of Religion," Harvard Theological Review, I, No. 4 (October, 1908), pp. 435-454. The first definitive survey of the psychology of religion. Being not far removed from the state of affairs, Pratt's description of the new science at the turn of the century is generally valuable; Orlo Strunk, Jr., "The Psychology of Religion: An Historical and Contemporary Survey." Psychological Newsletter, IX (1958), pp. 181-199. Placed the literature within delineated periods in the field, the "Pioneer period," from the 1880's to about 1930, and the "period of application," from 1930 through the 1950's; Orlo Strunk, Jr., ed. Readings in the Psychology of Religion (New York: Abingdon Press, 1959). See especially Chapter I, pp. 17-111, for a relatively comprehensive overview not only of the events but the literature as well. The best single-volume selection available of both classical and contemporary literature in the field.

For generally more limited surveys which attempt to bring an original classification or interpretation to the literature see: Edward L. Schaub's three articles surveying the development and status of the psychology of religion near the end of the first quarter of the twentieth century: "The Present Status of the Psychology of Religion," The Journal of Religion, II (July, 1922), pp. 362-379; "The Psychology of Religion in America During the Past Quarter-Century," The Journal of Religion, VI, No. 2 (March, 1926), pp. 113-134; "The Psychology of Religion,

(Limited to a part of the field)," The Psychological
Bulletin, XXIII, No. 12 (December, 1926), pp. 681-700.
Of special significance to our study is the second
article which discusses the primary role that America
plays in the development of studies in the psychology
of religion during the first quarter of the century.
Schaub points out that the psychology of religion in
America is still characterized abroad by an approach
to the study through the use of questionaires and biographical materials, and that Starbuck is to be mainly
credited for the former; David M. Trout, Religious
Behavior: An Introduction to the Psychological Study
of Religion (New York: Macmillan Co., 1931). A classical division of the field into decades, 1901-1910,
1911-1920, and 1921-1930, with references to the literature being made in the context of the highlights
of these decades; Vergilius Ferm, "The Psychology of
Religious Experience," First Adventures in Philosophy
(New York: Charles Scribner's Sons, 1936). Selectively surveys the psychology of religion in terms of the
methods used to secure the data for the field; Edwin
Diller Starbuck, "Psychology of Religion," Encyclopedia of Educational Research, Walter S. Monroe, ed.
(University of Illinois, 1941), pp. 865-869. The most
extensive consideration of the variety of methods used
in the field with an attempt to classify the literature accordingly. It should be noted, perhaps as an
indication of the general disappearance by this time of
the original momentum in the psychological study of
religion, that this particular article on the subject
of the psychology of religion was deleted from the
1950 edition of this encyclopedia; Vergilius Ferm, A
Dictionary of Pastoral Psychology (New York: Philosophical Library, 1955). A limited survey of the more
important works, although the article is valuable
especially for its insight into the impetus for the
therapeutic phase of religious psychology; Vergilius
Ferm, "The Psychology of Religion," Present Day Psychology, A. A. Roback, ed. (New York: Philosophical
Library, 1955), pp. 961-972. Classifies the literature and attempts to provide some reasons for the difficult times the field has encountered.

APPENDIX B

SELECTED DEVELOPMENTAL SURVEYS

For a brief historical survey of the development of the classical period by the pioneers themselves see: Edwin Diller Starbuck, The Psychology of Religion: An Empirical Study of the Growth of the Religious Consciousness (London: The Walter Scott Publishing Co., LTD. New York: Charles Scribner's Sons, 1899); James Bissett Pratt, The Psychology of Religious Belief (New York: Macmillan Co., 1907); Edward Scribner Ames, The Psychology of Religious Experience (Boston: Houghton Mifflin, 1910); George Albert Coe, The Psychology of Religion (Chicago: University of Chicago Press, 1916). Of these classical works, Coe's volume, by far, offers the most comprehensive bibliography, containing both an "Alphabetical Bibliography," by authors, pp. 327-345, and a "Topical Bibliography," pp. 346-355.

Of more recent origin are the following publications, which, though removed in time from the classical period in the field, during the first two decades of this century, offer in many ways a more seasoned perspective of the field: Vergilius Ferm, ed., Religion in Transition (London: George Allen & Unwin, 1937). The historical surveys in this book are in the form of autobiographical sketches by Edwin D. Starbuck, George A. Coe, and James H. Leuba. Ferm chose these three as representative pioneers in the psychology of religion, asking them to reflect upon the field as they were involved personally in its development, and to express some envisionment of its future. These are especially valuable resources in terms of surveying the literature as produced by the pioneers in the field, but we are given also a glimpse of the literature which influenced the pioneers as well; Karl R. Stolz, The Psychology of Religious Living (Nashville: Cokesbury Press, 1937). Though basically an apologetic work, designed to promote the use of psychological principles for religious purposes, Stolz includes an historical analysis of the emergence and development of the psychology of religion. In this chapter he discusses the place of

273

seven select pioneers in the field, among whom Starbuck is considered first; Charles F. Kemp, Physicians of the Soul: A History of Pastoral Counseling (New York: Macmillan Co., 1947). Kemp includes a chapter on "Pastoral Theology and the Psychology of Religion," which presents a brief historical perspective of the studies in the psychology of religion, including its relationship to pastoral psychology; Walter Houston Clark, The Psychology of Religion (New York: Macmillan Co., 1958). A revised and enlarged edition of a work first introduced in 1945. Written in light of the recent neglect of the psychology of religion, and in response to the need for a comprehensive up-to-date treatment of the field, Clark's text introduces the reader to the most important works and theorists in the field. In Chapter 1, Clark presents a history of the psychology of religion, surveying the major works produced during its development; Paul E. Johnson, Psychology of Religion (Revised and Enlarged, New York: Abingdon Press, 1959). Probably one of the most popular and useful treatments of the field, this book has been used widely as a college text. With an awareness of the development which has occurred since his first edition in 1945, and confessing changes in his own position since that time, Johnson has undertaken a major rewriting of a new psychology of religion. A rather thorough coverage of the literature is made in the context of traditional chapter headings. The first chapter deals specifically with an historical approach to the field. In comparison to other pioneers, Starbuck is given sizeable space in the relatively brief chapter; G. Stephen Spinks, Psychology and Religion (London: Methuen and Co. LTD, 1963). Wayne E. Oates, The Psychology of Religion (Waco, Texas: Word Books, 1973), Geoffrey E. W. Scobie, Psychology of Religion (New York: John Wiley and Sons, 1975), and H. Newton Malony, ed., Current Perspectives in the Psychology of Religion (Grand Rapids: Eerdman's Publishing Company, 1977). The most recent comprehensive treatments of the field, especially with regard to contemporary views.

For works which schematically classify or interpret the development of the field see the following: David M. Trout, Religious Behavior and Charles F. Kemp, Physicians of the Soul. Although these two volumes have been cited elsewhere they are included here by virtue of their classification of the growth

of the field into decades; Orlo Strunk, Jr., "The
Present Status of the Psychology of Religion." The
Journal of Bible and Religion, XXV, No. 4 (October,
1957), pp. 287-292. A brief but insightful article
dealing with three specific forces which Strunk
believes affected significantly the development of
the psychology of religion--the theological, the
psychoanalytical, and the psychological, in the form
of behaviorism. Instead of assisting in its developments, Strunk contends these forces affected the
field adversely. He attempts to offer some explanation for such an occurence, and lists four possibilities which lay before the field. He considers that
if the psychology of religion is to have a viable
future it must choose to redefine itself in terms of
the purposes of the earlier pioneers in the field
who viewed the psychology of religion as a branch of
general psychology; Orlo Strunk, Jr., "The Psychology of Religion: An Historical and Contemporary Survey," Psychological Newsletter, IX (1958), pp. 181-
199. Strunk's scheme simply divides the historical
development of the field into two major stages, the
"pioneer period" and the "period of application."
He thought of the former period as ending around
1930, and the latter period as applying to the development since 1930. Of special interest in this
study is Strunk's five year survey or research in
the field, which, although done at mid-century,
1950-54, would appear, at least by casual observation, to differ very little from the present situation. Strunk lists fifteen trends in the psychological study of religion during this period which reveal the shift which has occurred in the psychology
of religion, from its inception in Starbuck's day,
through his lifetime, and to a period just following
his death in 1947. Strunk's interpretation is that,
in general, the psychology of religion, as originally
understood by the pioneers in the field, had become
practically extinct; Seward Hiltner, "The Psychological Understanding of Religion," Crozer Quarterly,
XXIV, No. 1 (January, 1947), pp. 3-36. One of the
most thorough and perceptive analyses of the development of the psychology of religion. He interprets
the growth of the field in terms of varying foci
which were different from the original thrust of the

classical works, but still considers that these new foci have contributed to our psychological understanding of religion. He classifies these developments in terms of the main stream of "imitators" who follow the pattern of the original pioneers, the philosophical stream, which attempts to answer the question of religious validity or truth, the normative stream, which concerns itself with the educational implications of its studies, particularly as they pertain to religious education, the natural science stream, with a special concern for the scientific method, and the therapeutic or dynamic stream, which seeks to meet effectively the practical and clinical problems being faced.

Hiltner calls for a renewal of the efforts toward a better psychological understanding of religion, acknowledging that the original thrust of the psychology of religion which emerged when natural science was enjoying commanding attention has practically disappeared. According to Hiltner, it is clearly evident that the interests in the psychological understanding of religion have been kept alive mainly by the practical concerns of the pastoral and educational group. While contending that the most fruitful approach to the psychology of religion is by way of the practical field, in fact, particularly in terms of the therapeutic area, he concedes that the psychological understanding of religion has a significant and essential contribution to make to the theological enterprise and the philosophy of religion.

Finally, a more recent analysis: Benjamin Beit-Hallahmi, "Psychology of Religion 1880-1930: The Rise and Fall of a Psychological Movement, "Journal of The History of the Behavioral Sciences, 10 (January, 1974), pp. 84-90. A brief but important interpretative statement on both the rise and decline of the movement.

APPENDIX C

GENERAL QUESTIONNAIRE ON CONVERSION

I. What religious customs did you observe in childhood, and with what likes and dislikes? In what ways were you brought to a condition to need an awakening:--faulty teaching, bad associations, appetites, passions, etc.? What were the chief temptations of your youth? How were they felt, and how did you strive to resist? What errors and struggles have you had with (a) lying and other dishonesty, (b) wrong appetites for foods and drinks, (c) vita sexualis; what relation have you noticed between this and moral and religious experience? (d) laziness, selfishness, jealousy, etc.?

II. What force and motive led you to seek a higher and better life:--fears, regrets, remorse, conviction for sin, example of others, influence of friends and surroundings, changes in belief or ideals, deliberate choice, external pressure, wish for approval of others, sense of duty, feeling of love, spontaneous awakening, divine impulse, etc.? What of these or other causes were most marked, and which were present at all?

III. Circumstances and experiences preceding conversion:--any sense of depression, smothering, fainting, loss of sleep and appetite, pensiveness, occupation disturbed, feeling of helplessness, prayer, calling for aid, estrangement from God, etc.? How long did it continue? Was there a tendency to resist conviction? How was it shown?

IV. How did relief come? Was it attended by unnatural sights, sounds, or feelings? In what did the change consist?--breaking pride, public confession, seeking the approval of others, feeling God's forgiveness, sudden awakening to some great truth, etc.? How sudden was the awakening?

Did the change come through, or in spite of, your own thought, deliberation and choice? What part of it was supernatural or miraculous?

V. Feelings and experiences after the crisis:--
sense of bodily lightness, weeping, laughing, joy,
sorrow, disappointment, signs of divine pleasure or
displeasure, etc. How differently did you feel towards
persons, nature, ideas, God, etc.? Did you have
unfulfilled expectations or disappointments?

VI. What changes did you find that conversion
had worked out in your life:--changes in health,
habits, motives, conduct, and in your general intellectual and emotional attitude? Did you undertake
any private religious acts, as Bible reading, meditation, acts of self-sacrifice, prayer, etc.?

VII. Were there any relapses from the first experiences? Were they permanent or temporary? Any
persistent doubts? What difficulties from habits,
pride, ridicule, or opposition of others etc., had
you, and what methods did you adopt? Do you still
have struggles in your nature? Does that indicate that
the change was not complete? How have you, and how
will you, overcome them? What needed helps, if any,
were wanting at any time?

VIII. Did you always find it easy to follow the
new life, and to fit into its customs and requirements?
If not, how did you succeed--by habit, pressure and
encouragement of friends, a new determination, a
sudden fresh awakening, etc.?

IX. State a few bottom truths embodying your own
deepest feelings. What would you now be and do if
you realized all your own ideals of the higher life?

X. What texts, hymns, sermons, deaths, places
and objects were connected with your deepest impressions? If your awakening came in revival meeting,
give the circumstances, and the methods used. What
do you think of revivals?

XI. If you have passed through a series of
beliefs and attitudes, mark out the stages of growth

278

and what you feel now to be the trend of your life.

Source: Edwin D. Starbuck, The Psychology of Religion: An Empirical Study of the Growth of Religious Consciousness (London: Walter Scott Publishing Co.; New York: Charles Scribner's Sons, 1899), pp. 22-24.

APPENDIX D

QUESTIONNAIRE ON AGE OF CONVERSION

(1) Age of conversion
(2) Age of most rapid bodily growth
(3) Age of accession to puberty

(4) Health--
     (a) Before conversion
     (b) At time of conversion
     (c) After conversion

(5) Conversion occurred at--
     (a) Camp meeting
     (b) Revival
     (c) Regular Church service
     (d) At home or alone

(6) Was the effect permanent

(7) If there was a relapse--
     (a) How soon after the conversion
     (b) How long did it continue

(8) Present Age
(9) Sex
(10) Church
(11) Vocation
(12) Nationality
(13) Resident of what State

Source: Edwin D. Starbuck, The Psychology of Religion: An Empirical Study of the Growth of Religious Consciousness (London: Walter Scott Publishing Co.; New York: Charles Scribner's Sons, 1899), p. 26.

STARBUCK'S WORKS

A. BOOKS

Look to This Day: Selected Writings by Edwin Diller
Starbuck. Assembled and edited by the Staff of
the Institute of Character Research. University
of Southern California: University of Southern
California Press, 1945.

The Psychology of Religion: An Empirical Study of
the Growth of Religious Consciousness. London:
Walter Scott Publishing Co., 1899.

University of Iowa Studies in Character. Volumes I -
IV. Edited by Edwin D. Starbuck. Iowa City:
University of Iowa, 1927-1931.

A Guide to Literature for Character Training, Volume
I: Fairy Tale, Myth, and Legend. Edited by
Edwin D. Starbuck, assisted by Shuttleworth,
Frank, et al. New York: Macmillan Co., 1928.

A Guide to Books for Character, Volume II: Fiction.
Edited by Edwin D. Starbuck, et al. New York:
Macmillan Co., 1930.

Character Education Methods: The Iowa Plan. Edwin D.
Starbuck, and Research collaborators. Washington,
D.C.: Capitol Press, 1922.

Living Through Biography, Volume I: The High Trail.
Edwin D. Starbuck, and staff, compilers. Yonkers-
On-Hudson, New York: World Book Co., 1936.

Living Through Biography, Volume II: Actions Speak.
Yonkers-On-Hudson, New York: World Book Co.,
1936.

Living Through Biography, Volume III: Real Persons.
Yonkers-On-Hudson, New York: World Book Co.,
1936.

The Wonder Road, Volume I: Familiar Haunts. New
York: Macmillan Co., 1930.

The Wonder Road, Volume II: Enchanted Paths. New
     York: Macmillan Co., 1930.

The Wonder Road, Volume III: Far Horizons. New
     York: Macmillan Co., 1930.

B. ARTICLES

"A Child-Centered Religious Education." Friend's
     Intelligence Supplement, October 3, 1914, pp.
     38-48.

"A Decalogue of Free Speech." Look To This Day.
     Assembled and edited by the Staff of the Insti-
     tute of Character Research. University of
     Southern California: University of Southern
     California Press (1945), 384.

"An Empirical Study of Mysticism." Proceedings of
     the Sixth International Congress of Philosophy,
     Cambridge, Mass., September 13-17, 1926, pp.
     87-94.

"A New World and Its Values." College Bulletin of
     the Florida State College for Women, V, No. 3,
     September, 1912.

"An Untried Way of Human Improvement." Look To This
     Day. Assembled and edited by the Staff of the
     Institute of Character Research. University of
     Southern California: University of Southern
     California Press (1945), 197-198.

"A Philosophical View of Character." Interpretation
     of Physical Education. Volume III Character
     Education Through Physical Education. Edited by
     J. B. Nash. New York: A. S. Barnes and Co.,
     1932.

"A Study of Conversion." American Journal of Psycho-
     logy, VIII, No. 2 (January, 1897), 268-308.

"Backsliding." Encyclopedia of Religion and Ethics,
     Volume II, 1910, pp. 319-321.

"Centralized Authority and Democracy in our Higher Institutions." Popular Science Monthly, LXXVII, No. 3 (September, 1910), 264-273.

"Character and Science." Journal of the National Education Association, XV, No. 7 (October, 1926). 213-214.

"Character Education Seen in Perspective." Proceedings of the Midwest Conference on Parent Education, Chicago, February, 1928, pp. 46-55.

"Character Rating." Child Study, IX, No. 1 (September, 1931), 12-14.

"Character Training in the Public School." Washington Education Journal, IV, No. 5 (January, 1925), 141-143, 157.

"Climate." Encyclopedia of Religion and Ethics, Volume III, 1911, pp. 693-694.

"Confessions of Faith in the R. E. A." Religious Education, XXIII, No. 7 (September, 1928), 616.

"Cultural and Character Values of Fiction." A Guide to Books for Character, Volume II. Edited by Edwin D. Starbuck, et al. New York: Macmillan Co., 1930.

"Development of the Psychology of Religion." Religious Education, VIII (1913), 426-429.

"Double-Mindedness." Encyclopedia of Religion and Ethics, Volume IV, 1912, pp. 860-862.

"Doubt." Encyclopedia of Religion and Ethics, Volume IV, 1912, pp. 863-865.

"Fairy Friendships." The Wimp and the Woodle, Suttonshouse LTD, 1935.

"Female Principle." Encyclopedia of Religion and Ethics, Volume V, 1913, pp. 827-833.

"Fundamentals of Character Training." National Education Association. Addresses and Proceedings of the Sixty-Second Annual Meeting, Washington, D.C., June 29 - July 4, 1924, pp. 159-165.

"G. Stanley Hall As A Psychologist." Psychological Review, XXXII, No. 2, 1925.

"Home Influences in the Development of Character." Bulletin Ohio State Educational Conference, XXXI, No. 2 (August 15, 1926), 380-389.

"Hopeful Lines of Development of the Psychology of Religion." Religious Education, VIII, No. 5 (December, 1913), 426-429.

"How Moral Are the Movies?" Cinema Progress, II, No. 4 (October, 1937), 15-17.

"How Shall We Deepen the Spiritual Life of the College?" Religious Education, IV (April, 1909), 83-89.

"India and the Cultural Traditions." The Cultural World, III, No. 2, June, 1932.

"Institute of Character Research." Research News, Los Angeles: University of Southern California, Graduate School, II, No. 1, January, 1936, p. 1.

"Intuitionalism." Encyclopedia of Religion and Ethics, Volume VII, 1915, pp. 397-400.

"Life and Confessions of G. Stanley Hall." Journal of Philosophy, XXI, No. 6 (March 13, 1924), 141-154.

"Medicated Morals." Look To This Day. Assembled and edited by the Staff of the Institute of Character Research. University of Southern California: University of Southern California Press (1945), 125-131.

"Methods of a Science of Character." Religious Education, XXII, No. 7 (September, 1927), 715-719.

"Moral Training in the Public Schools." Moral Training in the Public Schools, Boston: Ginn and Co., 1907, pp. 89-121.

"New Techniques for Judging Literature." The English Journal, College Edition, XXIV, No. 5 (May, 1935), 396-403.

"N.K.E.C. Program Lauded by Prominent Educator: Splendid Address Given by Edwin Starbuck, University of Iowa, On Occasion of Ground-Breaking for New College." Our Guidon, IV, No. 3 (September, 1935), 7-8.

"Old Age." Encyclopedia of Religion and Ethics, Volume IX, 1917, pp. 458-462.

"Philosophy Functioning in Life." Southern California Alumni Review Supplement, No. 8, December, 1930.

"Professor Starbuck's Summary." Religious Education, XXII, No. 5 (May, 1927), 451-452.

"Psychology of Religion." Encyclopedia of Educational Research. Edited by Walter S. Monroe. New York: Macmillan Co., 1941, pp. 865-869.

"Reenforcement to the Pulpit from Modern Psychology: Part I Psychological Predestination." Homiletic Review, LII, No. 3 (September, 1906), 168-172.

"Reenforcement to the Pulpit from Modern Psychology: Part II The Doctrine of Original Sin." Homiletic Review, LII, No. 6 (December, 1906), 418-423.

"Religion's Use of Me." Religion in Transition. Edited by Vergilius Ferm. London: George Allen & Unwin LTD., 1937.

"Religious Education as a Part of General Education." Religious Education Association. Proceedings of the First Annual Convention, Chicago, February, 10-12, 1903, pp. 52-59.

"Religious Education in the New World-View." Bulletin of the Department of Religious Education, No. 2 (1913), 1-19.

"Religious Psychology and Research Methods." Religious Education, XXIV (November, 1929), 874-876.

"Resume." Interpretation of Physical Education. Volume III: Character Education Through Physical Education. Edited by J. B. Nash. New York: A. S. Barnes and Co., Inc., 1932, pp. 270-273.

Review of The Spiritual Life, by George A. Coe. Psychological Review, VII, No. 6, November, 1900, pp. 615-616.

"Scope and Significance of the Fairy Tale." A Guide for Character Training. Volume I. Edited by Edwin D. Starbuck, et al. New York: Macmillan Co., 1928.

"Self-Expression." Encyclopedia of Religion and Ethics, Volume XI, 1921, pp. 357-359.

"Should the Impartation of Knowledge as such be a function of the Sunday School?" Religious Education, IV (December, 1910), 424-429.

"Significance of the Fairy Tale in Character Education." Religious Education, XXII, No. 10 (December, 1927), 1004-1007.

"Some Aspects of Religious Growth." American Journal of Psychology, IX, No. 1 (October, 1897), 70-124.

"Some Fundamental Principles Underlying Religious Education." Proceedings of Sixth Annual Session of Ohio State Education Conference, April, 1926, pp. 417-425.

"Some of the Fundamentals of Character Education." School and Society, XX, No. 500 (July 26, 1924), 97-101.

"Stages in Religious Growth." Part V. Biblical World, XXXI, No. 2 (February, 1908), 101-112.

"Studies in Character at the University of Iowa." Religious Education, XXII, No. 1 (January, 1927), 48-49.

"Summary." Interpretation of Physical Education. Volume III: Character Education Through Physical Education. Edited by J. B. Nash. New York: A. S. Barnes and Co., Inc., 1932, pp. 90-92

"Symbols in the Development of Personality." Life - A Symbol. By Maurice H. Farbridge. Manchester: Sherratt & Hughes, 1931, pp. 3-26.

"Ten Commandments." Look To This Day. Assembled and edited by the Staff of the Institute of Character Research. University of Southern California: University of Southern California Press (1945), 199.

"Tests and Measurements of Character." National Education Association. Addresses and Proceedings of the Sixty-Second Annual Meeting, LXII, Washington, D.C., June 29 - July 4, 1924, pp. 357-361.

"The ABC of Character Education." Address delivered December 14, 1934, before the Tenth Annual Indiana State Conference on Supervised Student Teaching, Central Normal College, Danville, Indiana. Look To This Day. Assembled and edited by the Staff of the Institute of Character Research. University of Southern California: University of Southern California Press (1945), 135-154.

"The Challenging Epochs in the Life of a Child - Abridged." National Education Association. Proceedings of the Sixty-Fourth Annual Meeting, LXIV, Philadelphia, Penn., June 27 - July 2, 1926, pp. 147-152.

"The Child-Consciousness and Human Progress." Part I.
Biblical World, XXX, No. 1 (July, 1907), 30-38.

"The Cultural Equivalent of Religion in the Secondary
School Program." State of California Department of Education Bulletin, No. 12 (June 15, 1932),
34-44.

"The Dance, Mother of the Arts." Educational Dance,
I, No. 1, May, 1938.

"The Deeper-Lying Centers of Personality." Address
given December 14, 1934, before the Tenth
Annual Indiana State Conference on Supervised
Student Teaching, Central Normal College, Danville,
Indiana. Look To This Day. Assembled and
edited by the Staff of the Institute of Character
Research. University of Southern California:
University of Southern California Press (1945),
61-84.

"The Development of Spirituality." Part IV. Biblical
World, XXX, No. 5 (November, 1907), 352-360.

"The Feelings and Their Place in Religion." American
Journal of Religious Psychology and Education,
I, No. 2 (November, 1904), 168-186.

"The Forward Look in Philosophy." Address before
the Free Religious Association of America, at
its Sixth Convention and Festival, May 23, 1913.
Look To This Day. Assembled and edited by the
Staff of the Institute of Character Research.
University of Southern California: University
of Southern California Press (1945), 45-50.

"The Foundations of Religion and Morality: How
Far, and How, can the Foundations of Religion
be Laid in the Common Schools?" Religious Education Association. Proceedings of the Third
Annual Convention, Boston, February 12-16, 1905,
pp. 245-250.

"The Good Life Becomes the Attractive One." California Journal of Secondary Education, XV, No. 5 (May, 1940), 268-272.

"The Home: The Growth of the Larger Sense of Social and Civic Responsibility in Youth." Religious Education Association. Proceedings of the Third Annual Convention, Boston, February 12-16, 1905, pp. 339-343.

"The Human Animal that Thinks it Thinks." College of the Pacific Publications in Philosophy, Paul Arthur Schlipp, ed., I, Stockton, California: College of the Pacific, 1932.

"The Human Interest in Persons." Living Through Biography - Teacher's Manual, World Book Co., 1937.

"The Intimate Senses as Sources of Wisdom." Journal of Religion, I, No. 2 (March, 1921), 129-145.

"The Method of Evolution of Consciousness and of Religion." Part III. Biblical World, XXX, No. 3 (September, 1907), 191-201.

"The Moral Phases of Public Education: Iowa Moral Education and Training." Religious Education, VI, No. 1 (April, 1911), 84-93.

"The Nature of Child Consciousness." Part II. Biblical World, XXX, No. 2 (August, 1907), 101-110.

"The Play Impulse and Life." Recreation Round Table, I, No. 10, September, 1938.

"The Play Instinct and Religion." Homiletic Review, LVIII, No. 4, October, 1909.

"The Psychology of Conversion." Expository Times, XXV, No. 5 (February, 1914), 219-223.

"The Sources of Aesthetic Appreciation." Look To This Day. Assembled and edited by the Staff of the Institute of Character Research. University of Southern California: University of Southern California Press (1945), 303-313.

"The Vision Splendid." University Record: University of Florida, VII, No. 4 (November, 1912), 24-46.

"The Young Men of the World." Religious Education, XXIV (November, 1929), 872-874.

"Unconscious Education." Kindergarten Review, XXI, No. 3 (November, 1910), 129-137.

"What Can Religous Education do with Human Nature?" Religious Education, XVIII, No. 2 (April, 1923), 72-77.

"Theological Seminaries and Research." Religious Education. Edwin D. Starbuck, and Arthur E. Holt, XXIII, No. 5 (May, 1928), 404-406.

"Character Tests and Measurements." Bureau of Education Bulletin, Report of the Committee on Character Education of the National Education Association, Washington, D.C. Edwin D. Starbuck, Chairman. Arthur L. Beeley; T. W. Galloway; William H. Kilpatrick; Merle Prunty; A. Duncan Yocum; and Milton Bennion. No. 7, 1926, pp. 35-48.

"Report of the Commission Appointed in 1911 to Investigate the Preparation of Religious Leaders in Universities and Colleges." Religious Education. Edwin D. Starbuck; S. C. Mitchell; Harry E. Fosdick; L. L. Doggett; and Artley B. Parsons. VII, No. 4 (October, 1912), 329-348.

C. Unpublished Materials

"A Guide to Books for Character." Brochure printed but not published.

"A Guide to Books for Character." Informational monograph promoting the use of Volume I: Fairy Tale, Myth, and Legend, and Volume II: Fiction. Printed but not published.

"Anna Diller Starbuck: Concert Pianist." Brochure printed but not published.

"Institute of Character Research, Inc." Affiliated with the University of Southern California, Los Angeles: George Rice and Sons Printers. Brochure printed but not published.

Lecture delivered at the Conference of Religious Workers at the Summer School, University of Iowa, 1918.

"Living Through Biography." Promotional brochure put out by the World Book Company. Printed but not published.

"Look To This Day: Selected Writings by Edwin Diller Starbuck." Book jacket.

Memorandum of the Committee on Conference and Study Groups on Practical Christianity and Reconstruction after the War appointed at Mass Meeting, Commercial Club, Iowa City, February 21, 1918. (Typewritten.)

Memorandum of the Second Meeting of the Committee on Character Education, Hotel Montrose, Cedar Rapids, April 3rd and 4th, 1918. (Typewritten.)

"New Developments in Philosophy in the University of Southern California." Brochure printed but not published.

"An Introduction to a Sociology of Religion." Lectures under auspices of Institute for Comparative Research in Human Culture, Oslo.

"A Philosophy of Character Education." Brochure from the Editorial Office of World Book Company. Printed but not published.

"New Developments in Philosophy." Brochure about the School of Philosophy, University of Southern California. Printed but not published.

"The Wonder Road." Brochure printed but not published.